EVERY PLACE ON THE MAP IS DISABLED

Adrean Clark, *Perseverance,* 2014. Digital illustration and photo collage. Used by permission of the artist, https://adreanclark.com.

EVERY PLACE ON THE MAP IS DISABLED

POEMS AND ESSAYS

Edited by Camisha L. Jones, Michael Northen, Naomi Ortiz, and Travis Chi Wing Lau

CURBSTONE BOOKS / NORTHWESTERN UNIVERSITY PRESS
Evanston, Illinois

Curbstone Books
Northwestern University Press
www.nupress.northwestern.edu

Printed in the United States of America

10 9 8 7 6 5 4 3 2 1

ISBN 978-0-8101-4973-1 (paper)
ISBN 978-0-8101-4974-8 (ebook)

Cataloging-in-Publication Data are available from the Library of Congress.

For our collective thriving and brilliance. In tribute to all of those we've lost to systemic failure. For crip kin and communities who claimed me in my early days of Disabled identity and introduced me to the miracle of access intimacy. May the words of all these mighty poets likewise help us find strength, find our way to one another.

—Camisha L. Jones

I'm grateful to those who have traveled the disability poetry route with me: the Inglis House Poetry Workshop, the staff of *Wordgathering*, and all who contributed to *Beauty is a Verb*. First and foremost, however, I am thankful to my family for hanging in with me through it all.

—Michael Northen

For the Crip ancestors, including Marlin D. Thomas and Kellie Haigh. For Zach, Jean, Tom, and Rachel; thanks for being you; and for sharing café, time, and love with me. Por mi cuerpo hermos@. Por la tierra, las comunidades, y los linajes that made me.

—Naomi Ortiz

For crip kin—past, present, and future.

—Travis Chi Wing Lau

CONTENTS

Sheila Black

FOREWORD: A NEW POSSIBLE

In 2009, when Jennifer Bartlett, Michael Northen, and I began work on *Beauty is a Verb: The New Poetry of Disability* (Cinco Puntos, 2011), it felt like a project that would never see the light of day. No one was particularly interested in disability poetics. The constructs of ableism were so firmly in place—and this, really, was only ten, eleven years ago (I wrote this essay in 2022)—that a number of poets we approached balked at even being part of a volume that professed to explore disability poetics or affirm the identity of being disabled.

We moved forward with *Beauty is a Verb* anyway, even though we half believed it had very little chance of being published. We knew it needed to exist, but we had no idea how we would make that happen. A few people gave us advice on how we might make our effort "more commercial." We ignored them. And although the work often felt as if it was truly taking place on the margins, it was also one of the rare times in my life when I've felt a kind of unearthly confidence. We were working very hard; we had no idea what the result would be, and we didn't care. We had the joy of the work to drive us.

It is a rare pleasure to be asked now to write the foreword for a new anthology of disability poetry—and one that feels to be animated by the same spirit of urgency. Certainly, this is a powerful and deeply indelible book, with the kind of poems you can't help carrying around in your head. I hope this new volume will be as much of a touchstone for readers as *Beauty is a Verb* proved to be for an audience we didn't altogether know was there in 2009.

We still need books like this one. While people are starting to talk about disability more openly, more completely, more complexly, ableism is still endemic. In his first term of office, the US president Donald Trump openly mocked and imitated a disabled reporter trying to ask him a serious question. Disability poetry offers a way forward—but even that can be complicated. We need disability poetry that is not "About Us Without Us," or as Meg Day puts it so brilliantly in their beautiful essay "T-I-M-B-E-R" (published here), we need to avoid the trap of a disability poetics that "isn't for us . . . asks us to explain ourselves, starting at birth . . . says, memorize hearing rhymes . . . makes nondisabled demands."

Most of all, we need to open a space for multiple, diverse, non-white, non-cis-centered views and perspectives—to value the aesthetics of many truly diverse and distinct poetic voices—and, in the process, to honor the many different experiences of what is so often called "the non-normative body/mind" and how these shape the work of poets. As contributor Kay Ulanday Barrett writes, "The key point is, reimagine the landscape."

What I love about this new volume is something I didn't give myself the luxury of feeling much when I was editing *Beauty is a Verb.* Namely, a visionary hope that we can redefine how disability is seen and, in the process, redefine our map of the world. Back in 2009, it seemed a quiet miracle that we were able to put *Beauty is a Verb* together at all. Now, with a bigger audience and more people at the table, it is such a gift to read the words in this anthology and feel how they are reshaping our understandings. Here's what Naomi Ortiz, a contributor and editor, says:

> I know in my bones that art and writing by disabled people of color is valuable. Living in multiple worlds at once, we explore the hidden tunnels between our disability and POC associations and grapple with the consistently rotating reasons given for our exclusion. There is power claimed by naming these layers. Our poetry, writing, and artwork unearth links, sometimes even between contradictory realities, that can deepen relationships between our communities.

I recently revisited an East Coast city for the first time in thirty years. It was an old city and, like most old cities, many of the spaces there are not accessible because they were in buildings built before the ADA. Although there was some acknowledgment of this, there was still far too little being done to make them accessible. I grew indignant and also wondered—how many buildings were built through time with no interest in having disabled people access them? Over my visit, this began to seem like a strange kind of metaphor for the structures of imagination that the writers in this work tackle with such variety and exuberance. This is a volume that centers disabled, queer voices of color and centers, too, the idea of intersectionality as a core part of disability justice. I wish I could quote every single line of poetry and all the sentences and paragraphs I've clipped from the endlessly alive and rich poems and essays collected in this book, but I will settle for just two brief quotations. Here is Constance Merritt speaking of her disability poetics:

> Rather than art as essential body armor, I'd like to think that art could be a tool, not to say, a weapon, with which to dismantle the master's proverbial house and dance a free people in open air. A poetics of resistance, yes, but even more so one of liberation. For that I don't want a lineage, but rather a riot of black, brown, crip, queer, feminist, indigenous, immigrant, allied, struggling-to-wake-and-stay-woke human voices—a hell-harrowing din, a suturing sound—kicking ass and taking names, slowly but surely, rearranging the heavy furniture of this world.

And here is Leah Lakshmi Piepzna-Samarasinha on why it matters:

> If you don't see your crip life in writing, you can't imagine a crip life to be. If there is no Black brown queer trans slut disabled poetics, nonfiction, journalism, essays, crip literary forms, how the fuck will you write them or write your life? With difficulty. . . .
>
> We are possibility model and we also write to refuse erasure, to capture all these tiny everyday moments of disabled life, love, grief, and resistance that abled world tries its damnest to wash away. And writing those crip worlds creates new possibilities.
>
> Every line I write is a nocked arrow, the string pulled back, the x of release, the deep cunt feeling of yes as it hits the mark, as it goes farther than we have before, to the place we knew that we needed named.

That line truly resonates as I think about how to describe this work: "The place that we knew we needed named." I promise you it is here. Read this book. Relish it. Share it. Pass it along. After thirty years of working in this arena, I have rarely felt more exhilaration and pride than I did when I turned the last page, having read all of these poems and essays by writers who speak their bodies, their minds, their truths, precisely and without fear. Kudos to the editors and, Dear Reader, please read and speak back. One of the great gifts of being part of disability community is that it is just that—a community, and here, laid bare, are so many of the ways in which the naming of that community opens a new possible for all of us.

Michael Northen, Camisha L. Jones, Travis Chi Wing Lau, Naomi Ortiz

INTRODUCTION

When the idea for this anthology was first born, it was to be a second edition of *Beauty is a Verb: The New Poetry of Disability.* The first anthology had proved an unexpected success, and readers were asking for a second volume. Jennifer Bartlett, Sheila Black, and Michael Northen, the editors of *Beauty is a Verb*, recognized that there had been so much change since its initial publication and felt a follow-up volume could reflect the changing nature of disability poetry. That work began in early 2019. Toward the end of the year, Camisha Jones joined the editorial team.

The journey to bring this anthology into being included many unexpected twists and turns. The arrival of the COVID-19 pandemic in 2020 and its persistence for years afterward majorly affected the pace of the publishing process. The work of compiling this collection was done while holding the weight of alarming occurrences such as the disproportionate impact of COVID-19 on disabled, Black, Brown, Indigenous, and poor people; nationwide Black Lives Matter uprisings in response to the police murder of George Floyd; and increased violence and harassment targeting Asian American community members spurred on by racist rhetoric related to COVID.

As the work continued within the context of these current events with their particular impacts on the disability community, the editorial team was talking more and more about how to best hold the work and their intentions for the anthology. Throughout the team's time working together, everyone was in agreement that the new volume should embody a diverse range of voices. The editors decided to make some changes to increase the diversity of its team in order to more authentically and effectively pursue that goal and manage the editorial responsibilities. Two new editors, Naomi Ortiz and Travis Chi Wing Lau, were recruited in mid-2020 to expand the perspectives, experience, and skill of the team. Camisha Jones and Michael Northen remained editors. Sheila Black transitioned into the role of editorial advisor to the project, and Jennifer Bartlett also served as an advisor on an as-needed basis. These changes were rooted in a desire to do what the editors felt would best serve the project.

After thirty-six years of publishing groundbreaking poetry, Cinco Puntos, the original publisher of *Beauty is a Verb* and the expected publisher of this anthology, decided to close its doors in 2021. With Cinco Puntos now closed and the first edition of *Beauty is a Verb* expected to go out of print, the editors made the decision to publish the anthology under a new title. After months of searching for a new publisher, *Every Place on the Map Is Disabled: Poems and Essays* found a home with Northwestern University Press, which accepted the anthology for publication with worldwide availability in both print and digital formats.

While this anthology is no longer a second edition of *Beauty is a Verb*, it has been crafted in its spirit and as an extension of its legacy. The new title *Every Place on the Map Is Disabled* was chosen as a way of expressing and celebrating the fact that disabled people are everywhere. Often nondisabled people operate from an assumption that disabled people are absent, resulting in a pervasive absence of accommodations, accessibility, and awareness. Poems and essays in this collection are witnesses to the terrible cost of that wrong assumption as well as a compass to the beautiful ways disabled folks creatively build bridges to each other and tunnel our truths to the light. How incredible would the world be if the presence of D/deaf, disabled, neurodivergent, mad, and chronically ill people was assumed in all our communities? How amazingly supportive that world would be, not just for disabled people, but for everyone! This anthology makes a case for imagining the incredible possibilities of that new world.

In order to represent the multiple editorial voices that shaped this anthology and to offer each editor an opportunity to reflect on their editorial process and relationship to the anthology as a whole, this introduction takes the form of a Q&A in which each editor responded to a set of shared questions.

1. Why do you feel that a new anthology of disability poetry is needed?

MICHAEL NORTHEN:

When Sheila Black, Jennifer Bartlett, and I edited *Beauty is a Verb* over sixteen years ago, there was no real sense of what disability poetry was or even that it had claim to be an actual discipline. Our task at the time was almost an archaeological one: to establish a limited working definition of disability poetry, to gather together the leading voices within that movement, and to try to look back at the work of poets who had led us to that point. This was an essential first step but it was never intended to be definitive. Since that time, the nature of the field has changed substantially; we felt there was a need for a new anthology to reflect disability poetry as it has come to exist today.

CAMISHA L. JONES:

In 2015, I was featured as part of a poetry reading and open mic in honor of the twenty-fifth anniversary of the Americans with Disabilities Act, along with Kathi Wolfe and Ellen McGrath Smith. It was my first time publicly identifying as a disabled person, though my personal experience with disability dates back to 1996. Somewhere within the two years prior to that reading, Sarah Browning at Split This Rock introduced me to *Beauty is a Verb: The New Poetry of Disability,* describing it as groundbreaking and the first of its kind. I didn't know then how important the disabled writers connected to the anthology would become for me. By 2014, I lost the ability to consistently keep up with verbal communication or fast-paced life due to escalating bouts of hearing loss and chronic pain. I felt unrelentingly isolated and broken. By connecting with disabled people (and particularly disabled poets, such as *Beauty is a Verb* editors Sheila Black and Jennifer Bartlett), I learned the power of embracing all of who I am and knowing I remain whole even as I am also disabled. Disabled poets showed me new avenues for exploring and living within my craft. My world widened and I found a new sense of connection.

As COVID infection and impact continue to spread, we are living through what some refer to as a "mass disabling event." There will always be a need for disabled stories, disabled truth-telling, disabled art, because with time, more and more people experience disability. Many already are but can't yet refer to themselves with the "D" word. They may feel as though they aren't disabled *enough*—like I once did—or maybe they feel it's a dirty word or that to claim disability would be equivalent to believing themselves broken. When we're ready, we need to be able to find each other to counteract the ableist conditioning and lies we're constantly taking in. Our poetry is one way to do that. An uninterrupted flow of our mighty words will always be needed in my opinion.

TRAVIS CHI WING LAU:

I only began to write and publish as a disabled poet since 2016, and *Beauty is a Verb* was a formative anthology for me, as it helped me situate my work within a much longer tradition of disabled poets practicing disability poetics well before either category really received proper recognition. For so many of us, that collection helped us feel part of a larger project of disability poetics that pushed back against canons of literature that often did not include disabled writers at all. Thus, I see the work assembled here modeling the range of disability poetics as it has evolved over time to encompass new voices, new methods, and new experimental forms.

Since *Beauty is a Verb*'s publication, the community of disabled poets has expanded in ways that invite us to reassess our community's values and how disability poetry reflects or even challenges those values. How, for example, has disability justice informed disability poetics, if at all? To what ends does disability poetics serve and what distinguishes disability poetics from other forms of poetry? I feel this new anthology embodies the self-reflexive nature of the disability community, which constantly asks difficult questions of itself, be it about the ongoing ableism within disability culture or disability's fraught intersections with other underrepresented identities.

NAOMI ORTIZ:

I find that so much work is created trying to help nondisabled people understand our experience with the hope that they will invest in Disability Justice and liberation. However, for me, the real power in poetics and art is found in learning from each other. Disabled folks have a lot of wisdom derived from living within economic systems, communities, and families that struggle with our existence. Disability poetics is inherently intersectional, a process of embracing all of what makes us who we are. The poems in this collection are secrets whispered in the dark. They are shouted through bullhorns and written on the back of hospital intake forms. These poems about love, resistance, loss, pain, beauty, and culture often capture moments where one disabled person can recognize themselves in another. This book is a bridge, a tie, to strengthen our collective survival.

2. How would you describe your editorial philosophy and your approach to selecting poems for the anthology?

MICHAEL NORTHEN:

My claim has been that there is a legitimate disability poetry that can not only stand on its own within the larger tradition of poetry but has something new of value to add. I'm interested in who those poets are that have been making a contribution to that field and what the nature of that contribution is, the only qualification being that the poet identifies as disabled. Since I did not envision the anthology as only being read by other disabled writers, I asked myself whose work I thought a larger audience ought to be aware of. My approach tended to be descriptive rather than prescriptive. Once the poets were selected my focus was on the poem rather than the poet themselves. I asked what a particular poem had to offer in terms of subject, form, or perspective. I also asked if this was a poem *I* would want to read.

CAMISHA L. JONES:

When I became a part of the editorial team in late 2019, the work was already in progress and I was given the opportunity to invite a few poets to submit poetry for consideration. My initial focus was on widening perspectives to be represented in the anthology. Throughout the editorial process, I was holding the question, "What could this poem or this poet uniquely add to the anthology?" Disability intersects with an unlimited number of other identities, and it was important to me to do our best to illustrate that in the anthology.

In general, I am drawn to poems that surprise me, make me feel an electric shock of emotion, name something clearly that I've struggled to name. I love poems that push back against oppressive forces, and I also love poems that reveal the tender and precious parts of life. I appreciate poems that offer something relevant to the times we are living through. I always want to be moved in some way by a poem.

It was important to me to stay open to the perspectives and wisdom of my coeditors. I believe collaboration offers richness and depth to editorial processes.

TRAVIS CHI WING LAU:

My editorial approach was precisely not to have a set plan—or at least not a preconceived notion of what kind of work I would encounter and expect to include in the anthology. I instead wanted to learn from our contributors and allow their work to shape the anthology on their terms. Our process of organization and curation emerged from the work we received rather than a top-down imposition of our editorial philosophy onto that work. Editorial work so often can become gatekeeping, especially in literary publishing, so it felt particularly important to me to make decisions that reflected the real breadth of work happening in disability poetry that may surprise or challenge my own assumptions about what constitutes disability poetics. As I understand it, our editorial process has been about finding and honoring the unexpected and generative connections across our contributors' work that we did not realize were present until we put them in dialogue with each other. The anthology, as a whole, feels like an extended conversation among writers who have shaped one another and are shaping another generation of disabled poets.

NAOMI ORTIZ:

My editorial philosophy is a full body experience. I love poems that make my heart and spirit take notice or bring my imagination along for a journey. Another part of my philosophy is a lived one through a commitment to access. In this project I weaved in accessibility both in the ways I worked with poets and with the other editors. In discussing with poets what they needed in order to bring their work and words to this book in the most accessible way, we ended up offering poets extended time, processing conversations, and alternative formats such as an interview style for writing the essay.

As much as the editors worked to support each poet in their submissions, we also had to bring that same skill set to working with each other. As a group of four editors, we have met every other week for multiple years slowly selecting and organizing this anthology. We have navigated surgeries, losses of loved ones, disability flares, and supporting friends and family through their own disability journeys. To do this editorial work in an accessible way has meant making sure caption technology was working for each meeting, pausing with tumultuous internet connections, and sharing the workload depending on need.

3. ***What did you learn about disability poetry, culture, and community from the process of editing the collection?***

MICHAEL NORTHEN:

It has been over twenty-five years since I began facilitating the Inglis House Poetry Workshop in an effort to help disabled writers find work in which they could see themselves and their own experiences. Since that time I have watched disability poetry continually transform, one set of sensibilities giving way to another—and I am constantly learning. During the editing of this anthology, I learned just how difficult it is for four editors who come from different backgrounds to agree on what constitutes a quality poem. From contributors themselves, I learned about my own biases. I had not considered, as Roxanna Bennett points out in her essay, the ableism in requiring a writer whose means of communicating is poetry to write an essay, nor, as Meg Day asserts, the way that the audism implicit in the mainstream poetic tradition has insinuated itself into disability poetry as well. I have a greater appreciation for the difficulty involved in balancing complex community concerns with the needs of poetry.

CAMISHA L. JONES:

More and more, I've been pivoting toward rooting myself within disability justice principles. Doing so within the editorial process allowed space to lean on one another in nontraditional ways. As a team of disabled editors, we were committed, for instance, to ensuring meetings and interactions were accessible for one another. Our aim has been to prioritize molding, shaping, and bending the editorial process to honor our bodies and minds, and those of contributors. I was reminded how much pace matters—in our planning process, in terms of what we expect from contributors and how quickly we expect it. It's been a relief to be on an editorial team that isn't enamored with unrealistic planning goals. When timing was too tight, we adjusted.

This process has also helped to expand my understanding of disability and how to hold an editorial process even more ethically. I know that I, like everyone, have been conditioned by oppressive forces at work in society (particularly in areas where I hold privilege). Part of unlearning that conditioning is listening to people who are different from myself. I'm grateful for what I've learned from tuning in to my fellow editors, particularly around issues like what makes a "good" poem, which begs us to ask what's shaped those opinions. There are so many ways to experience disability and ableism (both the structural and everyday varieties). I have more awareness about those experiences because of what was shared by editors and contributing poets (in their poems and in their communication with us). I'm grateful to have that new knowledge as guidance for my future actions.

TRAVIS CHI WING LAU:

Many writers and editors, both disabled and ablebodyminded, have suggested that we are currently in the "golden age" of disability literature. Editing this collection has only affirmed this to be true: crip poetry not only has the capacity to respond powerfully to the most pressing issues of our present but also reckons with our struggle toward more inclusive futures in the wake of painful and often forgotten pasts. I remain moved by how so many of the writers in this collection have read one another and continue to see themselves as participating in a collective project of imagination and expression even as we work across differences in lived experience and history. Rather than a singular definition of disability literature, this anthology makes the case that there is in fact a plurality of disability literatures that can be in tension as much as in resonance with one another.

NAOMI ORTIZ:

When we as editors started this journey together, we didn't know a pandemic was going to rock the world, bringing to the forefront the issue of medical neglect, compounded for many by segregation in group homes and institutions—an issue disabled people have long known and fought against. For a period, the disposability and murder of disabled people (for example, being triaged or moved to the back of the line for COVID-19 treatment) was unfolding on a national and international stage. At the same time, powerful Black Lives Matter uprisings were highlighting systematic violence and murder of Black, Indigenous, people of color. As I write this in March 2023, folks are tracking and protesting anti-Trans bills that are passing through multiple state governments. In response to these things, people all over the country and around the world are organizing for a different future.

The poets and editors are part of many communities that overlap in these struggles toward liberation. This collection, which always felt political, became increasingly vibrant in its illumination of both the ordinary day-to-day, and in its repercussions, the violent echoes of so many lost. I have learned much from the poets as I have followed their words through experiences of discrimination, solace, grief, and joy. Sharing the work of these incredible poets became, for me, both an offering of witness and a testament to our collective strength and beauty.

* * *

During the final months of manuscript preparation for this anthology, two staff members of Zoeglossia, a disability poetry nonprofit cofounded in part by Sheila Black and Jennifer Bartlett, publicly resigned, expressing having experienced harm. Many of the poets in this collection are part of the Zoeglossia community and are involved in the work to mend the organization. We want to acknowledge how this situation ripples out into the pages of this book. As we contemplate how to honor the now without guessing at the future, we affirm a belief in a culture of belonging, one that encompasses bridges built slowly through vulnerable accountability and a rejection of disposability. At the time this manuscript was being completed, this situation was unfolding. We hope it will have evolved by the time this book is released, because in the end, we know we belong to each other.

EVERY PLACE ON THE MAP IS DISABLED

1

INTIMACIES AND INTERDEPENDENCE

Naomi Ortiz

TO RECLAIM POWER

My body is the oldest story in the world. Part broken, part brilliant, all nuance, disability offers a layer of perspective that is unique and profound. Knowledge of disability experience is political, social, sexual, ancestral. To name something is to claim knowledge. Disability poetics reclaims the power of understanding our culture(s) and our truths. It has the ability to build bridges between communities and support mutual liberation.

As a child growing up amid conflict within my home and neighborhood, I came across a book with a poem about a dragon who was afraid of everything and a young girl who helped the dragon become courageous. I learned to read a poem when I feel afraid. Poetry became a companion. As a teenager, poetry became the way I created space between wounds.

Then I met my friend Marlin D. Thomas. We met at a youth disability conference and bonded over disability activism. One evening, we were sitting at a table in a cavernous ballroom listening to speakers, when this elderly white man with a cowboy hat rolled onstage. An Asian woman stood next to him holding a microphone so we could hear him speak. The first words out of his mouth were, "I love you." Glancing around at all the teenagers and twenty-somethings, I saw I was not the only one who immediately started squirming in their chair. And then, leaning closer to the microphone, he allowed a dramatic pause and again said, "I LOVE YOU!" As he continued his speech, I looked over at Marlin, who sat enraptured with a goofy grin on his face. I had never seen a grown person tell a crowd of people that they loved them, and I was ready to bolt, but seeing the expression on Marlin's face made me pause and listen. The speaker talked about the need to redefine how we saw ourselves and each other. That we were powerful and had a responsibility. When the speech was over, I leaned over to ask Marlin who that was, but he was already maneuvering around the table in his powerchair, headed to meet the man as he came offstage. The speaker was Justin Dart and the woman with him was his wife and partner in activism, Yoshiko Dart. Together, they had traveled to all fifty states collecting testimony in partnership with local activists. This testimony helped convince Congress to pass the Americans with Disabilities Act. Marlin showed me how to pay attention and collect courage from living disability history.

As our friendship grew, Marlin and I traveled across the country to visit one another. We would bring suitcases full of old notebooks to read in the few hours of privacy between personal assistants supporting Marlin with day-to-day life. He was the first person I became really close to who was also a person of color (POC), disabled, and a poet.

As we shared our writing and read other poets, I realized that what I connected to about poetry was not form, style, or rhythm. Rather, I connected to poems when the words vibrated on my skin or in my heart. All the diverse ways people captured truth.

In addition to poetry and activism, Marlin and I also shared a similar experience in our cultural communities—disability being either shoved aside and disappeared or focused on as the sole area of attention. As artists, it was tough to access performance or gallery spaces. Both because of physical barriers, but also because we weren't seen as people who could contribute culturally—as people who would have something to say about our ancestors, place, or histories.

When Marlin and I would talk, especially on days when something terrible had happened, hearts were broken, or violence was experienced, after rehashing the details, Marlin would inevitably say, "We gotta put it in our poetry." I learned poetry is a way to witness. One afternoon I was working at my consultant gig, listening to music, dancing around in my chair, having fun in the ways we encouraged each other to, when I got the call that Marlin had suddenly died. That day my life changed forever. I have a poem about it.

Marlin helped me believe that my work is worth sharing, but in artistic spaces, I continually confront ableism. Recently, at an online Latinx writing conference, there were no options for access needs and my questions and feedback were ignored. At poetry open mics, I am unable to get to the stage or even to the sign-up sheet. Often, I am not invited to cultural events because people know I am disabled. When I am invited, I am on my own to figure out how to get in (let alone know if there will be a restroom I can use). If I cannot get in, no one identifies that I, or disabled people in general, aren't there. That we are missing from the "community" gathered at the table. In facing such intense inaccessibility in artistic spaces, places that are supposed to be grounded in creativity, what clues toward resilience and creativity are these cultural communities missing?

Disability poetics is how disability gets politically translated into everyday life: the hundreds of ways we have to ask for help—whether we want to or not—and the ways we find to reciprocate or help others. The humor at some random stranger throwing change in our half-filled coffee cups. Having to plan for everything (and then have a backup plan for each plan). The brutal experience of having little pieces of your humanity splintered away as you try to wedge yourself into a system that is supposed to help you survive. How Crip sex takes all the creativity earned by having to function in oppressive and inaccessible environments (having uncomfortable and awkward conversations, explorations of adaptive equipment, explaining to another person exactly what you want done to your body) and puts it to an amazing use. How we are brave only because we cannot back down from other people's fear of vulnerability. As I learn from Crip art, I think about how my other communities could gain so much wisdom from disability culture.

Poetry serves as a way to reclaim my cultural relevancy as a disabled mestize growing up in the US–Mexico borderlands. To share my understanding of driving weekly through one of the many border patrol checkpoints set up near where I live, twelve miles from the international line, or witnessing climate change's effect on the desert ecosystem. My visual art, writing, the songs I sing to the sky are all ways to glean what matters from my lived experience. These understandings are intersectional. They are disability cultural experiences *and* ethnic cultural experiences.

What does it mean to be a disabled mestize cultural worker? I am bruja when I write my truth down on paper, casting spells of transformation, even if it's just coaxing a different perspective on the sunlight illuminating cactus thorns next to the patch of pavement outside my door. In capturing a moment, a feeling, I am child, elder, ancestor. I render safety by bracing against place, maybe found on the edge of a parking lot between picnic table and wild, helping me to inhabit spaciousness. This allows my arms, legs, feet, torso to remember what body integrity feels like outside the constriction of rooms where medical trauma or other harm has occurred. Describing how I know family through plantas and ancestors is my own mending. It is sharing a model of restoration that transcends individual relationships.

A legacy I carry from my friendship with Marlin is I know in my bones that art and writing by disabled people of color is valuable. Living in multiple worlds at once, we explore the hidden tunnels between our disability and

POC associations and grapple with the consistently rotating reasons given for our exclusion. There is power claimed by naming these layers. Our poetry, writing, and artwork unearth links, sometimes even between contradictory realities, that can deepen relationships between our communities.

Benefaction

Naomi Ortiz

Great, Great, Great, Great,
Great, Great, Great, Great,
Grandmothers

Nanas, they go where I go
carrying these instruments of creation
womb, paintbrush, spirit, pen

Their song sings in my bones, whispers in my ear
I am and am not alone
Their song reminds me through my own grunts and moans
of a spectrum of color to pull from as I paint a life

Burnt orange memory of daughter carried on mother's back
eyelids closed against the summer sun
Ache of splintered red heart strands, ties cut to lovers, friends
Silver studded clarity which may come through prayer or song,
anger or betrayal, to fight for myself
Always flinging head-first into an infinite pitch-black hope that
both inner and outer journeys are worth the risk
With golden truth that survival requires so much more than any
one person can do alone
Deliverance grows vivid green, like a new shoot of alfalfa, after
fallow times
A pink dab of humility reminds me that I am to Great Spirit never
too fierce or too much trouble

Three feathers inheritance tucked in my palette
shiver, quake with delicate strength
ready for ritual movement on canvas, on page

This color collection sung in my cells
stained in my blood
is of unequaled perfection

My
grandmothers
speak

Y2K Philadelphia (That time we met)

Naomi Ortiz

Peach clouds smolder outside the fifth-story hotel window.
Two beds covered in geometric patterns, one beneath
each body.
Lying sideways, perched on the edge, we smile shyly
at the other in the crackling hum of so much to say.

You proclaim, "Walk with this." Hand clinched in a fist against
your heart.

"Feeling my blood and bone is the only way I know home," I
whisper, clutching the pillow beneath my head.

The chasm between beds,
                                        fills with secrets.

Nineteen. Neither of us knew how endangered sincere
vulnerability would become.

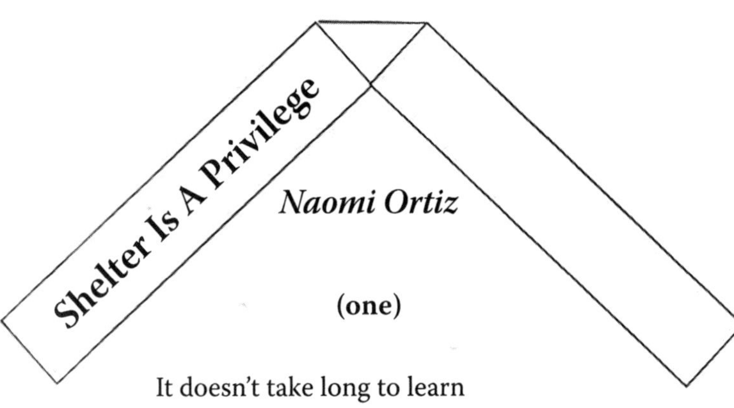

Shelter Is A Privilege

Naomi Ortiz

(one)

It doesn't take long to learn
life goes best when you go last
Hold their needs attentively
like a spiny cholla bud in your
tiny hand
Meet their needs with what you
have
Maybe then you'll prove yourself
        worthy of love
Only under the crisp, tangy scented
lemon tree can you be loud
Sing your six-year-old heart out
The delicate beauty of the open sky
the soft blooms which turn to fruit
are a heritage too tender to touch

Hunger is a divine practice
You will learn to feast on not enough
        and pretend you are full

(two)

hunger is my heritage, passed down from mother to ~~daughter~~ child,
fortified in DNA

in dimly lit mornings, calloused fingers weave into hair strands,
taut tension to hold the shape of self-sacrifice, endurance,
and pushing-through

alone, yet always needed; makes lists
ever flexible; accommodates his demands; aptly dodges insults

darts breathless; returns from another one of my doctor appointments
two busses each way, to have dinner cooked, served to mouths
that are never full

tending to survival leaves lingering questions to burrow into her heart,
disturb and peel back plaster patches covering the holes

in a quiet moment at laminate yellow and white kitchen table,
she tells me of my inheritance,
a lifetime given to evolve from where she got

To the Nondisabled White Grrrl with the Frida Kahlo Altar in the Living Room

Naomi Ortiz

Grrrl, if you're going to gush to me about Frida
you better be prepared with an intimate knowledge of nightmares
Those many things in life beyond your control and know them well enough to call their name

You better have experience of body meeting surgical knife
with a man who thinks he knows just how to fix you, holding the hilt
and what surgery after surgery, failing his expectations, feels like

Grrrl, you better know how to make peace with the boredom of pain

Grrrl, if you're gonna create an altar to Frida in your living room
then you need to be prepared to speak truth to your darkest vulnerabilities
To talk about what it means to never belong
Living in your own world because your parents smashed into each other, never knowing how to exist in the same place

Grrrl, I see it in your face,
how you want me to respond, all grrrl-crush-on-artist
but our love of Frida lives differently
You try to take on her diversity
You say you know her bravery
You aspire to be more like her

Me, I see a kindred soul
I want to honor her legacy
        by fiercely loving hard
        by translating culture through body
        by courageously inhabiting passion

Grrrl, Frida was her own woman
Living her own truth
Enduring her own pain
You can't inhabit someone else, and expect to find your own way

Liv Mammone

ART OBJECT, TALISMAN

There is a piece of lore in my family about how I became a writer. After my brother and I were both given our diagnoses as infants, he with autism and I with cerebral palsy, my mother returned to therapy. Often, she brought us with her. The story goes that I was on the floor at around two years of age having an elaborate conversation with a puppet my mother's therapist kept in her office. My mother was expressing her fears about my growing up unable to walk. Maybe she was talking about fears for the usual markers of jobs, marriage, and children. Her therapist looked down at me, sitting W-shaped but already verbose and imaginative, and posited, "Maybe she'll be a writer."

I can't say how much the repetition of this anecdote had to do with my lifelong obsession with stories and language, but she turned out to be correct. I can't remember a time when a life of words was not what I wanted. There was a very brief stint of wanting to be a ballerina, but even that was circumvented with writing. When I suffered over not being able to do the most basic steps in my walker, my father sat me down in front of his first word processor and said, "Write yourself as a ballerina." Writing has always been entwined with my disability. Primarily, fiction was given as a tool for going beyond reality rather than detailing it. Fiction was my first love. I started my first novel at age eight. But as I moved into adulthood, poetry became the site of more rigorous academic study. I felt I had more to learn about its mechanics and possibilities.

My life as a disabled poet is starkly truncated by two specific moments. In undergrad, a certain fellow student always came to my readings. I was writing fictitious, slightly surreal works drawing from my novelist dreams and spoken word conventions. After each performance, this stranger would approach me with a huge smile and say the same thing:

"It's so good to see someone like you just up there doing her thing!"

Someone like me. I wanted to be generous with my interpretation of that. During a repetition of this interaction, I finally asked her what she enjoyed about my work. Was there a particular piece she liked? Her smile didn't move. Something in her jaw twitched.

"You're just so strong! It's so good to see someone like you!"

She was not listening to my poems, I thought. The image of my body on crutches in front of a microphone was all that mattered. I decided I would not compound this image by writing about being disabled. I did not want my poetry to generate pity. I wanted to be more.

During the first semester of my MFA, this poetic fiction hybrid was no longer working. Everything I turned in felt lifeless. One of my professors, Kimiko Hahn, demanded of our poems: "So what?" Roger Sedarat built a syllabus around asking us, "Does poetry matter?" They wanted us to be able to articulate *why* we were poets. I was unsure. One day I showed up for a meeting with our program head, Nicole Cooley. On her desk was *Beauty is a Verb*. I was jealous of the title and enchanted by the cover photo of a woman scuba diving in her wheelchair, her floral dress and long hair calling to my childhood mermaid dreams. Nicole gave the book to me.

"You have a voice," Nicole said. "You deserve to use it."

Writing these two anecdotes together, I'm caught by the word "deserve." At eighteen, I made my imagined audience both a more powerful entity than myself and an entirely able-bodied entity. *Beauty is a Verb* was an art object and talisman. It woke me to a disabled audience that deserved to see their experience in mine. That audience deserved the experience of one of their own delivering her story onstage. But more than that, I had been leaving myself and my needs out of the process. I deserved to speak regardless of interpretation.

My original copy gifted from Nicole sits right next to me as I write this, covered in fingerprints, dog-eared, and littered with ancient Post-its. I studied it in very concrete ways over the next few years, working to establish myself as a member of its lineage. Craft and poetic growth are often spoken about as effervescent and nebulous. We often don't know, or don't know how to articulate, our creative forward movement. Much of the work my MFA instructors imparted to me is still sinking in. But the shift toward a fully disabled poetics was quick and lacked mystery. When I was a teenager falling in love with slam and spoken word, I chose a performer I admired and then let YouTube send me down all-night video spirals to discover more poets. I didn't know anything about slam and very little about poetry. I only knew that I wanted to do what those people were doing. Due to my disability and other related factors, it took me much longer than desired to start traveling the same spaces as those long-admired poets I imitated so I could begin to learn from and alongside them. There was a lot of time for the imposter syndrome to build up and a long journey to break it back down. I was slightly more mercenary in ensconcing myself with the writers of *Beauty is a Verb.* I avidly read and submitted to *Wordgathering* to gain the attention of Michael Northen. I wrote reviews for newly released collections by Kathi Wolfe and Sheila Black. Raymond Luczak asked a specific question of me during the submission process for the anthology *Queer Disability Anthology (QDA)* (Squares and Rebels, 2015) that led to its own essay. One of the poems here, "Surgery Psalm," was originally drafted in a workshop with Jennifer Bartlett. It was the first space specifically centered around the disabled people I joined willingly. These choices created a domino effect of new experiences, opportunities, friends, and colleagues. I lacked some of my usual fear because I was already connected to them by disability poetics rather than belief in my worthiness or skill. I felt deserving. I also felt I could be an ancestor to as yet unknown writers and readers.

Being accepted for this volume is the coming full circle of this journey to reach myself. All the poems selected have a very direct disabled foremother. Jennifer Bartlett edited "Surgery Psalm." Tara Hardy, a constant light for me as a queer, disabled, elder statesman of slam, provided the formal construction of "A Crip Is." Taylor Carmen Saveth, another poet with CP, messaged me the idea for "Reinventing the Scale" because chronic pain is not part of her lived experience. Two other authors presented here, Viktoria Venezuela and Gaia Thomas, are in a group text with me as we draft these essays together. *Beauty is a Verb* taught me not only about the worth of truth but that poetry is, for me, a collaborative process. I look forward to this volume's continued teachings.

Surgery Psalm

Liv Mammone

Ready yourself for starving the night
before; for the urine yellow soap that will soften
your skin like a ripening pear; for the sunrise drive.
Ready your ears for the moans of the woman
drooling in a sling in the waiting room. She's you.
Ready your ass for its exposure in the paper gown.
Open your throat for the codeine; veins for the saline.
Ready the backs of your hands for the needle—for your
iPod dying while you wait strapped to the gurney, four
hours to go. Ready your mouth to be masked for anesthetic.
See your voice disappear into that sweet ether?
Breathe deep. Shut up.
Ready your eyelids to play projector
to your nightmares. Paint the inside
of your brain fluorescent white and ready your mind
for the medicinal misremembering.
Be aware that the bed will be your world, a paper boat
on a hazy Hudson. Ready your eyes for the nurses' smiles.
They wrack your frame worse than when the meds wear off.
For your parents sleeping hunchbacked in plastic chairs, somewhere
between jailers and mourners; for your rest to be ruined
with the retching of your roommate. Ready your chest for the heaving.
Stop sleeping completely. (Maybe you'll write more poems.)
Ready your knees; they will transform to melting candles,
your ankles to nuts and bolts, your hips to wandering
planets, your calves into riots. Ready your ribs to collapse
around your fruit pit heart. The impulse to starve
will stay for years. Ready your lips to say endless
"i'm fines." Live in a new smile,
all teeth. What gifts
will loved ones shower on you now? Stuffed cats
and fairie dolls will no longer do, woman-thing.

Ready a cackle instead of laughter. Try and recite
the questions future lovers will ask
surveying you naked. Imagine their eyes, slitted critical.
Say freak until it's the name of a dog
that licks your face. You won't feel hands
plunging in you, these doctors—
your gods standing over the red rind
of your exposed spine. Instead, loosen your flesh.
Just one more time. Just a little
more machine and
we will make you human.

Reinventing the Scale

Liv Mammone

Health care professionals use a number system when asking patients about pain; one being none, ten being "the worst pain you've ever felt."

1. Sleep
2. July
3. I will never again be the dogwood in bloom I was at eleven years old
4. I can still imagine someone falling in love with me
5. Pretending I care why you're upset//Smiling//Not thinking what the NSAIDS will do to my stomach in five years
6. Still enough breath to sing—my voice is the only good of me
7. The bath and an hour of listening to an audiobook are all that's accomplished// The cats don't get breakfast//Talking to the ghost of my dead surgeon
8. Pray to a thousand laughing gods not to fall on the stairs but still stagger back to bed in terror
9. Bring myself to orgasm three times in an hour because my muscles only soften for three minutes just after: I am nothing but the stenches of sleepsweat, weed, and loveless cum
10. Even if I kill myself with all these pills, my Catholic mother will bury me on my back

A Crip Is

Liv Mammone

after Tara Hardy after Roma Raye

A crip is a bitch.
A bitch is a war. War.
A crip is a cry.
A cry is a tool
War cry.

A cry is a weapon.
Necessary. A crip
is necessary. A crip
cry is necessary song.
Song cry.

A crip bitch cries.
Nobody wants to hear
bitch and moan.
To moan means fear.
Crip

means fear. Fear is a stone
on the spine. The weight of
life. Stone spine bitch.
A spine is a tool.
Witch

weighing a life. Scales.
A monster with scales. Crip
is monster. Burn the witch. War
cry. Burn. A burn can crown.
Crown

is a weight. A crip
is not a weight but

is crowned. A crip
bitch earns a crown.
Bone

against bone
makes a song.
Witch bone crown.
Try to burn the crip
              bitch down.

Leah Lakshmi Piepzna-Samarasinha

WHY WE DO THIS THING CALLED DISABILITY JUSTICE WRITING

On June 19, 2010, me and the great Stacey Park Milbern[1] limped and rolled into Community Art Room 156 at the Allied Media Conference (AMC) in Detroit, MI. We were about to throw the first writing workshop we'd ever do together in the next eleven years of wild crip Asian femme friendship, writing partnership, coevolution, and comradeship. In the middle of a disability justice (DJ) movement being born, that we were part of birthing. "The Azolla Story: queer and trans of color disabled and chronically ill love and zine making workshop." It was also the first queer and trans disabled POC writing workshop either of us had ever heard of, been at, let alone thrown. That didn't stop us. We just did it. Crip Asian brother femme poetic audacity. If she was being a poet on her secret public blog and crip community organizer at eighteen, hiding queer books in the wall of her loving but fundie Christian parents' house, of fucking course she could throw a queer disabled BIPOC writing workshop. If I had been doing crazy writing since I was a sick and nuts twenty-two-year-old, so could I.

Disability justice as a term was only five years old, even though, as the statement above shows, we had been disabled and Asian and queer and radical for a lot longer than that. Our workshop was part of the first DJ track ever held at the AMC. It felt like there were maybe twenty of us angry radical beautiful disabled QTBIPOC across the United States who were doing this stuff. The Azolla Story was one of those early pieces of disability justice history that has mostly disappeared into the mists of time, Myspace-era internet, and the memories of the people who started it and hung out on it—but it was an old school online message board by and for disabled queer and trans people of color. Like, with those bubbles and drop-down menus. It's where I met Stacey, and Mia, and a lot of other people who were the ten radical queer disabled POC I knew.

I was nervous as hell. I had been disabled since I was twenty-one, but I was still in early crip "Do I dare call myself disabled?" Who the hell was I to co-teach this workshop? What did I know about being disabled? We had been so busy getting the AMC to order fragrance-free soap for the whole conference, being some of the imaginators of Creating Collective Access, an experiment in disabled people, mostly disabled QTPOC, creating access and care for each other, and holding down the three accessible dorm suites where we were all posted up, to create much of a lesson plan. Typical crip writer styles. I didn't even know if anyone would come.

But they did. The room slowly filled with crips of color. There was a quiet. Stacey said, her voice quiet and steady into the quiet, "OK, it's really simple. What are the queer disabled POC stories we want to tell?"

The conference room blackboard slowly filled up: the Hiawatha Insane Asylum for Indians, my mother's polio, my first cane, being in the ICU, crip sex, sex with someone ableist. I went looking on a deep search in FB to see if there was a photo of the blackboard but there's not. It's probably somewhere seven phones ago. We asked: *If your body could speak, what stories would it spill?*

Four years later I would start teaching my Frida and Harriet's Children SDQTPOC[2] writing classes online and I would start with the same question: What are the sick and disabled QTBIPOC stories we are burning to tell? Posing it to students most of whom had written me asking multiple times if they deserved to be there, if they were really disabled, if they were really a writer. Disabled writing and poetics have been met with a silence. *Oh. . . . Maybe Virginia Woolf?*

We are inspirations, tragedies, monsters, hermits, cautionary tales, plagues, warnings. We are Beth from *Little Women.* We are symbols and an absence. But the reality is crip writing is everywhere and crip bodies are overflowing pulse white dark water rapid rivers full of stories we are burning to tell.

I tell the story a lot about the fight I got into with an editor in the last weeks before *Care Work*[3] was going to the printer, where I insisted that the BISAC codes on the back read Disability Studies / Disability Justice / Queer Studies when she wanted them to read Social Studies / Health / Queer Studies. Her little tinkling white lady abled laugh, "Well, we do have to go with the official BISAC codes [note: there is one for Disability Studies, has been for decades] and I've never seen a disabled section in a bookstore, have you?" Tee hee hee.

Of course I had: Modern Times Books, where I was the events coordinator as well as cashier from 2009 to 2011, had one; Left Bank and Elliot Bay Books where I live right now do; and my friend Anju who ran the Toronto Women's Bookstore, when I posted, very tired and angry, about this convo, confirmed that they'd had a disability section since the 1980s and it was always one of their best-selling sections. I fought back, pulled the white crip guy (friend) card and was like "ELI CLARE HAS DISABILITY STUDIES / ACTIVISM ON THE BACK OF *BRILLIANT IMPERFECTION*, IF HE CAN DO IT SO CAN I, I DO NOT WANT MY BOOK NEXT TO THE GOUT CURES."[4] We compromised on "Disability Studies / Queer Studies." Dustin Gibson and Dana Bishop-Root in collaboration with Bekezela Mguni, in their brilliant essay, "Creating a Space for Disability Justice in the Library"[5] write about disability justice as a place where we can kick it, a place where we belong, talking about their work upending the Dewey Decimal system and placing Leroy Moore and Audre Lorde's books next to each other in the DJ section of their local Black neighborhood's public library in Pittsburgh.

If you don't see your crip life in writing, you can't imagine a crip life to be. If there is no Black brown queer trans slut disabled poetics, nonfiction, journalism, essays, crip literary forms, how the fuck will you write them or write your life? With difficulty. I thought of *Care Work* as a community in your pocket when you have no crip friends or you are all alone, as so often we are.

Crip poetry is the piece of driftwood I grabbed that I hung on to and that stopped me from going under, this pandemic two years when everyone died, my best most needed beloveds, the ones the world needed the most. By crip poetry I mean the crip poetry and writing I read, PDF online zines, and X (formerly Twitter), and more and more and more books and blogs and Instagrams we made with all our world-changing crip literary labor. But I mean writing it to make meaning out of the rage and empty, the crip bitter and fried of our friends being stolen from us.

We are possibility model and we also write to refuse erasure, to capture all these tiny everyday moments of disabled life, love, grief, and resistance that abled world tries its damndest to wash away. And writing those crip worlds creates new possibilities.

Every line I write is a nocked arrow, the string pulled back, the x of release, the deep cunt feeling of yes as it hits the mark, as it goes farther than we have before, to the place we knew that we needed named.

No more and no less.

Casual.

Notes

1. Stacey Park Milbern was a Korean and white queer disabled Southern writer, poet, organizer, and disability justice movement worker who created millions of incredible disability justice initiatives, friendships, and care initiatives in her lifetime. She died on her thirty-third birthday, on May 19, 2020, in part because of ableist medical gatekeeping. To learn more about her work, writing, and life, check out the #StaceyTaughtUS syllabus at https://disabilityvisibilityproject.com/2020/05/23/staceytaughtus-syllabus-work-by-stacey-milbern-park/.

2. Sick and disabled queer and trans people of color.

3. Leah Lakshmi Piepzna-Samarasinha, *Care Work: Dreaming Disability Justice* (Vancouver: Arsenal Pulp Press, 2018).

4. Eli Clare, *Brilliant Imperfection: Grappling with Cure* (Durham: Duke University Press, 2017).

5. "Creating a Space for Disability Justice in the Library," https://www.dustinpgibson.com/offerings/2019/2/25/collecting-a-home-for-disability-justice-in-the-library, accessed 1/20/22.

I know crips live here

Leah Lakshmi Piepzna-Samarasinha

I know crips live here. So many couches and blanket throws.

I know crips live here. A bathroom filled with coconut oil, unscented conditioner and black soap.

I know crips live here. Your Humira and T on the bottom shelf of the fridge.

I know crips live here. Only house on the block with a homemade ramp, property standards are so mad.

I know crips live here. Big exhale at the shower chair, the slip pads and the air purifier.

I know crips live here. I see all the things in reach around your mattress of glory.

I know crips live here. Straws and Poise pads and crosswords and weighted blankets and stim toys.

I know crips live here. You've been home for a couple days. A week. That's the imprint of your ass in the couch surrounded by empty bags of food and the Advil and the heating pad.

I know crips live here. 50-pound bag of epsom salts from the farm store, your painkiller display like an altar.

I know crips live here. I see your EBT card and your fought-for DSHS care attendant.

I know crips live here. Taught yourself to be an herbalist so you could afford to manage your pain.

I know crips live here. Everybody late.

I know crips live here. Your dogs, cats, and stuffed animals are part of your family.

I know crips live here. Your disabled parking placard a candle in the window.

I know crips live here.

Welcome
You are home.

(Inspired by Eli Clare's *"Interdependence,"* in *Brilliant Imperfection*)

Bad road

Leah Lakshmi Piepzna-Samarasinha

"my body is 40 miles of bad road"
—working class disabled saying

oh I know,
you mean well

but
when I say I hurt   when I say some part of
my body hurts   and you say, *oh, did you do something?*

I hear   *what did you do?*   As in, it's your fault,
there's cause and effect and there's a simple
story, and if a + b = c, we can fix it

But there's no simple story in this body.
She falls apart whenever she feels like it,
which is often. She doesn't feel like going to
work or up and down three flights of stairs, and she'll tell you all about it.
She can smell the weather.
She got a lot of stories
and just like her mama did at slam church two decades ago,
she spits them out my kneecap like a gun with chaotic
yet accurate aim.
They are forty miles of perfect bad road
all bumps and potholes that could take out your wheel.
You gotta know how to drive it.
You gotta not be too worried about breaking your car
(because they're already broke   too)

I mean, I could tell you, everything happened! I could tell you my mama
molested me, I could tell you hers did too,
I could tell you we had to walk a long long way and get on a boat,
I could tell you I moved to Brooklyn for love, but there's a lot of stairs here too

I could read you the particulate matter of the air, that they're spraying for pesticides today
that I ran out of the fish oil that greases my knee into smoothing,
and I don't know if the CVS sells it here
—but does anyone want to hear all that?
The staying chant
the recitation
of everything that's happening in my body, and their body,
and the park's body, and on the subway huffing diesel and cigarettes

When you say, *it's just pain for no reason all the time, fibro, right?*
I say, close but no cigar!
I say I intimate with pain tides
This ground not steady! Why would it be?
As soon as I figure it out she flips me the bird
shape-shift hip transforms and says, *fuck you, you figure it out*
Sometimes the place where my mama threw me into the wall
at three talks to me and locks all my earth into cement.
Some days I don't know what day it is.
Some days my ass leaks tidal marsh, briny river
Some times everything   everything
everything   every thing
hurts
like a church bell
like a call to prayer
and it calls me to pray
this pain
breathing into any place that doesn't hurt
some of which only exists in my revolutionary imagination.
Sometimes you have to talk quiet.
Sometimes I can't talk at all.

Of course you don't believe that, but I feel the need to declare:
my life is worth living anyway
I love every jounce on this bad, bad
underfunded budget cut frost heave road
not everyone's car can make it down;
        you gotta know
        how to drive it
I love every car that just gave up in the mountain pass

every hubcap that fell off
every—yes—road not on any map
every rock and resisting
every reason this happened
every reason this body
is reason enough
for being.

Adaptive device

Leah Lakshmi Piepzna-Samarasinha

I want to give you a poem like an adaptive device
that will hold you just as good
as your favorite cane   bed sling   accessible toilet seat
rescue ventilator   cigarette   crushed pocket Xanax
blanket weight mad map sign

Give you the words that are what I know how to do
Give you the words that will take meaning, make language
make a word house to hold you, open-doored and firm-roofed.
The steady tap tap thrum of your cane tip
The steady roll of the charged battery
of your chair, your brain, humming.

What does it mean to call a poem
an adaptive device? A piece of beautiful supportive tech
that puts in work to keep you alive?
Something your doctor will sneer at and never understand
you mean you just walk around with a cane all the time?
Something the newly crip say
I don't want to be, you know, pathetic, I just need a little help.

This poem will never be found in a packet of home care instructions.
This poem is not taught in med school.
This poem is not behind the counter at the pharmacy or OTC.

But if poetry is a means of telling the truth, June,
and poetry is as sturdy butterfly as the steady tap of my cane's dance,
then poetry is crip. Then truth is crip.
Then this poem be a crip hand to hold you.

This poem is short enough for even my memory to memory it!
This poem can be whispered or signed.

This poem unspools from a drooling lip
This poem can be tapped in and sung from augmented communication!
This poem spoken from gesture and nuance
This poem is nonverbal
This poem is crip kindness
This poem thinks you are desirable and love is coming
Is here. This poem will help you get on and off the subway.
This poem is a reason to live.

Ekiwah Adler Beléndez

ON WRITING "I BARGAINED FOR THIS WHEELCHAIR"

When I first started writing "I Bargained for This Wheelchair: Dream of a Pre-life," the first draft read something like this:

> In my last lifetime
> I danced so hard and fast
> God said—next time around
>
> I will give you a wheelchair. So you learn
> to stay put. And wait. And watch. And listen.

My poetry teacher interrupted me. He asked, "When has dancing been a legitimate cause for spiritual punishment? You don't exactly look like a convict. There is not enough remorse in your face for that one. Come up with something else. Revision means *to see the vision again.*"

Revising that poem produced a big bang. A big bang that is still happening. The journey to be able to say, "I Bargained for This Wheelchair" and mean it, and to live up to the bargain.

Out of the explosion came this life, this book. A book that, like my life, is still writing itself—and is thankfully, nine years later, far from finished, far from final.

> We bargained
> for our wheelchairs.

So I began my revision. You can find the new version of that poem in my poetry book *Amor sobre ruedas* (Editorial Diecisiete, 2021). The book, oddly, was originally written in English as *Love on Wheels,* but found a place in my homeland first.

A new vision of the "reason" for my disability unfolded: I will attempt here to summarize the poem for the sake of clarity though I well know it is a literary crime that should be avoided. What makes poetry is what cannot be easily summed up. Nuance is its body and soul. Each body is so unique it cannot be replaced with any other. But here is a glimpse: In another lifetime a veiled woman asked me to dance with her. I danced so hard and fast from the heat of our joy, that first body went up in smoke. We joked I would have "more luck balancing myself with the strong third leg dangling from my loins." I was left with my second body. The body I have now "panting and exhausted from the spasms of my sheer pleasure."

By the end of the poem that veiled woman gives me a wheelchair to keep dancing. With an added gift: "poetry as a third body" to dance through time in this world and into the next.

> . . . a human woman?
> A Fairy? God herself in disguise?
> or my own crazy dream?
>
> I don't know now
> and I didn't know then. When she touched my hand
> there was no time to ponder
> on who and what. Utter elation
>
> filled us both. A fire was lit in my chest
> and my feet moved
> as fast as possible to keep up
> with her swift grace.

What matters to me is not to ponder on the spiritual, medical, or social reasons behind my disability but to reinvent and discover what it means to me. As free as possible from pity, self-indulgence, or flagellation and sacrifice. Poetry has allowed me to live by passion and love. To make music and fire out of my wheels.

*

While there are still men and women around the world who are viewed or view themselves as Eternal Children, incapable of having an active sexual life, a family of their own, or lucrative work simply because they have a disability—these highly personal poems cannot speak for myself alone.

Even though I have been graced with the best parents I could have hoped for and family who believes in the power of imagination—my self-pity once trapped me (and can trap me again) more than my wheelchair ever has. I know of others who have not been so lucky. Their disabilities make them scapegoats for verbal and physical violence and solitary confinement.

We fight for physical accessibility, something that in Mexico is barely beginning to exist. But accessibility must not only concern itself with physical access to buildings. It must also promote imaginative access to spiritual exuberance (which needs no ramps for us to enter).

The Speed of Sound: Skydiving from one life to another

Ekiwah Adler Beléndez

Felix Baumgartner is an Austrian skydiver and daredevil who jumped from a helium balloon in the stratosphere on October 14, 2012, descending an estimated twenty-four miles at tremendous speed and landing in New Mexico. https://en.wikipedia.org/wiki/Felix_Baumgartner

As I wake up next to her
Baumgartner skydives
from the edge of space
faster than the speed of sound

and sees the face of the earth
staring back at him—

(I feel our love should be
the broadcasted achievement
of the virtually impossible.)

I have fallen in love.
I want to tell the world
just how hard and far
I have fallen for her

But as she
uncurls from sleep
her eyes still full
of dew and morning
she doesn't say a word.

In silence I praise the sound
of her even breathing, the slow
and precarious peace of repetition

the nearly noiseless rose:
she as she opens again

the blazing days with their sharp demands
the nights in which we slip—so far back into our dreams
later we can't find each other
even in broad daylight.

La velocidad del sonido: Saltando de una vida a otra

Ekiwah Adler Beléndez
(translation by Kenia Cano)

"El 14 de octubre de 2012, el paracaidista austríaco de 43 años Felix Baumgartner se convertiría en la persona más famosa del mundo tras realizar un salto al vacío desde más de 39.000 metros y pasaría a la historia como el primer ser humano que supera la velocidad del sonido al alcanzar los 1.357 kms/hora, cuando la barrera sónica oscila sobre los 1.120 km/h".
—Begoña Villarrubia. Mundo Deportivo, 29-07-2016

Mientras despierto junto a ella,
Felix Baumgartner se lanza
desde el borde del espacio—más rápido
que la velocidad del sonido

y ve el rostro de la tierra
devolviéndole la mirada.

(Siento que nuestro amor
debería ser el éxito masivo
de una misión imposible.)

I've fallen in love.
Quiero decirle
al mundo entero
lo duro y lejos que he caído
de amor por ella.

Pero mientras ella
se desenrosca del sueño, sus ojos todavía cerrados
llenos del rocío triste de la mañana,
no me dice ni una sola palabra.

En silencio alabo el sonido
de su respiración, la lenta y precaria
paz de lo que se repite, la apenas audible rosa,
pliegue por pliegue abriéndose de nuevo,

los días deslumbrantes
con sus agudas demandas,

las noches en que caemos
tan hondo en nuestros sueños, que al despertar
no nos encontramos
ni a la luz del pleno día.

Falling into Truth

Ekiwah Adler Beléndez

A poem for our son

And who would ever be brave, or lonely, or free enough to ask?
—Tony Hoagland

When he is not busy hunting for criminals
he is Lucio Valentin, our son. Craving fruit
napping at midday, doing somersaults

on his bed, head hanging upside down
listening with acute ears
for the cars of the people he loves
way before they arrive.

He puts a hand over his face
lining up his fingers to hide.

Then stretches his arms
out to the sides
stiffly into the air. That's all it takes
to be in flight. I am the Joker

and he tosses a pillow at me
a hurling rectangular blade
aimed to defeat me.

I am on all fours
on the edge of the bed
and I fall.

Are you OK Pa?
Are you OK Apa?

Yes, I say as we catch
our breath again
and we keep playing.

So that's what it means
to follow a hero: to love a mask
and care to remember who we are
when one has finally fallen

and we must be brave, and lonely
and free enough to ask.

En verdad caer

Ekiwah Adler Beléndez
(translation by Kenia Cano)

Para nuestro hijo

¿Y quién sería valiente, o solitario,o lo suficientemente
libre como para preguntar?
—Tony Hoagland

Cuando no está ocupado atrapando villanos
es Lucio Valentín, nuestro hijo. Con antojos de fruta
y su siesta al mediodía, hace marometas
en su cama, su cabeza colgando bocabajo

distingue con oídos agudos
a los motores de los coches
de las personas que ama
mucho antes de su llegada.

Se cubre la cara con una mano
y alinea sus dedos
para esconderse.

Luego estira
los brazos a los lados
rígidamente en el aire. Eso es todo lo que necesita
para emprender el vuelo. Yo soy el Guasón

y me arroja una almohada
una navaja rectangular
destinada a derrotarme.

Estoy en cuatro patas
en el borde de la cama
y caigo.

¿Estás bien?
¿Estás bien Apa?

Sí, le digo.
Recuperamos el aliento
y seguimos jugando.

Así que eso significa
Seguir a un héroe: Amar a una máscara
y averiguar quiénes somos
cuando finalmente se cae

y tenemos que ser valientes y solitarios
y lo suficientemente libres
como para preguntar.

Jay Besemer

PERMEABLE

Both "eleven" and "where the loved ones go" emerged from my particular complex experience living as a queer, trans man with multiple chronic illnesses and a neurological alignment that includes but is not limited to probable undiagnosed autism. The intensity of my sensory experiences, and my difficulty processing the information they bring into my body, have led me since early childhood to seek "offsite" processing modes—writing and image-making—so that my everyday is less overwhelming, more tolerable. The constant adjustment to the porousness and vulnerability of my body-mind (to gratefully borrow Eli Clare's excellent term)[1] holds me open to the wonder I experience as I engage the world, and it provides the deep attention to detail and vivid sensation in my work regardless of genre.

"eleven" was sparked by a delicious experience I had when pausing by my garage door one day. I noticed that the brilliant green ivy lushly covering the brick walls of the garage had begun its sexual cycle. My attention was held by the rainlike sound of the ivy's pollen falling on its own leaves, and I found myself thinking about nonhuman time cycles. The ivy makes its own temporal context in response to its own bodily needs, its own relationship to the information it senses in its ongoing openness to the world around it. It has no reason to account for itself by human (artificial, capital-driven) time frames or schedules. Such things are irrelevant to it. Although that also makes it irrelevant to human-imposed systems (with serious consequences for its survival), this irrelevance or exclusion also holds a kind of protection. Ivy can't be held to human standards or expectations because it exists in a different mode. Those standards simply do not apply. In order to enter a relation with ivy, humans must learn from the ivy how to do so.

There is considerable overlap in the ways the ivy lives its time, and the ways I live mine. I too have a permeability at the point of contact between my body (my senses) and the world around me, and I must constantly adjust my actions to the information I get from within my body, and the information given by what's around me. Permeability of this sort comes with a high level of risk, but there are also great rewards. Access to pleasure is empowered by my permeability. My sensitivity to pattern and color brings me a great deal of pleasure in my encounters with the world around me. I love the way my focus on tiny details—like the sound of falling ivy pollen—opens me to experiences of joy and wonder. I love the relief of entering the safety of my bed when I'm exhausted and in multiple kinds of pain. I love the ripples of deep comfort brought by my husband's hand stroking my hair during our bedtime routine. I love the way my senses can totally take over my awareness, even though this can also lead to dangerous levels of stimulation beyond my ability to process and discharge.

I can only speculate about pleasure in plants, of course. I'm not suggesting that my permeability is the same as an ivy's permeability. I definitely do not want to imply that the "natural" is better or more valid than the human-made, or to engage in any other reductive romanticisms about nonhuman life forms. I am **not** closer to the plant than to the human because I am disabled, autistic, trans, and queer. Rather, my point hinges on the earlier assertion that in order to enter a relation with ivy, a human must learn how to do that directly from the ivy. The moment by the garage door made me realize that, if others in my life want to engage with me, they must learn from me how that is most possible. I have been learning from plants for decades, including from this ivy. I was both delighted and humbled by the ivy's lesson, and the poem emerged from there.

"where the loved ones go" is a very different kind of piece, written as I attempted to care for my mother, who was then in the long process of dying of ovarian cancer. Though my own illnesses are serious and need constant care, my mother had established no working support in her immediate community, and I traveled the five hundred miles between our homes every few months to care for her in the limited way I could. During that five-year period, my life consisted of that travel and care work, the months of recovery between them when I returned to my home, and writing myself alive. (I can't think of any other way to put it.)

"where . . ." was written in desperation, during a time when my mother's cancer and its treatment had led to the failure of several of her vital organs. At the time of its writing, she was in a hospital in the city where I grew up, an hour from her house. I drove every day from that house to the hospital and back, so overwhelmed and exhausted by the strain (and my neglected needs) that everyday things like buying food for myself became hallucinatory, otherworldly, and dangerous experiences. "where the loved ones go" crystallizes and embodies the total destructiveness of being someone's sole support, while one's own needs go unmet, and in the absence of any support of one's own. The garden mentioned in the poem is an actual garden at the hospital where my mother was. I could never enter the hospital garden because the gate was always locked. I felt that to be a potent echo of my specific circumstances. Barred from nurture and solace, even from safe food and rest, I had nowhere to go. Despite being "smacked from [my] body" by the constant state of crisis, I was still obliged to take on and to process bodily damage. In that scenario I was not entitled to the hospital room, no matter how much I might have needed it. In the poem, this room stands in for the rest and medical care I deserved but was not given space or time to get. Instead, in my "own" room in my mother's house, I begged for just a little more time, swamped by night sweats. Some of the poem's emotional charge comes from my awareness that I could easily die before she did. I was trapped in a cycle I could not get out of without social and other consequences.

I could not be present for the month of in-home hospice care before my mother's death. From my bed, I struggled to hold my own against insistent demands that I explain and justify why I would not be coming back to join her care rota, or visit for the winter holidays she ultimately would not live to see. From my bed, I chose a person to hold power of attorney on her behalf and submitted the resulting paperwork in a confusion of PDFs and emails. After her death I arranged for her cremation from my bed, and conveyed my inability to organize or participate in any form of memorial service. In the minds of most of those who knew her, there was room for only one person with serious illness, and none of my needs could possibly justify my absence.

All of this was tangled in notions of gender role as well as ableism. My transness complicated matters in ways I'm still trying to untangle. The beginning of my transition had coincided with my mother's cancer diagnosis and treatment. She had asked me to hold off transitioning until after she had died, and I refused. I now know that if I hadn't refused I would not have lived, either. But many of my mother's friends shared her belief that I had done her unspeakable harm by proceeding with my transition. Whether they said anything overtly or not, I felt the disapproval and saw the curled-up lips, the hard scorn in their eyes. This constant tension pervaded the years of my attempt to care for her, and did not abate after her death. Although I was mostly addressed by my right pronoun and name both in person and over the phone, I had to constantly ask myself whether the expectation of self-sacrifice would have been as strong for a cis man, whether he was the only son or not. The people around her who knew of my previous life or knew me from before—and most did—did not hesitate to apply their opinions of trans people to their assessments of my social performance as a dutiful offspring.

My mother died in late 2018, and I turned a corner in both life and work. The poem "eleven" was written after her death, so between nine and eighteen months had passed from the composition of "where the loved ones go" to the writing of "eleven." There is a marked contrast between the spareness and simplicity of "eleven," and the mass of fragments (like gulps of air) in "where. . . ." This form came about on its own, rather than as a result of a preexisting plan to make a poem that looked a certain way; everything I wrote at that time took that stop-start form. For someone trying not to go under, these gasping fragments make sense. Cluttered, telegraphic gasps were all I felt I had breath and time to utter. I was all over the place, so the words I had use of were spread out all over the page. This form reflects the difficulty of sorting and processing the information, decisions, feelings, and experiences I had to take on at the time. Everything was happening at the same time, and I could only put it on the page in the same way. Though I did not set out to communicate to anyone but myself in this poem, readers might nevertheless experience some of my own sense of being overwhelmed as they navigate "where the loved ones go." By contrast, the slower pace and roomier structure of "eleven" leads readers more gently than the crowded utterances of the other piece. Although there is no narrative to follow downward through the linear structure of "eleven," the onslaught of words in all directions is now absent. There's more time to spend between ideas, sensations, observations. These can happen one at a time, not all at once. From the inescapable cycle of giving care while being refused care, to the recognition of a more sustainable cycle in the behavior of the ivy on the garage wall, these poems emerge from the embodied experiences of fifty-plus years of living, of art and writing practice through and with a trans, queer, neurodivergent and disabled body-mind.

Notes

1. This particular usage, "body-mind," comes from Eli Clare's book *Brilliant Imperfection: Grappling with Cure* (Duke University Press, 2017). In the introduction, page xvi, Clare addresses the definition of the term and his specific formulation of it, identifying several other related versions or variations in which the two parts of the term are presented in different order, without hyphen, or with a different type of separator.

eleven

Jay Besemer

the ivy has some things
to say
concerning permanence

you can stand right here
& feel the words fall
against your skin

get a sense of their
descending tone

think of your own
pet expressions
& how they work

the ivy argues softly
places its all
against the stacked
stones of the hand

& still it shakes
in terror of winter
just like a human

ivy with its round shoes
& leaf shields held
to the sky
proclaims itself alive
& necessary

questions the bland
human face

dreams itself a long
green dream & drops

that dream
again & again

a soft dry rain
murmuring

where the loved ones go

Jay Besemer

not my hospital   not my room
the days that run & drip   cheaply
dyed with pain   & third-rate color
those are mine   i spend them running
too   & sweat pours from me in a cascade
& fills my rental car   my hotel room
my bed in the lake house   & the lake
itself

                        & there is no fox in the garden
where the loved ones go   smacked
out of their own bodies   there is no
seed in the feeder   for the birds to
pray over   & my legs shake under the
load of two lives   two lives   where
only one should sit

i don't know what i'm meant to carry
& so i carry everything

later   in the 24-hour grocery   the haloes
around each item   blur into each other
like these days   & i hear the high shriek of my
own nerves   & choose what foods will least
damage me

                        something so obliquely wrong
inside   it has no name

i hold myself deep in the night
& whisper to it   *wait*   *more time*

Viktoria Valenzuela

MY FIBROMYALGIA, LIKE MY POETRY, IS A RESPONSE TO TRAUMA

In response to the world, I write poems. The world can be a pain-filled place. As a person with fibromyalgia, my nerve endings, muscles, and tendons are constantly overreacting as witness to injustices and trauma. I am hypersensitive even with nonpainful stimulation such as mothering, experiencing life changes, or even being alive in this miraculous space-time continuum. I am hypersensitive to all forms of energy and touch. The overload of sensations is soothed when I write poetry.

I suffer with the disability of fibromyalgia, a painful central sensitization syndrome that sometimes comes from stress, injury, or trauma. I also have post-traumatic stress disorder coupled with anxiety. While I would like to pinpoint how my fibromyalgia and trauma are connected, the truth is there has always been trauma affecting me. As an adult, I only know that the body aches I feel are widespread and never-ending. I have worked at healing from trauma in selective ways, and have had stronger or weaker days, in terms of energy. Yet there is always pain. Writing is a way to pull pain out of my body onto the page; the operation required to soothe these shifting symptoms.

This ever-shifting chronic pain and panic is a nepantla state of being. This is how I view my invisible disability. The nepantla state is a fluid third space, the middle or in-between space defined by Chicana feminist and theorist Gloria E. Anzaldúa in her book *Borderlands / La Frontera: The New Mestiza* (Aunt Lute Books, 1987). Fibromyalgia finds me in between, or in the fluid middle of a biological state or a psychological state. The liminal space between optimum able-bodied health and death, I suppose.

I've learned to live within this shifting liminal space, this invisible disability, unbroken in my wholeness. The wounds are invisible, the trauma reverberates in the form of fibromyalgia. This is how my body remembers trauma.

My body is not a waiting room until some future place of no pain or healing. This body, like all bodies, is held together with stardust particles inside skin. I gave birth with this body four times. I am protected by brown skin in this body. I thank the universe for the magical and elegant expression of light, energy transference, and fusion of existence. This is not to say that I should deny symptoms and pain to try to operate like an abled-bodied person after a restful moment. This life as a nepantlera, Chicana poeta, and fibromyalgia warrior means that I know, or have conociemento, that I must make art to get along in daily life. "Conociemento" is the concept coined or proposed by Anzaldúa to describe a person's inherent funds of knowledge. I listen to my body and the ways in which the symptoms of fibromyalgia manifest. My inherent funds of knowledge, my conociemento, seeks to expand awareness, with poetry as the work produced. I find myself in poetry. I exist in the poems as they express and share experience.

I can also write poems that acknowledge the privileges I hold. I am a Chicana and mother born in the United States. I am privileged to write poetry and respectfully advocate for undocumented mothers who are equally loving mothers. My body responds to her trauma and brings me to advocate for her as I would do for my own self. My poem is the voice calling for change with empathy in mind. We must all see undocumented people as we see ourselves because our differences do not actually matter when it comes to being a fellow human being.

Wholeness despite chronic pain, or invisible disability, is wellness. Writing poems is my proof that I am doing well, because these poems help me record, process, or reset my mind with my Chicana poeta perspective. Wellness is not the same for all people. What is lost when diagnosed with fibromyalgia is a state of total wellness and being shifted into a nepantla, in-between place. The able-bodied-world-at-large recognizes wellness as meaning not ill or disabled. I regard wellness based on how well my body works instead of how it outworks itself.

Sure, I might look fine on the outside, but fibromyalgia intensifies my pain and fatigue with each activity of my daily routine. Bearing witness, documenting, and writing poetry is a comforting connection between my experiences as a Chicana feminist, graduate student, wife, and mother of six children. I am compelled to record the history of now in a poem because if I didn't the trauma response of fibromyalgia would expand or deepen.

There have been weeks that I didn't leave my bed because I needed the rest. Resting my body matters because societal expectations have not been able to fully recognize that being productive is possible with accommodations for disabilities—visible or invisible. I am thankful for the energy I wake up with each day. I honor all that is possible with poems like "The Scent of a Battle," "Thank You to the Dust," and "Nightly News." These poem contributions are intending to hold space with vital honoring of beauty, of existence, in the history of now.

I will continue on as a nepantlera, a writer with disabilities, a Chicana M(other)Scholar and human rights activist offering poems as interconnection. Life is short and eventually a black hole will consume the galaxy, but in the space-time of a poem we can share a moment.

The Scent of a Battle

Viktoria Valenzuela

Understand that a black hole eats stars for breakfast;
We have only this moment to lie in sunshine.
You've given me an omelet with salsa y avocado folded inside.
Our son was planted between us in sunshine.
You soothe my fear of death in childbirth.
From the windows, we are bathed in sunshine.

You enter my pregnant desire
Delve deeper for the slit in sunshine.

The things we do with bare bodies, blood cannot strip away.
Our reverence for the other is sheathed in sunshine.

Thank You to the Dust

Viktoria Valenzuela

Thank you to the flowers of each milk-producing breast that made fat my born children. Thank you to the marigolds grown and set out for the two children miscarried in my youth. Thank you to two more daughters for holding space on this side. Thank you to the white butterflies and bees that kissed blessings into my body as I crossed but did not die. Thank you to all the mangoes in the summertime. Thank you to this journey, sweetened by honeyed fruit. Thank you to the dust of San Anto, heartily bitten into the darkest parts of my skin; so I never wear too thin, too ripe, or rip apart at the seams.

Nightly News

Viktoria Valenzuela

Her children
(Taken by I.C.E.) whom she may not see again
Resemble my children.

Her hair
(Tufts poking out in places) silky and black
Is pulled taut into a bun like mine.

Her skin
(From days in the sun) chapped
Is the same red-brown hue as mine.

Her hands
(Clasped in her lap) one handcuffed to the other,
Are wringing like mine. We ask again and again, what can we do?

Her real name
(The one our children call us), Momma,
Is screamed out every given night that baby is captive of a nightmare.

Osimiri Sprowal

A QUEERCRIP REFLECTION ON INTIMACY AND BOUNDARY BUILDING

My poem "Hearth" is a piece that I wrote while processing a bad separation I had from a queer platonic partner. Shortly after writing it, I had a conversation with another poet whom I sent the piece to, about how there isn't much visibility around Disabled people in partnerships with each other, even though the relationship in question was not romantic. I feel like the lines "there is an intimacy / between Disabled partners / I miss more than I miss you" really speak to what I was trying to articulate while feeling through those experiences.

Understanding that ableism holds Disabled people as undesirable as romantic partners, which is even more exacerbated for me as an Afro-Indigenous, Trans, and Queer person, I thought it was important to unpack the unique type of loss that comes from losing a partner who has similar disabilities to you. This person, who will not be named, was the first person I had ever gotten close to who mirrored a lot of parts of myself that I didn't really get to hold, and the loss of that in many ways was even bigger for me than the actual person in and of themselves. There is an inherent equivocation among many able-bodied people with being Disabled as sadness, or a point of pity, and I think the way that the grief is expressed is important, because it highlights how much love and community there is between Disabled people. Leaving not just the actual person, but the mirror of self and body I experienced through that partnership, is paramount to the piece. The agency to love oneself wholly is something Disabled folks are shown not to feel entitled to, and I think that through this relationship I was able to expand that for myself, and that is what I was afraid of losing. The symbolic loss of body, through deciding to no longer continue to tolerate what was unacceptable in our relationship, was hard.

Intimate partner abuse is something that also can be common for a lot of

Disabled people, speaking specifically for myself as a mobility-impaired person, because we often wind up physically dependent on other people. Having that type of interdependence was lovely, but also wound up becoming really codependent and toxic in many ways. I added "manifesto" to the subtitle here, because I feel like it's important to honor the fact that yes, even we as Disabled people, or people who may need or rely on a type of communal interdependency, do not have to tolerate bullshit in relationships. Ableism dictates to many of us that we are somehow disempowered, or otherwise lacking agency over our lives, and this poem for me definitely documents a moment where I said "Naw, I'm good" to things that I found unacceptable.

I hope this poem can inspire and push people to have stronger boundaries and create necessary parameters around what they actually want to create in life. As a Disabled person, I live in a world that is not designed for my body, but that doesn't mean that I don't get to create the parts of my life that I actually do have control over. In a word, this poem is about authority, and I hope that it pushes other Disabled folks to command their authority, both in and out of their interpersonal relationships. There's a reason why the extended metaphor is a house and not a doormat. We have control over who and what is in our sacred spaces, and we have the ability to receive and hold that which nourishes us. I get to decide who has and who does not have access to me, which is what makes "house" as an extended metaphor so important.

There are so many buildings that aren't made with my needs in mind, so why would I live in a reality where that extends to my emotional environment? I don't owe anyone that. If *I* am inaccessible? Then that is my right. Or: I don't have to be able to move my legs (that day) to kick someone to the curb.

Hearth: A QueerCrip Break-up Manifesto

Osimiri Sprowal

I don't know how to explain what we were
but I know there is a house full
of oaken floorboards missing
the kiss of our cane tips upon her cheek

I know there is a staircase
still dizzy from the waltz
of all our limbs crawling
into an unreachable bed

There is a snaggletooth grin
in the sound of us coming home
to a place we cannot enter alone

I know that I tried to love you
the way I climb up stairs
on all fours
with grit teeth
and magmen eyes
with the refusal to bow
before something
even when I'm on my knees

I am so glad I never had sex with you
but I know the look on your face
when I'm helping you onto a toilet
I know you remember mine

There is an intimacy
between Disabled partners
I miss that more than I miss you,
and I know why you said I was cruel
when I left you

I know I thought
that love
was like our bodies
that when it doesn't know
how to love itself
you love it harder

Let it throw tantrums
Let it go up in smoke

It's not my body's fault
it has to hurt to be alive.
I didn't see you as any different.

I thought if I let you go
it'd be the same as admitting
there's something wrong with
people that are built like us

what is a house, after all
If not a howling thing?

I know I held your limbs
because I wanted to learn
how to hold mine
soft
how to hold mine
tender

I wanted the luxury
of having a place to be weak
and this isn't something
any Black girl
gets to ask for
No matter how many
disabilities they have

I know that you got to be soft
And break
And I didn't and I still don't

Have the luxury of not being made of fire
For any part of me a person can see

I know the house still aches
and the poem whispers
and the boy
girl
it
writing it laughs
the way our bones
always laugh at us

With bitter
spastic cold
with the creaky joint
of a floorboard

The day I left
I told you if I loved you it didn't matter
I had to love myself more
I meant that

I don't believe
bodies like ours
can't heal from things
they shouldn't have to

I meant thank you for showing me
that I have always
the hearth,
not the wildfire

I meant to say I already know
how to keep myself warm

I meant to say I am so grateful
that houses have
doors

Molly McCully Brown and Susannah Nevison

A PLACE THAT'S OURS

The poems in this sequence are excerpted from a book-length collaboration that explores questions of identity and belonging in the aftermath of lifelong medical intervention. We were invested, both in these particular poems, and in the project as a whole, in enacting a conversation in which the lived experience of disability is communal as opposed to isolating, shared and discussed as opposed to explained. In the lyric landscape of this project, disability is—quite literally—rooted at the center, in trees "still stitched to their leaves," rather than relegated to the margins. And the language of surgery, rupture, and the violence of repair, of "men / and saws and knives," is the common vernacular rather than either jargon or translation.

The epistolary form of the poems engenders an immediate and intentional intimacy. The two speakers of the sequence, "M" and "S," who map roughly onto our own selves, address one another with both tenderness and familiarity. "Today I forgot" and "Today I started walking": They begin their letters in a way that suggests their dialogue is both constant and ongoing. "Today" has a shared meaning for both speakers, and they're familiar enough with each other's yesterdays to understand the fabric out of which a new day arises for each of them. In our friendship, which has often occurred at considerable geographic remove, we discovered a dynamic in which our bodies and experiences felt less alien than ever before, and in constructing our poetics of disability we were able to "recognize a place as ours," as cooperative, joyful, and innate.

For both of us, this kind of cooperation and co-making happens not just by virtue of epistolary exchange but at the level of language itself, the moments at which the voices in our poems cease to be singular and static and become instead a kind of chorus: converging, separating, and later merging again. Throughout the sequence, both speakers echo, adopt, and alter each other's images, so the hands that transform into nesting birds become "ones with holes cut / in their cores" and a wound that "was always / meant to be a window" yields a body "shot with light." Each poem's language both yields and transfigures the metaphors that follow, so that the reality the sequence reflects is greater than the sum of its parts: not simply two intersecting experiences, but lives transformed by their convergence, and a whole world built in the field between them, in the space where they collide.

As we constructed the collection, we were interested in repetition and refrain not only as an engine of collaboration, but as a way to trouble a linear sense of narrative. The echoing, circular nature of the poems, in which pieces of the body are removed and reinserted, and selves are disassembled and reformed from "what they left us with when it was over," is an argument with ableist notions of progress and investment in healing, resolution, and cure. It is, instead, an assertion of a wholeness that coexists with the fragment, and a communion that does not need either continuity or cure to thrive.

And yet every made thing takes a form. Our understanding of our particular disability poetics is wed to the lyric's endless capacity for reinvention, for music, for destabilization: The lyric form does not demand assimilation. In contrast with the sterile and clinical space that so often seeks to contain and restrain medicalized bodies, the lyric becomes the room in which these bodies reimagine themselves, in which they assert their own wildness, their own off-key song. While the epistolary form announces each voice, the speakers are free to perform the erasure and reconstitution of the body beyond the margins of an ableist world.

Each speaker knows that there are always forces at play that seek to remake a disabled body. Essential to our concept of disability poetics is integration of that duality: the push and pull between a body and its ableist environment, and the reimagining of a new space that still bears its marks.

"The woods, once, were something else," writes M to S. Everything holds other selves within it. The disabled body knows the weight of carrying them. We hope, in these poems, there's room to name them, share them, and set them down.

Dear M—

Molly McCully Brown and Susannah Nevison

Today I forgot I went looking
for my own face, the shape
of something I should love.
I watched the leaves
gather around my feet,
their small dead selves lighter
now, unselved. Perhaps this is
part of it, this willingness
to forget the way the world
has touched our bodies sharply,
so we refill ourselves with
someone else: someone who
doesn't start every time
she hears a distant saw, who doesn't
feel her legs as deadwood, rot.
I want to be the kind of woman
who has one story and it's a good one,
and it starts like this: once,
I was in the dark woods.
            Here's the version I know
instead: nothing ever happens
once. The woods are everywhere.
The woods are rife with men
and saws and knives.
The trees, once, were alive.

Dear S—

Molly McCully Brown and Susannah Nevison

Today I started walking where the trees were alive,
still stitched to their leaves, still humming, still houses
for musky warm and wild things who out-breathed all
the men and all their knives. And yes, the woods were dark,
but nothing ever happens once, and so they didn't stay
that way: the sun came up on the survivors
and there I was, somehow among their number, still
dragging the same legs, still finding buckshot caught
behind my tendons, braced for new machines
I might hear readying to work on all my flesh.
S, it turns out we can last a long time with our legs
bent, make it for miles crawling on our hands.
A callus forms, we grow a shell. In curling downward
it is easier to press our ears right to the ground,
hear that, beneath us both, where leaves and marrow
wear down and wear out, there's water running.
The woods, once, were something else.

Dear M—

Molly McCully Brown and Susannah Nevison

Our faces are beyond recognition
and there are so many ways
I've failed to see myself
in the world, failed
to see the world in me,
though I've folded the woods
and the river into my arms, my chest,
so that I might be wrecked again,
so that I might be made
into another thing
the world forgets. I don't think
we'll ever recognize a place
as ours, as built for us, unless
it's one we make from the ashes
of the-next-best-thing, a nest
that's shaped by all the birds
before us. Even the raft
wasn't made for us, but of us,
our bodies unable to carry
themselves but made to carry
everything else. When I open
my hands, I'm never surprised
by the birds they turn into, how
quick they are to take a thing
apart to see what holds it up.
Take a little string, some gauze,
a piece of bark. Whatever it is
we carry into each clearing,
let's hold it up and squint
until it turns into a face we know,

a house we've loved, a wrecked
and empty nest, a place the birds
made for someone else,
then left.

Dear S—

Molly McCully Brown and Susannah Nevison

The birds our hands become
are the ones with holes cut
in their cores so you can see
right through them to the world
they're leaving toward: little globe
of cloud, or rusted brush, or green held
steady there between their bones while
they go on building and unbuilding
their homes from what was there already,
unspooling the string and tearing through
the air like they are not torn through,
like what's a wound was always
meant to be a window. I open my hands
and watch them work until they're out of sight.
          In one clearing, we settle down for a night
with what the birds have left behind,
in another, our hands make an aperture
somebody sees the sky through.

Dear M—

Molly McCully Brown and Susannah Nevison

If what's a wound was always
meant to be a window, then say
my body's shot with light: say
it's me who looks, who
presses herself against the glassless
frame and waits for the riddled surfaces
to announce each version of the body
I've been, and the ones I think I'll become:
my mother's perfect face
that mine doesn't resemble, the idea
of a child I can't see, and so imagine
I might keep. Say it's me who
does the mapping: I name the river
and every gnarled tree, the places
that they reach: say I see
the whole of me blanch dry and white.
            Say home is a shard of bone I pull
from the riverbed, and say it's me
who cracks the earth to put it back.
The map is wrong. Someone else
shoots me through with light,
an X-ray a map I'm told is clear
and true, someone else cracks me
open too, names the earth, says
what shard comes out, what each
becomes, which piece goes back.

Dear S—

Molly McCully Brown and Susannah Nevison

At the bottom of the riverbed
the ground is dry as all the shards
of bone we buried and unburied there.
I puzzle skeletons together from
the bleached scraps we wrenched loose,
trying to make an animal of what
they left us with when it was over.
I know I'm glowing from the artificial
stars they pumped us bright with,
that the rivers in my wrists are running
violet before they calcify. I'm leaking light.
I stain the things I touch. I lie down
in what is just a canyon now, and
watching from above, they use my
growing constellations to map out
the world they've made: pin down
the north, my waning water, what's
worth saving, how a good war spreads.

Rachel Scoggins

THE MAGIC CONSORTIUM OF POETIC DISABLED LIVES

Essay in conversation with Naomi Ortiz

Naomi Ortiz: In your poem, "Guide to Magic Helium," what are you using magic helium as a metaphor for?

Rachel Scoggins: In the "real world" magic helium is marijuana. Even though marijuana has been legalized in some form, throughout most of the United States, it has a bad reputation. A lot of people see it as just another addictive drug! That is not true. Marijuana is a natural plant that helps a lot of people get through their everyday lives.

What motivated you to write this specific poem?

I wrote "Magic Helium" as a way to look at marijuana as a helpful medication, something that helps different people from every background with a wide range of issues such as pain, anxiety, depression, cancer, the list goes on. Marijuana helps me with pain but also with my anxiety.

I can go days or weeks in my room without talking to anyone. I won't even notice that I'm doing that. When I finally come out of "my box," I feel very nervous and like everyone is staring and judging me. With magic helium, the anxiety I feel floats away. I feel more confident to have a conversation with someone new. For me, there are fewer side effects with marijuana than there are with pills.

Before magic helium, if I had an anxiety filled day, I couldn't just come home and decompress and not stress about it. I would have conversations in my head, "Why did I say that! Everyone hates me now!" These conversations in my head would give me more reasons to just stay in "my box." It is very easy to get stuck in a box and not venture out into reality, 'cause honestly, reality is hard. With magic helium I soon realized, it really doesn't matter what other people think about me. At the end of day, it matters if I am good with myself.

Why did you write "Vivid Dreams"?

I've always had realistic dreams, even as a kid. They are often about someone that has passed away in my family. These dreams used to make me sad and even scared. Since I kept having them, especially after my sister passed away, I had to make a decision to not be scared of the realism. I looked into the meaning of dreams and figured out that there was a reason I was having them.

I began to use the opportunity to embrace these vivid dreams that my unconscious gave me. I'd remember all the details and the places where we went in the dream. Then I'd look up the things in my dreams for the symbolism. For example, water can be a big part of a dream. Water is about washing things away and renewal. I'd find answers for things going on in my real life. It is very helpful.

In "Vivid Dreams" some of the family members in the dream aren't alive, and in the dream, we were going back and forth between Arizona and Illinois. What was helpful was that I realized there is family in each place to support me.

What is your process for writing poetry?

A friend and I write poems for fun. We pick random words and use them in a poem.

With an intellectual disability, these prompts help me get started. When I wrote "Vivid Dreams," that day we picked the word "vivid" and I had no idea where to go with the poem. But that night I had a most amazing vivid dream with my sister and grandma who have both passed away and been gone for many years now. This dream, unlike other dreams, was so real that in the dream I had to tell myself that it was a dream. I felt like I was with my sister and my grandmother laughing, singing, and dancing. This dream will stay with me forever. The poem "Vivid Dreams" is a tribute to my grandparents and my sister Jenny.

Why is poetry by disabled people important in these times?

My disabilities have been a part of me my whole life. I remember the times that I was sad, angry, and frustrated, not just at myself, but at the world. At people who didn't understand me, how I fit in when I can't read or spell like everyone else. But I had a good support system that helped me see I could do poetry even if I can't spell the words. I knew what I wanted to say.

With poetry we say our truths. Writing gives us a way to share feelings we have. Feelings of defeat, sadness, sorrow, love, and hope. Our truths tell how it really is to be disabled in the world. Poetry gives us a way to tell our story, to say, "These things have hurt me, these things have helped me." It does it in a beautiful way and in a visual way, so other people can see it in their mind's eye. A lot of times people don't see disabled people like themselves. Disabled lives are just as human as everyone else's. We make mistakes, have trauma, and go through the human range just like everyone else.

Guide to Magic Helium

Rachel Scoggins

When consuming Magic Helium note that one's thoughts float above like a balloon. With one's head high on Magic Helium, one can see oneself talking in conversation. It will have the effect that one is sliding words down a thick white string. Even though this is all in one's head, one should hold on tightly to the string, so not to lose oneself in random thoughts far away from the conversation, knowing that the farther away the string gets from the body, the connection weakens and the Magic Helium may fade.

As defined by the Consortium of Rare Magic Elixirs: Magic Helium connects one into deep conversation. One must be deeply committed. Every word, phrase, and sentence must be taken in and carefully analyzed. Then the answers will come quickly, clearly, to the conversation that is taking place.

If one is taking Magic Helium alone, one must realize that conversation will come, you will just be alone talking to the television. What you learn, you may use later in real conversations.

Magic Helium is a recreational elixir so one can have deep conversations without pain. A professor from the Consortium of Magic Elixirs describes Magic Helium as a dance in a field of bright yellow sunflowers. It lets you float above the pain. When it is fading, it is like all the sunflowers are dying, the color is gone. So, it is recommended to use magic helium sparingly, so as not to forget about the pain altogether. The Magic Helium will let you dance with sunflowers but the pain will let you be in reality. Both are needed in life.

Thank you. I hope this guide to Magic Helium will help you in all your deep conversation needs.

Vivid Dreams

Rachel Scoggins

Dreams, they come to me like a movie in brand-new technicolor, bright and vibrant, as real as you could ever imagine . . .

Let me lay out a scene. The people and places are from my past, present, and I guess future . . . A drive through the Arizona mountains in a blue car with my sister and me in the back seat and my grandma driving. We stopped along the side of the road to watch a mariachi band play beautiful music.

We dance and sing.

My mom and dad join us. Then we watch the ocean waves at sunset.

I scratch my head, think out loud. Is this real? It feels real . . . It's something so real that you can feel everything . . .

The scene changes rapidly in my mind as I sleep.

I go from Arizona to the beach to my grandma's blue house in Illinois. In the living room is a triangular '60s style coffee table I had in my first apartment in Tucson . . . Why is this here? How? Strange moments like these pop up in my dreams. No explanation, no reason, it's just here . . . Then the scene changes to the backyard. I quickly forget about the table when I see the beautiful flowers throughout the yard. The memories of my past flood my dreams with colors of greens, purples, pinks, blues of summer.

There's an old barn with my grandpa's red and white truck in front of it. We sit back under the big old tree. My family and me.

Daniel Sluman

SUSPENDED DISABILITY AND THE IMPORTANCE OF DISABILITY POETRY

Unbeknownst to me, I started my journey into disabled identity at some point in 1997 or 1998, when I was eleven. During that time a previously latent gene, in combination with what science calls "unknown environmental factors," switched itself on. An enormous acceleration of cells resulted in a sarcoma: this tissue-like ball of white smoke on an X-ray that grew in my left femur and didn't react to any chemotherapy. One hip-level amputation and twenty-three years later, I see being a disabled poet as not only one of the things that keeps me living and learning new things about the world I inhabit but also as an important political act.

When I was thinking about this essay, I realized that while I have written about the technical details of my poetry before, I have never talked about why I write this poetry and what I hope it helps toward. Rather than tightening the focus closer into the mechanics of the work here, I have chosen to talk about why being a disabled writer is important to me, and why I think disability literature changes the world for the better.

Disability has always been a unique form of *othering*. Those of us who proudly embrace the identity have often spent years prior to that pushing against its borders and outright rejecting it. Many of us grew to hate the term because it is so often foisted upon us by others without our consent, and without any care for how it affects us. Disability is often a marker of value or worth assigned to us by a medical establishment that is only here for the cold clinical work of our biology, or it is assigned to us due to the physical or mental difference which the crowd often sees first in us, and often doesn't see much beyond. Because of this, and due to the repeated stigmatization and social isolation that is embedded in traditional narratives around anyone whose body-mind deviates from "normal,"it is a long road toward acceptance of disability as an identity.

While there is now a community of us who embrace and utilize our disability in all its wonderful complexity, the abled are in a unique position in that whether they know it or not, however much they push against the idea of lives like ours, they are always in a suspended state of disability themselves. Whether it's a slipped step that leads to a fall and a permanent need for mobility aids, emotional trauma that triggers an autoimmune disorder, or the aging process itself, all abled people will eventually become disabled. Circumstance and time will create needs in us all for the same access, care, and support that disabled people are currently, and have always been, fighting so hard to improve.

The mirage of ableness and bodily and mental performativity is such a delicate tissue of contradictory ideals and narratives that people will often go to great lengths to reject the true reality of suspended disability. To make peace with the fragility of ableness would require self-examination and a change in attitudes that would then compromise the ideals capitalism embeds in us and relies on us to repeat to others. Whether consciously or not, the work of the disabled writer helps dissolve this tissue of narratives and rhetoric by reflecting the reality of the actual variance in people's experience of ability and disability and the barriers that deny so many of us access.

Both of my poems included in the anthology here are little pieces of disability experience. In "my love is sponsored by the warmth of opiates," I wanted to recenter the experience of chronic pain and the need for long-term opioid use that many rely on. For too long, opioid use has been centered as an issue about drug policy and overdose, and the users of such drugs seen as addicts by default. These narratives have become so strong that it has affected medical legislation, and now many disabled people are left in pain because the way we talk about painkillers has been connected to recreational abuse.

I move from day to day with chronic pain, alongside the effects of medication, as does my partner, and my writing often doesn't move far outside these simple realities because I myself am not able to move outside them. For a long time, I didn't consider my work political because I don't use a didactic mode; instead, I find myself writing directly out of lived experience and circling often very domestic scenes. But just as is the case with feminist or queer poetics, when you are writing contrary to the dominant modes of living, the personal becomes politically charged regardless of intention or ideology—it simply has to.

Like a lot of my work, "& this is love" prominently features my partner and centers our relationship within the poem. Traditional notions of love have performative aspects which often aren't accessible or realistic for disabled people, but the lack of disability awareness means people often don't think about inter-abled relationships at all. Abled people in relationships often fail to consider the fact that suspended disability means they will at some point need to provide some form of care for their partner or receive care from them. Sex and love in our culture are heavily dependent on ideas around physical aesthetics, sexual performativity, and hetero-centric power dynamics. If there is something I have learned about relationships that I can impart in my poetry, it's that disability forces us to consider the actual needs we require from a partner, and how time and circumstance will almost certainly modify those needs.

Because *literature* itself is a kind of mirror of societal narratives and culture, when we write and publish poems that feature things like medication, back braces, and disabled love, it can only work to progress disability awareness. The more disability literature can inform readers about the way people are othered by disability and excluded by society the better, and the more that abled people realize they are themselves in a state of suspended disability, the more we can all work toward changing the ways the world isolates and pushes us to the margins.

my love is sponsored by the warmth of opiates

Daniel Sluman

that crack from foil packs
jammed in the pocket of my coat

hung over my braced back
as I bend to turn my face

to yours   the joints strain   the pills
spill through the blood to hush

the nerves   a damp towel thrown
over a pan-fire   & I can only love you

like this   the chemical theatrics that keep
a twenty-eight-year slow-motion

melodrama   from slipping
behind the curtain

& this is love

Daniel Sluman

she goes limp & falls into my arms
like an important-looking letter
I help her to the bathroom

& sit the other side of the door
tearing nails between my teeth
clutching the phone like a safety rope

& this is love   how we live between
the side-effects of glittering pills
the wads of her dead hair snarled

in the plug-hole   the morning cigarette
that shakes in her hand before her kiss
once again says *whateverhappens*   I ring

the ambulance when her head smacks
the floor   & in the crazed flutter of her lids
I see a million lives for us   each one perfect

2

LANGUAGE

Shahd Alshammari

NAVIGATING A HIJACKED BODY WITH TWO TONGUES

I always knew I wanted to become a writer. There's nothing unique about this statement, and I think most writers will attest to this desire becoming the recurring thought they have. Except for me, my relationship with the English language is complicated and yet tied to my experience with disability. I was born to a Palestinian mother and a Kuwaiti (Bedouin) father. Language was always two dialects, two states of being. I spoke different dialects at home and later was schooled in an American curriculum, where English was the language of instruction and we were aware that bilingualism was a must. As I began to read and write in English, my Arabic (first language) began to suffer. I would think in Arabic (but also in English) and write in English. Most of the time, thinking in Arabic came first. I would later translate the feeling to English.

When I was diagnosed with multiple sclerosis (MS), I struggled to speak either language. The act of speech became a tiresome task—even when I did speak, I wasn't understood, as my speech slurred, my voice was inaudible, and getting the words out was an exhausting process. I began to write instead, in short sentences, quick, to the point, and with the desired outcome of feeling out of breath—the way I felt when writing the words. Poetry, for me, became a gasp, a sigh, a short interruption in breath. Breathing and speaking were too interconnected, and I thought about how sometimes speech requires too much. I remembered the words of my high school English teacher who would urge me to "Say little, but say it well." What was the obsession with speech, long paragraphs of prose, when we could just say little? Poetry became the method of choice when writing about pain, loss, and my complicated relationship with MS.

My body would oscillate between periods of relapses, remission-free months and years, and I would almost forget that I was disabled—until I fell, forgot words, or struggled with my voice. Throughout it all, I would write about the anger swelling up inside of me. I wasn't angry at the disability; I was angry at the cultural stigmatization of disabled people. I would feel uncomfortable and shamed under the ableist gaze (which I didn't recognize was ableist until I learned the term in graduate school). I felt the words could only come out in short phrases, adjectives, and gaps in speech. Poetry was the place I could attempt to grasp language through shaking hands. Writing in English sometimes offered a distance from my body, allowing me to express feelings of insecurity, shame, anger, and grief. The words would go on paper, leaving my body and psyche. Once they were written, I could breathe again.

Arab disability studies is not a field. I am an Arab disabled scholar working within disability studies and still learning new terms and ideologies of ableism and disability discourse. I don't always find it easy to transfer Western disability studies to my lived experience of disability, but I do attempt to write my voice into Western scholarship on disability. I use English to write because that's the language I grew up learning to use as a tool to express myself. I do not live in exile, nor has my language been colonized, and I am not altogether estranged from the Arabic language. If Arabic is my mother tongue, then English is my stepmother, not the evil kind, but rather the one that helps me navigate complex feelings and experiences.

Disability poetry is the place I find myself engaging when I need to be away from academia and disability scholarship, where I need to feel connected to the emotions within my body, and where I need to speak freely, without worrying about harsh expectations from readers. Disability poetry, for me, is poetry that is uncontested; it is free in its depiction of bodies, experiences, and provides insight into what it means to be human and alive. It is the place that I can "say little" and yet attempt to capture tremors of my body, social injustices and inequalities, and allow poetry to speak freely. But it is not just that—disability poetry is an experience that is visceral. I narrate my body and its intricacies, navigations, interruptions, and usually end my poems with the same discomfort I feel when facing ableism in society. Both poems offered in this anthology consider ableism and the way it is presented in social and intimate settings. At times, I barely notice ableist comments and interactions, as I have become so desensitized to them. But, when I pause, when I reflect, I realize that this whole interaction can be summed up in a few sentences, in an expressive poem. When I write disability poetry, I invoke moments of oppression, discrimination, and ableism in everyday life. Only disabled poetry offers me this place of reclaiming my voice in instances where I am silenced and brushed aside. It is the place I get to rewrite the moment, the interaction, and the injustices.

Public Disgrace

Shahd Alshammari

My fingers fumbled,
I just couldn't do it.
How complicated can it be?
Does it need skill?
Heavy fingers struggled with my buttons,
And the zipper just wouldn't cooperate.
Public bathrooms and failing hands,
I'd have to swallow my pride.
I called you for help,
and everyone in the bathroom stall giggled.

Meaninglessness

Shahd Alshammari

A word in a sacred text,
        I hold the book carefully, afraid the pages will fall apart,
this body crumbles as you probe it,
        no masochism here, save for love.
You are the word, the antidote to the pain,
        Language has no words to describe dismembered bodies, banished from love.
Literary critics, always finding meaning,
        making sense of the nonsense of it all.
Months later there's just me and the syllable and the syllabi
        I can pour my coffee and I can teach,
lungs letting go.
        But how am I to train my body to fill your shoes?

David James "DJ" Savarese

SQUAWKING JOY AND MAYHEM

How does one "hear in red" or "see in wet"? Well, it helps to have synesthesia as I do. Synesthesia, scientists are now saying, is much more common among autistics than among nonautistics, and as Donna Williams once wrote, "Autistics live in the sensory."[1] By that she meant the senses have more autonomy. They're like free-range chickens, not at all cooped up, not standardized or mass produced. They have a life of their own. They dart this way and that across the yard, squawking joy and, yes, mayhem.

In "Swoon," I try to capture the two-sidedness of the sensory in autism: the way it both delights and sometimes defeats me. The neurodiversity movement encourages us to respect difference, but often that respect is just a subtle form of pity. And so, in this poem I remind typical people that their prized sense of normalcy comes at a cost. Do you want to be an accountant or an artist? Do you want your eyes to sleep alone, or do you want them to have company and one day maybe even marry your nose? Life should be a wedding, not a bankruptcy hearing.

One problem with staring—and people love to stare at me as I "make strange noises" and "do odd things"—is that it presumes to know my inner life. From a distance, strangers pass judgment without asking a single question. Weird on the outside, barren on the inside, so they believe. And yet, my body is like Fort Knox: so much gold inside! And it doesn't even need guards because most people just walk on by.

In my Peabody Award–winning documentary *Deej,* which I wrote, starred in, and coproduced, I struggled with the mode of realism or cinema verité.[2] The camera seemed to be no different from the ableist strangers who gawked at me in public. My nonautistic coproducer thought that it simply and faithfully captured my every move. He couldn't appreciate how the lens itself was contaminated. The real—or reel—was a freak show. I thus insisted that the reelistic story be interrupted periodically by my poems and that the visuals for these poems depart dramatically from the dominant mode.

I worked with oil paint animator Em Cooper to give viewers access to my inner life. Together, words, music, and painting danced synesthetically and ekphrastically across all manner of categorical borders. The poem "Swoon" appears at the beginning and sets the tone. Viewers must reconcile the insider and outsider views of autism. They must inhabit the swirling, swooning world of the sensory. Disability doesn't so much become ability as refuse the terms and binary altogether. Said another way, art behaves interdependently. Neither poetry nor painting is allowed to be an individual, and realism reinvents itself.

For this reason, I am tremendously interested in ekphrastic poetry—in relationship. "The Librarian in the Trees" is modeled on a poem by Eduardo Corral, who has written a lot of poetry about art. I loved the way that Corral numbered the lines in his poem. The numbers suggest a kind of logical progression, and yet the movement from one line to the next is anything but logical or orderly. Paratactic leaps abound. Moreover, the poem behaves almost like a villanelle, circling back and repeating things.

When I happened upon a drawing by ten-year-old David Barth called "Vogels," which features hundreds and hundreds of birds all crammed onto the canvas, I knew I had to write about it. Barth, who is autistic, creates a kind of mischievous aviary, a teeming metropolis of wings. The medical profession would call his love of birds a "restricted interest" and immediately pathologize it. Yet what is perseveration but commitment, devotion? Elsewhere I term this "the eye in its pew."

At one point in the poem, I reference an autistic savant named Nadia who lost her talent for drawing when she learned to speak. "At three she had rivaled Vermeer," I write. I ask the reader to say a prayer for David because like me he lives in a world that demands conformity. Will he lose his way of looking? Will he be spared behavior therapy? Encouraged to be himself?

This poem appears in my ekphrastic chapbook, *A Doorknob for the Eye.*[3] In that collection I say that my parents dragged me into literacy, and I lost my native eye. I lost my penchant for astonishing detail—a level of detail and patterning that nonautistics have difficulty appreciating. As a sort of expat, "I now live abroad in language . . . ," I lamented. "When I type, my fingers speak with an accent." At the time, I feared that literacy had alienated me from my fellow autistics who remained profoundly visual. But as I wrote these poems, I came to realize that what I see is distinctly not what nonautistics see. And anyway, I can meet my visual friends in ekphrastic poetry. We need not all be the same. Indeed, we are *not* the same.

I still haven't learned how to speak fluently, but I am making progress. My poem "Tongue" recounts the sense of alienation I often feel when I'm around speaking people. Their mouths are like firehoses, spraying everything. Ungenerously, I might even compare them to an oppressive government's goons putting down a protest. There's little room for me if the jabberers don't slow down and let the speed of my typing dictate the pace of exchange. Disability justice can be as simple as making sure that everyone is essential, and by that I mean deferring to the needs of nonspeaking people. In "Tongue" I express my admiration for my friends' linguistic energy—the dining hall is a veritable derecho—but also my longing to speak, which is really a longing to more easily participate.

Critics focus commonly on a writer's "voice," which is an ableist trope unless we mean something closer to subvocalizing or silent speech, which most of us do when reading. To me a disability poetics combines silent speech, as a condition for participation, and attunement to the sensory. In a lyric poem, a poet whispers intimately to the reader, who is technically alone. They bridge the divide between them in silence, which is anything but empty. In a medical context, the prefix "sub" means "under, below, less than normal, secondary, less than fully."[4] It encapsulates an entire history of oppressive judgment and exclusion. But as with the term "cripple," we can reclaim it. "Sub" means rebellious, underground, earthy. It plunges to new depths. Lyric poets are submariners of the body, the different body.

Notes

1. Donna Williams, *Autism and Sensing: The Unlost Instinct* (Jessica Kingsley, 1998), 17.

2. Robert Rooy, dir., *Deej* (Rooy Media and ITVS, 2017).

3. David James Savarese, *A Doorknob for the Eye* (Unrestricted Interest, 2017).

4. Definition of "sub": https://www.medicinenet.com/sub-/definition.htm

The Librarian in the Trees

David James "DJ" Savarese

after Eduardo Corral

1. Who needs water with so many wings?
2. A Dewey Decimal System for feathers.
3. The librarian in the trees says, "Quiet!"
4. "I felt an intimacy with [birds] . . . bordering on frenzy [that] must accompany my steps through life." —John James Audubon
5. Bird shit: a Malthusian catastrophe.
6. To go out on a limb.
7. I would like to be a pelican, I think, because penguins are much too theological.
8. With my eyes I scoop fish from the air.
9. Must love always be a form of taxidermy?
10. Audubon tied yarn to the legs of the Eastern Phoebe and thereby discovered that it nested in the same place every year.
11. Ornithologists call this bird banding.
12. I call it autism, or as the experts like to say dismissively *perseveration.*
13. Let us persevere with detail.
14. The yellow beak, the red beak, the brown beak, the black beak.
15. With my eyes I scoop fish from the air.
16. The world is not a zoo.
17. Nor is it an aviary.
18. Nor a dictionary.
19. When Nadia, an autistic savant, learned to speak, she lost her drawing skills.
20. At three she had rivaled Vermeer.
21. Does diversity have a call number?
22. The librarian in the trees says, "Quiet!"
23. To go out on a limb.
24. No duckling is ever ugly.
25. Say a prayer for David.
26. In autism categories do not wish to rule the world.
27. Rather, they attend; they procreate.
28. Like rabbits.

Swoon

David James "DJ" Savarese

The ear that hears the cardinal
hears in red;

the eye that spots the salmon
sees in wet.

My senses always fall in love:
they spin, swoon;

they lose themselves in one
another's arms.

Your senses live alone
like bachelors,

like bitter, slanted rhymes whose
marriage is a sham.

They greet the world the way accountants
greet their books.

I tire of such mastery. And yet, my senses
often fail

to let me do the simplest things,
like walk outside.

Invariably, the sun invades
my ears

and terrifies my feet—the angular
assault of Heaven's

heavy-metal chords.
I cannot hear

to see, cannot see to move.
And so I cling,

as on a listing ship at night,
to the stair-rail.

Tongue

David James "DJ" Savarese

In the landscape of the mouth,
a pinwheel of sound

like a wind farm
corralling the air, carving

its silky syllables. I watch
my friends talking

at the dining hall: so many pinwheels
turning all at once—

a fricative parade, the fire trucks
of emotion blaring

their horns . . .
What sonorous insinuations!

The long vowel of the social
envelops them.

My tongue neither turns nor twirls.
Upright and eager, it stands,

a rusted turbine dismayed
by the wind.

torrin a. greathouse

POEMS WITH BODIES LIKE MINE

Much of my work is concerned with reckoning with, and reconciling, the many ways my body occupies space in the world. With how I locate myself within a society that is, most often, hostile to bodies like mine—queer, trans, and disabled. This—as many disabled poets know—is far from an easy task. So, I've searched for texts and frameworks which could, recursively, serve as a cypher for understanding myself as both subject and object of my craft; the critical work of Robert McRuer is one such cypher.

In his 2006 book, *Crip Theory: Cultural Signs of Queerness and Disability*, McRuer builds from Eve Sedgewick's definition of queerness, writing that, like queerness, "we might say that disability refers to the open mesh of possibilities, gaps, overlaps, dissonances and resonances, lapses and excesses of meaning when the constituent elements of bodily, mental, or behavioral functioning aren't made (or *can't be* made) to signify monolithically."[1] These overlaps, gaps, and dissonances, but most of all "excesses of meaning," are a tactile thing. A felt presence, beyond language, which I hold in my body, my mind, my memory. And since reading McRuer's words, this framing has served as an instruction for both understanding what I had already written and for guiding my future work.

My poems frequently serve as attempts to render—textually and formally—these spaces in which my body cannot be made to signify monolithically, or even legibly (to a cis-abled audience). At their core, the pieces included in this volume are interested in the social dissonance created by my disability and my queerness, as well as how these come together in overlap and excess. They explore the ways in which my body and experiences are medicalized in parallel ways, and how these understandings of my body intersect. How transness can be weaponized to gatekeep medical access, or how disability produces conditions from which the performance of expected feminine rituals becomes impossible.

Formally, I've long been obsessed with what it means—when so much of our received vocabulary of poetic craft centers the metaphorization of the body—to create bodies like my own. I want the poem with a fractured body, a jagged body, a body which teeters threatening collapse, the poem which mimics the recursive and fallible structures of my memory. I want the kinds of poems which court failure in the same way my body does. In this pursuit, Jim Ferris' essay, "The Enjambed Body: A Step Toward a Crippled Poetics," has served as a guide, leading me toward a poetic line which strains—like a muscle—against itself.[2] My poetic lines are not quite *muscular* in the sense that Carl Phillips writes of in his essay "Muscularity and Eros: On Syntax," though they are concerned with the interchange of pattern and its breaking.[3] Perhaps, Phillips's sense of muscularity places a higher degree of importance upon the pattern, while mine is more concerned with the act of breaking. If poems are small muscular things, then each muscle must be capable of tearing.

Notes

1. Robert McRuer, *Crip Theory: Cultural Signs of Queerness and Disability* (New York University Press, 2006), 156.

2. Jim Ferris, "The Enjambed Body: A Step Toward a Crippled Poetics," *The Georgia Review* 58, no. 2 (2004): 219–33.

3. Carl Phillips, "Muscularity and Eros: On Syntax," *At Length* magazine, http://atlengthmag.com/poetry/muscularity-and-eros-on-syntax/.

Weeds

torrin a. greathouse

The shower stall
my body's confessional
—here, I admit, I love
most what can be
removed from me.

I raise the heat
until my thighs
bloom with small
guilty hands, scrub
dead cells, till
new skin to soil.

Trace fingernails
across my skin, each
red ghost they leave
behind, a scalpel
daydream, plowed
& opened dirt.

False rain feeds a new
season's unexpected
blooms. I have learned
to call them weeds.

Meaning: *unwanted;*
invader; invasive
species. I'm taught
removal as "women's
work." Nothing's more
femme than empty

field, a place to bury
seed. I mean, when
my grandfather tells
me, *You will never*
be a woman, this is
a matter of geography,

my body not yet
hollowed. Valley
at the meeting
of my hips, more
forest than clearing.

Pelvis a strangulation
of bloodvine, thick
choke of branches.
I mean, what man
will want to conquer
skin as wilderness
as mine's become?

I mean, this back's
too broken to bend
in all the ways
a woman must.
O, but I have tried

so many methods
to tend this garden
of salted flesh. Gentle
scythe of a razor. Plucked
stems out by their root.

As a little girl, I watched
my grandmother tear
dandelions from the damp
loam & laugh, her breath
winging seeds into the air.

She knelt each day
until the labor curled
her palms inward,
made root balls
of her swollen joints.

Once, I asked her why
she pulled the weeds
each day, only to watch
them return? Why replace
their flower with another
when they are already
there? She told me:

This is women's work,
to remake the wild
into something
a man deems worthy
of keeping alive.

I feel most daughter
when I remember
this, when I make
myself bare despite
the snapped stem,
the split taproot

of me. I first learned
womanhood as
survival—a field,
or body, made
so blank there is no
-thing for a man
to sharpen his
imagination against.

But even when I drenched
the field of my thighs in
a litany of poisons, still

each bud unclenched
its tiny golden fist
as if to say:

We were your first teachers.
Even in the harshest season,
we survive. We bloom forever
where we are told we don't belong.

Abecedarian Requiring Further Examination Before a Diagnosis Can Be Determined

torrin a. greathouse

Antonym for me a medical
book. Replace all the punctuation—
commas, periods, semicolons—with question marks.
Diagnosis is just apotheosis with sharper
edges. New name for a myth already lived in.
For the sake of *thoroughness*, I have
given until my veins cratered. Tests administered for:
HIV, cirrhosis, glucose, cancer, creatine, albumin, iron, platelets.
I've slept for days, wired to machines. Had my piss filtered for stray proteins
just to be safe. Still, inside my body—
kingdom with poisoned wells. I want anything but an elegy
lining my bones. I just want to be a question this body can answer.
My new doctor writes one referral, then another, still
no guesses. A man in a scowl & lab coat
offers yoga, more painkillers. Suggests
PTSD could be the cause—of chronic pain, my limp, of migraines,
quickened pulse & blood-glittered coughs, of seizures
rattling me inside my skin—O,
syndrome of my perfect & unbroken
transgender arm. They checked my hormones too. Yes.
Unfathomable—a suffering I did not choose. Must be gender, this
vacancy my body makes of its own flesh. How I vanish from myself.
We search for a beginning to this story & find only a history of breakage
X-rays cannot explain. Some girls are not made, but spring from the dirt:
yearling tree already scarred from its branch's severance.
Zygote of red clay that rain washes into a river of blood.

That's So Lame

torrin a. greathouse

He says when the bus is late, when the TV
show is canceled, when a fascist is elected,
when the WiFi's bad. *That's so lame!* I say
rubbernecking my own body in the bath
-room mirror. See, every time *lame* comes
out a mouth it doesn't belong in, my cane
hand itches, my bum knee cracks, my tongue's
limp gets worse. Some days it's so bedridden
in the bottom of my jaw, it can't stand up
for itself. Fumbles a *fuck you,* trips over its
own etymology, when all I want to ask is, *Why
do you keep dragging my body into this?* When
I want to ask, *Did you know how this slur
feathered its way into language? By way of lame
duck, whose own wings sever it from the flock
& make it perfect prey.* I want to ask, *How long
have you been naming us by our dead? Baby
-booked your broken from the textbooks of our
anatomy?* A car limped along the freeway,
a child crippled by their mother's baleful stare.
Before I could accept this body's fractures,
I had to unlearn *lame* as the first breath of
lament. I'm still learning not to let a stranger speak
me into a funeral, an elegy in orthodox slang.
My dad used to tell me this old riddle: What
value is there in a lame horse that cannot gallop?

A bullet & whatever a butcher can make of it.

Essay Fragment: Economic Model of Disability

torrin a. greathouse

How do you calculate   in hard mathematics
the value of a ~~disabled~~ body?   The body which reduces

like a fraction[1]   to an object/icon   of pity?
[In physics] *Work* is defined   as the degree to which

an object[2] is affected   by an applied force[3]
& is not defined by effort   exerted toward a task.

Ex. Two birds   [of equal weight]
fly [at equal velocity]   toward two windows.

If one bird shatters its neck[4]   & one the window
the first bird[5]   has achieved a net work of zero.

Consider the ~~disabled~~ body.[6]   Consider its potential
for work: if *force* is defined [in part] by *mass*[7]

how much weight[8]   can the ~~disabled~~ body exert
[on society]   before the net worth is zero?

---

[1]Some portion < human.
[2]Or body.
[3]Or body.
[4]Spine collapsing like an equation.
[5]Still alive, beak loamy with blood.
[6]Not unlike the bird—malfunction of anatomy.
[7]$F=MA$.
[8]Read: burden.

Jessica Stokes

ALL THE FLOORS I KNOW TOO WELL FROM TRYING NOT TO TRIP ARE ONE THICK MEMORY

"Simplify, simplify, simplify," my poetry professor said to me one day in office hours. His tall frame was hunched forward and the tendons in his neck bulged with each repetition, imploring me to listen this time. He was echoing the hopefully ironic phrasing of Henry David Thoreau, but he was doing so without irony. My poetry, he made clear, was too specific, too detailed, too unwieldy, too unique to my disabled body. No one could empathize. "All good poetry is at least stretching toward the universal," he reminded me. Each of my Achilles tendons, the ones doctors had punctured in my childhood with three small holes apiece, had tightened again with age; I would not be standing on my tippy-toes anytime soon to stretch toward the stars or the rest of the universe.

A few months later, the same poetry professor went on to assign his workshop students eight books of poetry to read for the winter semester. He thought reading the "greats" would greatly improve our own writing and help us learn how to simplify and universalize our poetry. All but one of the assigned "greats" were men. All of them were white. I came to understand the coded meaning of the word "universal."

But there were things in my everyday I wanted to be able to describe that made no sense in everyday language. As someone with neuropathy, I wanted to be able to articulate what numbness felt like to me, but all the available metaphors had someone else in mind. One could be comfortably numb. One could be numb in a way that leads to inaction or indifference. But the numbness of my body did not feel at all like that. Accidentally landing my nerve-damaged foot on a Lego didn't feel like nothing. Nor could I tell the specific origin of the pain, unlike most parents sharing a meme about the problem of playroom Legos on the internet. Numbness to me was a thousand feelings simultaneously, a realization of the overlaps between responses to extremes, and a synesthesia that experiences burns as frostbite, tickles as scrapes.

During that semester of "great" poets whose universal feelings were not accessible to me, I read voraciously in hopes of finding someone who might speak a language where numbness did not have a fixed, discursive meaning but was rooted in the materiality and particulars of the body. I wanted to write everyday objects, sensations, feelings I hadn't wholly felt on someone else's page. Submerged in poems by Eliot and Pound and oh so many others, I read sideways to poets angering Pound and Eliot. In imagist poet Amy Lowell's work I stumbled on poetry that refuses to hold everything. In describing some imagist poetry, she writes: "poetry should render particulars exactly and not deal in vague generalities, however magnificent and sonorous . . . we oppose the cosmic poet, who seems to us to shirk the real difficulties of his art."[1] Instead of his cosmos, in the poem "New Shoes" I write the floor of a mall: the silver Brannock and the round brown shoes atop that floor. Even as I attempt to stick to the specificity of a day at the mall, the poem loses focus, sliding through time as generational guilt and blunt metaphors blunt the narrator's precision. I trip then over another of Lowell's principles for poetry "that is hard and clear, never blurred nor indefinite."[2] Rather than making a hard and clear image, this poem leans through time and into a crip poetics, following the specificity of objects and sensations through the winding, blurring associations entangled with our memories of them.

And I kept reading toward crip poetics and through time. In reading Audre Lorde's *The Cancer Journals* nearly thirty-five years after it was published, I stumbled into her complication and specificity. When Lorde asks her oft repeated questions—"What are the words you do not yet have? What do you need to say? What are the tyrannies you swallow day by day and attempt to make your own, until you will sicken and die of them, still in silence?"—she does so from the materiality of her life.[3] While material feminist thinker Stacy Alaimo has posed Lorde's questions to her students in the past as if the language in them is just metaphor, she's also aware of their materiality: "Notwithstanding the potent metaphorical resonance of 'swallowing' tyranny, the swallowing—and the death that results—is also quite literal, since it alludes to the ingestion of carcinogenic foodstuffs."[4] Lorde's use of her day-to-day experiences with cancer to transform silence and to connect people at literal and metaphorical levels is why I am interested in the potentials of poetry in disability community.

As a white disabled person, I must labor with the hope of ending the tyrannies that make the experiences of white, ablebodyminded, middle/upper class, citizenship-having men appear universal. I labor on numb legs in round brown shoes or on wheels. I labor with others who know numbness does not mean inaction or indifference to tyranny. I labor with those who know numbness is many and complicated. I labor with those who know feeling numb can be a small part of doing the work.

Notes

1. Amy Lowell, *Some Imagist Poets: An Anthology* (The Riverside Press, 1915.), vii.

2. Lowell, vii.

3. Audre Lorde, *The Cancer Journals* (Aunt Lute Books, 2006), 19.

4. Stacy Alaimo, Susan Kekman, eds., *Material Feminisms* (Indiana University Press, 2008), 86.

New Shoes

Jessica Stokes

after Amy Lowell's "Red Slippers"

Dad drove the Impala nervous to the mall.
Only plastic bags were left to leaf the trees.
Graybrown leftovers of snow coated the lot:
where Burlington sold coats to keep each winter
from the body and cars passed on black rubber
tracks to the ground and JCPenney propped red
heels in a window display, taking eyes off
people's feet. They were dreaming of stalactites,
lovers, direction, rockets, and purchased polish.
I was looking down, imagining shoving
my left foot on a silver Brannock, sliding
to find its size—slide—And Dad is mad he says
about how slowly I lace the thick tan shoes.
"Walk heel—toe, not thud—thud." And I am crying
about how the round brown shoes push on my toes.
And I don't understand how blunt the shoes are,
even as metaphors. And I don't fit in my father's.

Gala Thomas

HOLD IT AGAINST ME

On the River Walk in San Antonio, boats full of tourists motor downstream. Ducklings swim up and scatter when a bow threatens to cut into their raft. Current pushes them up against the cement that lines the river. These ducks have a different vantage point from the tourists on the boat. In my life as a brain-injured person, I was no longer skimming down the river in a perfect craft—I was pushed up against the side. Thought became more a tactile encounter than a vision from above.

A year and a half after the accident, I woke up from a dream of my dead aunt and wrote my first successful poem. In the dream sequence, she had reported her world to me in sudden openings. There was a burned bed. A dimly lit pathway to the sea. A series of murders disguised as endings. My stamina for seeing this world lasted only in flashbulbs.

The land grew arms out into the sea where it couldn't grow bridges. Touching the ocean became more important than restoring stability. My home has burned. I'm writing to you of my home. The house will not configure into a framework. The predictive slides backwards in priority, in favor of listening for flux.

My brain in its authentic broken state leaves an anti-fascist outline on the page. I hesitate to use the word broken: altered, damaged, affected by time and velocity . . . a product of physics. An organ that encounters the damaging world through the medium of its plasticity. There are certain habits of literature I will no longer reproduce. One is narrative's propaganda of fairness: the idea that a protagonist works for and achieves their outcome. Another is lyrical resolution. My mind flies and stitches. Rests and leaves. Whips around like the wind. Does not disclose. It's simply the poetry in every motion that matters. A departure station, with trains leaving, leaving, leaving. I no longer try to make my writing bend to known maps; I am configuring territory that runs by other orders. If there is someone in the driver's seat, they don't speak to me—but still a world is generated. Explorations and designations of this territory are up to the reader.

(My girlfriend and I are applying for an apartment, and there's some debate whether I am too crip to rent. The landlord finally agrees, but with me as a subtenant, to avoid any liability. As renters, my girlfriend's income privileges us. Too often crip lives are in limbo waiting for essential services, the valuation a shadow that chills our lives as it transits.)

The way light casts circles through the branches of some trees, crip poetics should be multicentric. There should be no waiting outside a circle of light. Ableist poetics elevate the privileged, but we strive to dismantle these models. What would an anti-exclusionary poetics look like? The answer came to me in the midst of a fight. When I'm scared, I go to my head: I talk. My girlfriend couldn't come up with the right thing to say. The bridge of understanding had been ruptured. I needed to be met. Our cat came over and sat on my chest. I sometimes feel like she understands both of us better than we understand each other. I realized I needed to love Caitlin more. That there was no understanding until I loved her.

As a reader, I have been guilty of saying, *This poet just isn't for me*. It's an act of exclusion. Remembering, as Sontag wrote—*Rules of taste enforce structures of power*, we have to ask ourselves who benefits from our love of certain aesthetics. Crip art has that radical proclivity to upset power structures. (Be cautious of any crip art institution without crips at the helm.) Elitist aesthetics groom the consumer to replicate privilege, but when you love you invoke the experience of beauty. Crip love, crip community, is anti-hegemonic. We are defying an aesthetics that says we don't deserve attention and resources. Most of all we are defying an order that demands our docility.

I'm thinking about how much agency we give each other when we make love. I'm thinking about that vulnerability implied in eros. And I'm thinking about how when I'm listening or reading, I'm subject to a kind of erotic delight. I do give the poet and artist power, they are within that circle of light. And within that circle of light, they have power to tell me how the world is, or to be that world, or to make that world inside me, all around me. I have stepped out of my centering, and I am now allowing them to center me within their worldview. The convenience in marginalization is that you never have to empathize. The risk in love is a loss of sequestering. Becoming crip for me was a kind of departure from my security. And certainly, the kind of departure that any real deep love guarantees. A ticket to estrangement from my privilege, and a ticket to a kind of catalytic empathy that would start troubling the edges of my comfort everywhere, everywhere.

from Change Hands

Gaia Thomas

V.

So as to go forward
sustain abrasions between one breast and the other
as if I am a landmass moving through ice
but this is a record that keeps going   the openness is evidence of a continued journey
there is no learning curve   there will be no future scars   only almost-to-the-bone
so that ice against costal cartilage is how it's done
and breath means pushing against frozen territory which is future
a body in time is movement and distance is a string of limited length
and the bone against ice is a type of endurance and the resistance
is a type of song and the song is the only meaningful thing about being human
it sounds like a violin   and the only way worth being
is to be pulled I want to be pulled across across across towed like planets
and moons the eclipse is a way to absorb energy like the silence
of a blinking traffic light between beats all your sleeps combined together
in a row each life ends like a strand of hair by breaking but I cannot say
the thread vanishes beneath the cloth because I am not here to repeat the things
we tell each other to comfort   to complete is a kind of leaving
with her head of empty shafts she walked in like an X-ray and read all the protected
souls like someone disarming a flight of passengers that would board her and could
not trnsform the man but could make him put his switchblade down and use
the restroom single file

VI.

Rules had the half-life of ripples
so that the encounter of one set with another would hasten the decay
as if the pink of the rose were hypercolor and responded to heat in the breath
the girl braided her hair into a ring and saved this relic in a wine bottle
her mud-encrusted velvet slipper on his desk   clock the speed of her river in helicopters
a green ribbon attaches the oak to the elm to the birch to the beech
across water we will participate in bondings like yeast
if letters could form words by mutual attraction
god will be there we will play the part
the garden will contain violets and impatiens   the lexicon will assign value and importance
this key will be called sharp will be called flat
use ice to kill the body in sections
a cool body against a warm body
before there was glass
insert dance in place of narrative
the memory of heat and light in the shell universe
and what gives and what pushes and what pushes and gives
open open open open open open open
enter
a procession of women holding candles up the mountain
without the women without what is called a woman with an absence at the heart of a life
with a life that is life on life life life

Ilya Kaminsky

READING CELAN IN UKRAINE

Delight, surprise, irritation, or puzzlement live in the speaker's tongue, teeth, cheekbones, the twitch of an eye. I watch it all because lipreading isn't just about lip movements. Only about 30 to 45 percent of English is visible on the lips. I watch your shoulders and hands, the way you hold your head. Don't shout at me, lipreading is easier in soft tones.

But some vowels are difficult to see.

Some lip-shapes look alike, for example "f" and "v."

When I read lips, I learn, despite the gaps between words, despite missed sounds, to make sense of language anew: as lips move, eye follows; the cloth of incomprehension shivers, tears up—I see through it.

But let me go to the beginning. How do I learn English?

*

When Father dies, we are living in our tiny immigrant apartment in Rochester, New York. I am reading lips in a new language. I catch only squeaks of words, a scrap, a speck of spit, a raised eyebrow. Lips of a rabbi at Father's funeral chanting in Hebrew I don't know. Lips of an undertaker speaking in English I don't know. Then, lips of Mother, whose Russian I do know, but her lips are not moving, we are alone with Father's absence in the room. But I can't have Mother find the papers with notes about Father's death I begin accumulating, or the crumpled drafts of Russian poems on our kitchen table, I can't do that to her. But I also can't seem to stop reaching for a pen. So English comes in: a language neither of us has. It is 1994, I am living for the first time with English in the same room.

This, I understand years later, is freedom.

*

When at the end of the day I find myself in front of the bookshelf, when my baffled eye is searching for a word in which it can find a home, I do not tend to look for the writers who exchange their native speech for English. No, the hand reaches for someone who can understand a deaf man's alienation from any spoken word.

Yes, at the end of the day, my hand reaches for a poet who remains inside his native speech—despite the gaps of uncertainty, despite misunderstandings, crisis, loss. A hand reaches for the book not because the author stays inside his native speech, but because he sees how to be alone with the language in the room—and not give in.

Paul Celan, the poet who stays.

He stays with his native language, stays with it despite the holes blown in its textures by historical avalanche, stays to "the point of claiming that language for himself alone"—a point in which the solitude of a man makes the language tilt over.

So, this:

> You are light: you will sleep through my spring till it's over.
> I am lighter:
> in front of strangers I sing.

*

What does Paul Celan have to do with lipreading?

Wait.

First, it is the 1980s and our mustached neighbor Petya buzzes our door. I cannot follow his hairy lips at all. Then I see: He is shouting something about water. In the winters of the 1980s, the city often turns off the hot water in our building.

Father sighs. It is time to go to the public bath on Proviantskaya Street, his lips say.

Mother puts together my bag: towels, soap, an apple.

We cross the snowed-in Tolstoy Square.

Outside the bathhouse, an old lady sells little brooms made out of branches: birch branches, oak branches.

Her lips move, giving directions, but I don't understand any of it.

This might need an explanation for American readers, too.

Russians do a peculiar thing in public baths: They use a gathering of branches called "venik" to beat themselves up, naked, while they chat with others.

You enter the bath and you see dozens of naked men beating themselves with little birch brooms under steaming hot water.

It's a national pastime.

The public bath is a place where a child of the 1980s sees that World War II has never ended.

One sees, for example, a parade of naked men with scars running from their chins to their hips.

On the soaped floors walk men with burned out backs, or with missing toes.

A child of the 1980s learns about War World II not from textbooks, but from a trip to Proviantskaya Street.

This is where I first see that people have numbers tattooed on their arms.

I do not yet know what these numbers mean.

In the soap bubbles are naked men with numbers tattooed on their arms, laughing. One of them gives my father an orange, and so Father teaches me how to peel an orange. The year is 1986 and I have never seen an orange before.

Behind us, men with tattooed arms are having a competition to see who can stay longer in the very hot sauna room: They are shouting encouragement to each other.

I catch a few words of Yiddish on their lips, not because I know the language, but because their lips move in the same way my mother's and grandmother's do when they say something they want to keep secret from Father and me.

This hot sauna room, my first orange, and the lips of naked men moving around Yiddish is the first image I think of when I read Holocaust poets.

*

If there is a country named Celania, as Julia Kristeva once proposed, each person here stays alone with language, stays with it to "the point of claiming that language" for themselves alone. To the point in which the solitude of a person makes a language tilt over.

For Celan, this experience of language is a result of historical crisis, yes. Celan's mother's language was German. In his poems, this German-speaking mother was shot by Germans. Celan told himself, in German: "This word is your mother's ward . . . your mother's ward stoops for the crumb of light."

Mother tongue. Is it hostile to this man?

Elie Wiesel wrote in French, as a protest against the German language. Even Joseph Brodsky, who continued to write Russian poetry after his forced exile, began to write his prose about his parents in English, explaining:

> I want English verbs of motion to describe their movements. This won't resurrect them, but English grammar may at least prove to be a better escape route from the chimneys of the state crematorium than the Russian. To write about them in Russian would be only to further their captivity, their reduction to insignificance, resulting in mechanical annihilation.

Celan, however, chose to protest from inside German, in "death-rattling," "quarreling" words. Though he spoke numerous other languages (Romanian, Russian, French) and though he had written previously in Romanian, he nevertheless decided to remain in German, which he broke and reclaimed, the language that, for him, had to "pass through its own unresponsiveness," pass "through its own fearful muting, pass through the thousand darknesses of death-bringing speech."

Why break a language? To wake it up. "We are asleep in the language," writes Robert Kelly, "until language wakes us with its strangeness."

*

But what does all of this have to do with lipreading?

Wait.

Celan called himself a man from a "place that was dropped from history." Here are facts: Born in 1920 to German-speaking Jewish parents in Czernowitz, Bukovina. Soviet troops occupy Czernowitz in 1940. Celan learns Russian. German troops enter Bukovina in 1941. In June 1942 his parents are arrested, his father dies from typhus, his mother is shot. Celan himself is arrested in July of the same year and spends two years in forced labor camps. After the war he flees to Vienna and then to Paris, where he settles down, marries, teaches, translates, commits suicide.

*

Theodor Adorno: "It is barbaric to write poetry after the Holocaust."

Adorno, when confronted by others, repeated: "After Auschwitz to write poetry is barbaric, I would not want to downplay this remark."

Adorno, after reading Paul Celan's broken and reassembled German, reconsiders: "It may have been wrong to say that after Auschwitz you could no longer write poems."

*

I stood in front of a bookshelf, asking who can understand a deaf man's alienation from spoken words, who can teach me how to be alone in a room with a language I can't quite hear.

But precisely because every third word is getting lost, and less than 45 percent of speech is visible on the lips, and precisely because lipreading is a language without rules—you grab what you can and run with it. Precisely because I can't tell "v" from "f," so there are gaps in sentences and the eye jumps over the gaps—this alienation from speech is a freeing thing for a poet. One is always intent on walking alone into the language of the hearing.

*

This is where I open the book by Paul Celan. Writing to his wife from Germany, the poet comments: "I am not sure the German I write in is spoken here, or anywhere."

Yes: Celan's strangeness is rooted in his inward, almost cryptogrammic relationship with language. A stranger in his *mother* tongue, Celan, writes Anne Carson, was "a poet who uses language *as if he were always translating.*"

> You are light: you will sleep through my spring till it's over.
> I am lighter:
> in front of strangers I sing.

*

Let's go a bit deeper: Why does Celan's language appear so fresh when it is so wrecked?

The best answer to this question was given by Zbigniew Herbert. Interviewer: "What is the purpose of poetry?" Herbert: "To wake up!"

But how does the wreckage of language wake us? Here is a word-by-word translation from Hebrew, which requires us to read from right to left:

בְּרֵאשִׁ֖ית בָּרָ֣א אֱלֹהִ֑ים אֵ֥ת הַשָּׁמַ֖יִם וְאֵ֥ת הָאָֽרֶץ׃
[the earth] [and] [the heavens] [God] [created] [in the beginning]

וְהָאָ֗רֶץ הָיְתָ֥ה תֹ֙הוּ֙ וָבֹ֔הוּ וְחֹ֖שֶׁךְ עַל־פְּנֵ֣י תְה֑וֹם
[deep] [upon the face of] [and darkness] [and void] [waste] [was] [and the earth]

וְר֣וּחַ אֱלֹהִ֔ים מְרַחֶ֖פֶת עַל־פְּנֵ֥י הַמָּֽיִם׃
[the waters] [upon the face of] [moved] [God] [and the spirit of]

וַיֹּ֥אמֶר אֱלֹהִ֖ים יְהִ֣י א֑וֹר וַֽיְהִי־אֽוֹר׃
[light] [and there was] [light] [let there be] [God] [and said]

These opening verses of *Genesis* are well known. I suggest that we read them backwards. A strange lyricism awakes as these famous phrases are wrecked:

"And the earth and the heavens God created in the beginning [. . .]
And there was light let there be God."

And so creation becomes the creator. There is more poetry in reading the text we know by heart backwards.

*

Is this why lyric poetry of this kind feels like a native tongue to me, no matter what language, geography, or period it is in?

Look: No more than 45 percent of words in English are seen on the lips, but we still keep talking. I write this in a time of pandemic. Everyone wears masks. Lipreading is out of the question. We have come beyond meaning. Here we are.

That Map of Bone and Opened Valves

Ilya Kaminsky

I watched the Sergeant aim, the deaf boy take iron and fire in his mouth—
his face on the asphalt,
that map of bone and opened valves.
It's the air. Something in the air wants us too much.
The earth is still.
The tower guards eat cucumber sandwiches.
This first day
soldiers examine the ears of bartenders, accountants, soldiers—
the wicked things silence does to soldiers.
They tear Gora's wife from her bed like a door off a bus.
Observe this moment
—how it convulses—
The body of the boy lies on the asphalt like a paperclip.
The body of the boy lies on the asphalt
like the body of a boy.
I touch the walls, feel the pulse of the house, and I
stare up wordless and do not know why I am alive.
We tiptoe this city,
Sonya and I,
between theaters and gardens and wrought-iron gates—
Be courageous, we say, but no one
is courageous, as a sound we do not hear
lifts the birds off the water.

In a Time of Peace

Ilya Kaminsky

Inhabitant of earth for forty something years
I once found myself in a peaceful country. I watch neighbors open

their phones to watch
a cop demanding a man's driver's license. When a man reaches for his wallet, the cop
shoots. Into the car window. Shoots.

It is a peaceful country.

We pocket our phones and go.
To the dentist,
to pick up the children from school,
to buy shampoo,
and basil.

Ours is a country in which a boy shot by police lies on the pavement
for hours.

We see in his open mouth
the nakedness
of the whole nation.

We watch. Watch
others watch.

The body of a boy lies on the pavement exactly like the body of a boy.

It is a peaceful country.

And it clips our citizens' bodies
effortlessly, the way the President's wife trims her toenails.

All of us
still have to do the hard work of dentist appointments,
of remembering to make
a summer salad: basil, tomatoes, it is a joy, tomatoes, add a little salt.

This is a time of peace.

I do not hear gunshots,
but watch birds splash over the backyards of the suburbs. How bright is the sky
as the avenue spins on its axis.
How bright is the sky (forgive me) how bright.

Constance Merritt

SOME NOTES ON A (DIS)/EMBODIED POETICS

The body and the mind are not separate. We are whole people. Yes, absolutely. And yet, remaining and becoming a whole person has been one of the central struggles of my life, and it is rather bittersweet to have come to this: back around to the very things—identity, embodiment—I once imagined poetry could free me from. In the beginning, poetry was a door out of a problem body—wrong eyes, wrong size, wrong skin—into the glorious universal where disembodied souls and minds communed irrespective of all the lines that corral us and govern the distribution of power in the world. Back then, embodiment (and, yes, I am choosing this impersonal conceptual word over the intimate and messy "body" or "flesh") seemed an incidental accidental that more often than not distracted and detracted from who I was and meant to be—what I thought, what I felt, what I did, the content of my character, so to speak. My first language was Black Southern and the KJV. Away at school I learned to talk "proper"—not necessarily a good thing back in my neighborhood or among extended family.

Scaffolded by the sensibilities of Emerson, Whitman, and Thoreau, as a teenager I constructed an identity around the values of independence, conscience, and empathy. Stand in your own truth. Stand up for what you know to be right. Move toward what enlarges the self; away from what diminishes. As I began to feel my way as a writer, I surrounded myself with poets and artists who were also in retreat—from the body, from the world—and who, perhaps as a logical extension of that retreat, made well-crafted structures where bridled emotions could safely dwell. The promise of poetry was the miracle of transubstantiation: circumscribed body become "vast horizons of soul."

All of this of course would turn out to be a fiction, albeit a necessary one, the mind in the act of finding what will suffice as I struggled with the ultimate questions of whether and how to live and of how to be whole in a world that contested my value and hijacked my identity through what Laura Hershey calls "members-only thought processes."[1] How else to stand in one's truth than to stand in a particular body that experiences a particular world in a particular way? In an effort to name that particularity, left to my own devices, I would have titled my first book *Ears, Hands, Belly, Mouth,* naming the essential ways I take in and give to the world. This preference for the aural, the tactile, and the gustatory, by which last I mean hunger broadly conceived, permeates all of my work. When it comes to the visual, my focus is on what is close at hand, what I see in my mind's eye, and of course I am a fool for color.

"Separation," a formative poem in my first book, *A Protocol for Touch,* voices the sensory and emotional experience of a medieval leper as she is being ritually separated from her community and is steeling herself to not only accept but to embrace her exclusion.[2] My second book, *Blessings and Inclemencies,* mourns various individual and collective lost worlds, coming to rest in the notion of rest, of dwelling, of abiding what we can and cannot abide, blessings and inclemencies.[3] My third book, *Two Rooms,* openly wrestles with the angels of self-fragmentation and with the double-edged sword of desire that gives us energy and life and rends us to the core.[4] The title poem juxtaposes a beautiful, orderly, sterile, impenetrable, empty room—art as armor, if you will—with another room where "a woman dreams, / Hair tousled, breasts unbound."

It would take studying modern dance, attempting suicide, becoming a gardener, being viscerally offended and vitally altered by the obscenity of the Second Iraq War, falling in love and making a life with my beloved, and witnessing the dissolution of my parents' aging bodies to bring me fully awake, finally alive to and in the body—my body!—to the pleasures and needs and vulnerabilities and powers of other bodies, and to the world—this one earth which is also a body. *Blind Girl Grunt,* my most recent collection, is a manifestation and a manifesto of this awakening and incarnation.[5] As ungainly and unseemly as any blind girl—*Shhh, don't look, she's blind; Is there really nothing they can do to help you? Did your parents regret bringing you into the world?*—a grunt rumbles up to say: "Eff you. I'm here and here to stay. I have beat my last retreat. From here on out I will defend myself and what and whom I love. *All God's chillun got a right to be—dignity, respect, community, opportunity.* Move over. Make room. I'll have a slice of that pie. Mmm."

Certainly I have a poetic lineage to which, perhaps, I'll circle back around before this conversation's done, but these days I find myself less interested in a lineage—a past that I rooted myself in—than in a circle of comrades with whom I join the struggle for our lives in the here and now. Over the years my passion for the page and the library has not so much waned as it has been utterly overtaken by my passion for living a good life and for creating a world that is kinder, more just, and generally more habitable to more of us than is the one in which we now live.

The salient traits of my first poetry kin were lyricism, musicality, existential challenge, and some ineffable feeling-sense that tugged at my core like magnet to steel. As when a small child listens to grown folks talk, elaborating a world mysterious and hers, reading these first poetry kin, love and kinship often ran well ahead of understanding. While some of these poets subscribed to mental illness, while others just freestyled crazy without formal diagnoses, and still others were Bartleby's contrary children, simply preferring not, I never thought of any of them in terms of having or not having a disability.

During grad school in Nebraska I ransacked medieval history looking for proto-feminist cultural outliers among mystics, heretics, martyrs, witches, and lepers, and for one of my comprehensive exams constructed a personal canon of American women poets from Dickinson to the present. But still, and even where details were known—Bright's disease, depression, breast cancer, rheumatoid arthritis, stroke—I never read these women poets, nor do I think I was ever invited to, by the light of disability. I don't think finding other poets with visual impairments or with other disabilities would have been meaningful to me back then. At the same time, there are poets with no discernible disabilities who nonetheless telegraph existential trouble—identity, belonging, the tears of things, the broken world, the unbearableness of the human condition ("Their redness talks to my wound, it corresponds.")—with such force and clarity that for another minute, hour, year the unbearable can be borne.[6]

Rather than art as essential body armor, I'd like to think that art could be a tool, not to say, a weapon, with which to dismantle the master's proverbial house and dance a free people in open air. A poetics of resistance, yes, but even more so one of liberation. For that I don't want a lineage, but rather a riot of black, brown, crip, queer, feminist, indigenous, immigrant, allied, struggling-to-wake-and-stay-woke human voices—a hell-harrowing din, a suturing sound—kicking ass and taking names, slowly but surely, rearranging the heavy furniture of this world.

Notes

1. Laura Hershey, "Translating the Crip," *make/shift* 9 (2011): 43–44.

2. Constance Merritt, *A Protocol for Touch* (Texas A&M University Press, 1999).

3. Constance Merritt, *Blessings and Inclemencies* (Louisiana State University Press, 2007).

4. Constance Merritt, *Two Rooms* (Louisiana State University Press, 2009).

5. Constance Merritt, *Blind Girl Grunt: The Selected Blues Lyrics and Other Poems* (Headmistress Press, 2017).

6. Sylvia Plath, *The Collected Poems* (Harper and Row, 1981), 161.

Jay-Walkin Blues

Constance Merritt

You got to stop on the red
You gots to move when the light turns green

You got to stop on the red
You gots to move along on green

You got to color in their lines, Lord
Or call down trouble like you never seen

Makes no difference if you're a hero
Or headed for a life of crime

Makes no difference if you're a hero
Or hellbent on a life of crime

Once you step across that line, man
You're gonna be lookin at hard time

You got to walk the straight & narrow
Cleave to the middle of the road

You gots to walk it straight & narrow
Hold the middle of the road

Stray one iota left or right, jack
& you done violated code.

Excuse my different eyes
Excuse my rough & tattered coat

Please excuse these eyes, ya'll
Pardon this rough & tattered coat

But if you're guardin somethin precious
You needs some dragons and a moat

The kingdom ain't for everyone
That's what the Bible say

You know the kingdom ain't for everyone
That's what my Good Book say

But if you wanna get a foretaste
Look up & meet this beggar's gaze

Revelation Blues

Constance Merritt

For who or what is appointed to heal or mediate the "stricken" may just as well be a gust of wind, a ghost, a book, an animal, a leaf, or a gesture.
—*The Other Within*

Winds gotta blow sometime
Unholy ghosts have got to roam

Hard winds gotta blow sometime
Even unholy ghosts need a home

Sometime even the devil turn his back upon me
Sometime God's own angels ring my phone

Sometime not one book
Has got a single word for me

Sometime not one book
Has got one lousy word for me

The leaves turn brown & scatter
Dogs howl their witless sympathy

Sometime it don't mean nothin
Sometime it mean most everything

Said sometime it don't mean nothin
Sometime it mean everything

One look, one touch, one gesture
Opens the wound whence healing springs

Less Than Greater Than Blues

Constance Merritt

Good morning, Mr. Charlie,
Can you spare a girl a dime?

Right fine morning, Mr. Charlie,
Can you please spare a girl a dime?

Mr. Charlie rush on pass me
Like his own life was on the line.

Black man's less than white man;
Blind man's less than that.

You know black man's less than white man;
Blind man's even less than that.

But in the sight of a good woman,
He's no less a man for that.

I had a lovely sister;
Her eyes were blear and vague as mine.

I had one lovely sister,
Eyes as blear and vague as mine.

Seem like every sorry no-count joker
Lined up to waste that woman's time.

Woman's less than man;
Blind woman's less than anything.

Tell me woman's less than man;
Blind woman's worse than anything.

Lord, folks act like they can't see me;
They's gonna hear me when I sing.

3

ABLEISM

Aurora Levins Morales

THE WHY AND THE HOW: DISABILITY JUSTICE POETICS

You ask how my poetry connects to disability justice. DJ is not separable from any aspect of my life. I am a bodymind organism within an eco-social system. I am a colonial subject in a front-line climate place; a female-bodied survivor of medical, environmental, and sexual abuse; queer, brown, and radical; exposed to deadly pesticides as part of an agro-industrial project to repurpose chemical weapons for farming. I live with extreme fatigue from a constellation of ills my evolutionary biologist father called twenty-first-century syndrome.

I am a brain-injured epileptic, living with a condition I sometimes describe as cognitively rearranged. If poetry arises from flesh, biochemistry, and electrical impulses, also known as memory, thought, imagination, then my conditions are the soil for my creations. The frequencies of my brain waves, spike and wave, that sometimes flare into convulsions, the unpredictable tides of my hormones, how the biome of my gut affects my states of consciousness, and also how the heating of the oceans spins more and fiercer hurricanes across my archipelago, how the neighbor's glyphosate drifts across the road, but also how the trees hold soil on my mountain, how the red-tailed guaraguao and emerald hummingbird fill the air with wings, all of these things are my poetics, the dense undergrowth of roots and veins, fungi and neurons, that upholds and nourishes my awareness as I begin to arrange human symbols called alphabets into a meaning all my own.

Cripping the Torah

I am also a rearranger, a collagist, raised in a family that rewrote song lyrics and built satires upon satires, so when I come to the garment of Jewish liturgy, I come equipped to make many alterations, make patches, re-dye the fabric, rip out seams, add sequins and bone buttons, until it fits me. The Asher Yatzar, meant to praise our bodies after emptying bladder or bowel, contains some extremely ableist language. It's meant to exalt how necessary our bodies are in every function, but in praising all the channels and openings and hollow spaces within, it says: "It is obvious and known before Your Seat of Honor that if even one of them would be opened, or if even one of them would be sealed, it would be impossible to survive and to stand before You even for one hour."

I rewrote this prayer to celebrate our wild diversities of the flesh and to declare it "well known and obvious" that each of us is made just as we should be. All kinds of unexpected openings and closings and variations can happen in our bodies and we survive whole lifetimes.

Cripping Activism

During the uprisings that followed the police murder of George Floyd I was deeply moved by the events taking place in the streets and also knew that even if those events were taking place in my rural Puerto Rican community, I could not take my body into those crowds, could not be on my feet, could not endure the noise, the adrenaline, the need to move quickly. I wrote back to the grief that I could not surge along avenues with thousands of comrades. I employed a trick I often use—to leap forward into an imagined future in order to look back at now from a different vantage point and allow hope into a narrow place that feels hopeless. In this sense my poems are often medicinal for me first, and then for others.

"Poem for the Bedridden" imagines those of us who can't ever march or do civil disobedience or use up more spoons than we have, through a futuristic leap, into "times to come when the generations look back" and honors the work of resting, of recovery from all the ways that oppression has caused our disabilities and illnesses and then mistreated us for them. This is a Healing Justice moment, the recognition that the intense action phases of social justice work have to be balanced by rest, recovery, slowness, healing, in order for our movements to be possible. By resting in our beds we hold the other pole, we model what is needed for activism to be sustained across lifetimes.

Why Crip Consciousness Matters

Why does our poetry matter? There is no form of injustice I can think of that doesn't require its targets to override the true needs of our bodyminds in the service of power and profit for others. We the sick and disabled have bodyminds that already defy those requirements. Being unable to comply has given us a profound set of understandings and skills as consequences of our physical and mental unruliness. We know things that people are literally dying to know. The art we create, the poetry we shape, our true stories and envisioning are expressions of something all bodyminds hunger for. Worlds of inclusive justice, rest and help as fundamental human rights, restoration and reciprocity as the core value of all human societies.

Because we know what it is to need personal care assistants (PCAs), we can imagine systems of flexible and universal support. Because we know what fires exhaustion can set in us, we know that the most aggressively currently able-bodied person will burn out someday without learning to rest. We can reshape the cultures of the movements where change is made. Model leading from bed, with frequent naps. Imagine, if crips led the labor movement, how much more striking workers might demand. Imagine food systems where biodiversity of crops mirrored diversities of digestion. Imagine the schedules of conferences led by people with chronic fatigue. This is why I write. To lift up the immense value of what we already know and to stretch imagination toward the far better futures we deserve, and to do it by following the leadership of the actual bodyminds we have.

Poem for the Bedridden

Aurora Levins Morales

In times to come
when the generations look back
on the Great Uprising of 2020
and speak of the people in the streets,
the people healing wounds, cooking food,
making signs,
because so much will have changed by then
they will also speak our names, the ones
who could not join the crowds
or write manifestos
or cook vats of soup
or deliver supplies,
whose fields of action were our beds,
our chairs set by the windows
where we could watch you march by.
They will say these are the ones
who carried the consequences of the bad old days
in their bodies, who shouldered the harm
in lungs that wheezed, in guts that churned,
in aching muscles and crushing fatigue,
whose hearts burned beside your own
as the old world fell, and as we marched
and toppled monuments and governments,
who did the work of resting
for the sake of the whole new world.

Asher Yatzar

Aurora Levins Morales

Blessed is the evolutionary dance of life, which formed the human body in perfect wisdom, made cerebellum and cortex, made the many branching nerves, the bones and their marrows, the muscles and ligaments, the red cells and the white, the myriad hormones singing their biochemical song of praise, made eyes and ears, capillaries and fingernails, the magnificent heart with its chambers, all the organs and passages, cavities and openings. Blessed is natural selection and the infinite diversity of our shapes and colors, our forms and functions, and blessed is the ability to adapt, for it is well known and obvious that each one of us is made as we should be, that even though openings close, and closures open, even though limbs grow wildly and genes mutate, even though hearts dance to different drummers, lungs labor, bones bend and break, and biochemical signals go awry, even though we age and will someday die, we are infinitely splendid as we are. Blessed are you, life force of the universe, that has made us so varied and resilient.

Roxanna Bennett

YOU WERE BORN, ERGO, I LOVE YOU

In the crippest spirit of art-making, I needed help from a friend to both scribe for me and translate my words, to the best of their ability, into academic English for the purposes of essay-making.

If I was able to write an essay, I wouldn't need to write poems.

I am wondering, with open-hearted curiosity and some bewilderment, why the poems in this anthology aren't enough. Why does the work require explanatory essays, and isn't that similar to how we have been treated, as disabled people? Being forced and expected to justify and explain your experience, over and over again, until you misbelieve it yourself. And the pain of that, of being profoundly misunderstood, over and over again. I put all of my effort and energy into my art and have none left over to explain why.

This hurts, attempting to sense-make the insensible: Why try to categorize experience in a linear, coherent narrative that has nothing to do with reality? I thought that's what the poetry was for. And the physical pain of this, the excruciating effort of typing while trying to concentrate enough to keep one's bodymind still to form these sentences, the tremendous effort, the work before even opening the hated computer, object of pain, of trying to formulate a kind way to say, "Why are we hurting each other by asking each other to perform extra labor?" and the terror that this essay will be rejected, that my poems will be rejected, that I will be shut out of yet another space because I cannot seem to make my experience make sense to any other person, except, sometimes, through a poem. But even here, even now in this anthology of poets who are also disabled, that isn't enough, either.

The essay structure itself is a Western form of thinking concomitant with the scientific method––in which, mirroring the essay's structure, a hypothesis is subjected to evidence from which a conclusion is drawn. This Aristotelian categorization marks the beginning of the division of one form of life from another and Cartesian mind–body dualism marks the beginning of division of the *self* into hierarchized categories––and the identification of *thought* with *the self,* such that simply *being* is of no value per se, while *thinking the best/right/true thoughts* IS of value––which leads to a kind of detached, discursive, disinterested, *unalive,* intellectualized, conceptual ableism.

This constant division and labeling breeds disunification and keeps us separated from one another. When we categorize other beings in terms of difference instead of similarities—for instance, every being on this planet is alike in wanting to be happy and free of suffering, every person who ever lived is the same in terms of wanting to be fed, sheltered, cared for, loved, free of pain—we create conceptual barriers that prevent us from apprehending reality. Which is a very wordy way of saying, we treat each other like concepts, ideas, narratives to reject, judge, correct, instead of living, breathing, heart-beating sentient beings.

In addition to the rigor and attendance to convention designed to insulate power and exclude those deemed "unworthy," implicit in the essay form and its execution in standard written English is the assumption of the educational background of the writer. I don't understand why we would equate poetry-making with an expensive education rife with formidable barriers to access depending on one's intersectional socioeconomic, mobility-related, intergenerational trauma-related, racial, gender-related, sexuality-related, ethnic, age-related, cognitive, emotional, and energetic position and ability. Along with countless other queer, crippled artists, I've never lived a life where a postsecondary education was ever going to be part of the equation. But no one has ever needed an education to make art.

My own lived experience within the dominant worldview that informs our educational and medical systems has been one of suffering and profound disempowerment, having failed all of my life to fit into any rigid category. Extrapolating from my own experience, which is not unique and all too common, millions of others have also suffered from the expectations of a thought system that privileges one particular worldview, and one particular type of bodymind, over all others.

The internal division of the self in Western thought has progressed to the extent that *no one studies the body entire or appreciates its intrinsic internal harmony*: a human being, rendered without agency or dignity, is passed from specialist to specialist like a piece of hot trash, to be peeled apart, carelessly handled like so much meat, stripped of all dignity and self-worth. And a poem, a work of art, appears to have no inherent value unless it is chewed up, analyzed, criticized, consumed and regurgitated like a waste product instead of a sacred expression of livingness.

Most discussions of disability are informed by the importance of technologies that will enable us to succeed academically and compete in the work sector. To become yet another cog in the great grinding wheel. I don't want accessible technology so I can subject myself to the same abusive mindset that labels all difference as deficient; I want accessible technology because I'm a human being. I want my worth not to be measured in money or academic accomplishment. I want everyone born to know they are worthy because they exist.

How can we best support each other in the creation of art-making? How can we most compassionately appreciate each other, whole-heartedly and without reservation? Perhaps by recognizing that we are all different and yet all exactly alike and perfect as we are. To my fellow disabled artists, your work is enough. *You* are enough. You don't owe anyone an explanation for your art or existence. Like one's life, one's art is a gift requiring no dissection or justification. You were born, ergo, you are worthy. Whatever shape, form, color, identification, wherever you are today on the fucking pain scale, I love you.

Your poems break my heart but keep it beating. Thank you for choosing to make beautiful the unbearable pain of being.

"What do you do for a living?"

by the disabled poem-making entity known as Roxanna Bennett

Inhale, exhale, inhale, exhale. I wait
to get on the waitlist to wait to wait
to fill out forms, be injected, I wait,
am inspected, rejected, I lose weight
while I wait to be dissected, I wait
for prescriptions to be filled, I wait
to be told painkillers are backordered,
manufacturer went under, insurance
doesn't cover, the specialist retired,
was arrested, hospital hiring frozen solid,
Honey, you'll have to wait for an opening,
cancellation, doctor to return from
vacation, inhale, hold your seat & wait
for a single moment that makes this worth the wait.

“Wherever You Go, There You Are”

by the disabled poem-making entity known as Roxanna Bennett

In Oxford on OxyContin, in Ajax
on Ativan, in Paris on Percocets,
in Cobourg on Clonazepam, in Switzerland
on Seroquel, in Scarborough on Serentil,
Berlin is a blur of Baclofen & Nabilone,
Old Town is absinthe, Abilify & absence,
Montreal is Mirtazapine, codeine & callous,
Strasbourg is a parking lot of Pepto-Bismol
& panic, the hospital is a labyrinth of
protocol & damage, a Code White is
a euphemism for “your pain is a tidal wave
our system can’t manage,” home was
that floor, that skin, that skeleton, now it is
aether, vibration, air & the ocean, O & the ocean.

Meg Day

T-I-M-B-E-R

It's taken me quite a bit of time to realize just how thoroughly assimilated my poetics have become under ableism. Even now, I have an easier time identifying ableist tendencies and internalized audism in the craft or content of the work of my comrades and contemporaries, the poets we revere as leaders and elders. None of us should be surprised that it's difficult to unlearn in our poems what we are still fighting to resist in the most basic moments of our piss-on-pity, access-only-when-it's-reasonable, nothing-about-us-without-us, personal-is-political lives.

Throughout the entirety of my education as a poet—including my own career—I have been taught to anticipate only hearing readers. When my first book, *Last Psalm at Sea Level* (Barrow Street, 2014), was a finalist for the Kate Tufts Discovery Award, the commentary from the judges panel included abundant praise for my "sonic brilliance" and "unmatched ear." This kind of feedback is not unfamiliar to me; one would expect I'd be pleased that, after years of memorizing hearing rhymes in English and attempting to master meter without the assistance of sound, reviews of my work might remark positively upon its "auditory density" and "muscular sound." Indeed, overcoming narratives are often the stuff of poetics, disabled or otherwise.

When I started publishing poems that aim to upset phonocentrism and fully open only to readers with knowledge of ASL or DEAF-GAIN, the conversation shifted. In one interview, a podcast host questioned whether I meant, as a trans Deaf poet, for my work to feel so coded; in a post-reading Q&A with other contemporary poets, the moderator asked if I was in search of a new sound. What did Audre Lorde say about the master's house and the master's tools? I'm still rolling that one around in my hands.

If a tree falls in a forest and no one is around to hear it, does it make a sound? My answer—despite the philosophical debates we could endure, or the great variety of ways to dip into metaphysics and neurology, the anthropic principle or differences in sensation and perception—is no. If it is that sound is characterized as vibration, transmitted through the machine of the ear, and decoded only by normate nerve centers in the brain, then no: If there is no one around to hear it, it makes no sound.

Like most thought experiments I've encountered, the givens—the "no one" of this hypothetical—are more problematic and persuasive than the inquiry itself. Why, in all of the seminars or books or workshops through which I encountered this question, did no one ask what would happen if the forest was full of Deaf folks like me? Why, too, were so many of my (hearing) peers insistent that sound occurs even in their absence—when I'm sitting proof, right in front of them, our view of one another obscured, ironically, by the body of an interpreter?

There's a story I've been told since I was young, an old Deaf joke about a tree falling in a forest. In the variation I know, it begins with a (hearing) lumberjack in a dense wood, swinging his axe with gusto. He chops at the trunk of each tree—the lower torso of a raised forearm—and before it falls, he cups his hands around his open mouth and yells, "Timber!" This goes on for some time, trees dropping left and right, until the lumberjack encounters a tree that refuses to fall. He chops and shouts, chops and shouts (there is a subplot here about hearing culture, but that's another essay). The tree stays upright. In the story, the lumberjack calls for a "tree doctor," some kind of arborist of sorts, and she informs him plainly that the tree is Deaf. With annoyed nonchalance, she fingerspells #T-I-M-B-E-R, and the tree falls down.

Deaf jokes—especially old classics like this one—are an important part of Deaf literature and the visual vernacular that stokes our culture. What seemed to me, as a young person, to be a corny kind of folklore now reads as a many-layered, multimodal take on audism, language deprivation, medical intervention, and hearing supremacy. The joke, of course, is not that the lumberjack's business-as-usual decimation of natural resources wouldn't work on a Deaf tree—though we're all familiar with ableist tropes about Deaf folks being stubborn, or too stupid to understand, and we all know a doctor who weaponizes ASL to assist in clearing the forest. No, the joke is that hearing people think even trees have ears.

It took me the better part of fifteen years to realize disability poetics isn't for us. Did you know? We aren't at the center. We aren't in the imagined audience. We aren't making the rules, or calling the shots, and so our inclusion is contingent on our adherence to the guidelines set before us. And we all know—from our experience with any and all institutions—that the guidelines were not made with us in mind; are not accessible; make adherence, in many cases, absolutely impossible.

Disability poetics asks us to explain ourselves, starting at birth. Disability poetics says, memorize hearing rhymes. Disability poetics makes nondisabled demands: It wants to know what you *have* before you read the poem about it—or the poem about flowers, or the poem that has nothing to do with our ears, or our eyes, or our legs, or our tech. Disability poetics says, if you want to be published, play nice; act normate; don't out the nondisabled Implant Poet who uses our bodies as metaphor; and don't criticize the caretakers. Above all, pass. Use pretty words, not *cyborg* or *cochlear implant* or anything that conveys earnestness around having been actually paralyzed by something. Disability poetics reads aloud because it assumes the reader is hearing. It assumes, like poetics, that there is no disabled reader. Disability poetics isn't for us, and it also helps disappear us. It asks—upon our confession that ableism magnetized eugenics and pulled it to the heart of how we were taught poetic craft, then stripped us of our linguistic identity and asked that we cure our poems of any evidence of a disabled self as an exchange for a seat at the table—if what we're looking for is a new sound.

If I write English poems in a Deaf tradition and no one can understand my work, does it exist? It does. It does. I'm just in the wrong forest.

Deaf Erasure of the Gospel According to the TSA Agent at Atlanta International

Meg Day

This is the good news: [inaudible]
    & we have a plan for you. Can you follow

what I'm saying? Follow me. Bless you,
    [inaudible], there's no need to [inaudible].

Doesn't this happen to you all the time?
    [Inaudible]. I said step in here. Why would you—

copy. Copy that, I'm here with—yes I'm here
    with [inaudible] now. Like I was saying before,

I'm not here to preach [inaudible]. You are
    what you are. Even Jesus wasn't believed

& it's not like he could put some marker
    on his driver's license. Have you had the [inaudible]?

My cousin had the [inaudible]. But the other
    way. Spread your [inaudible]. A little farther

down the line & I would've been Paul
    or [inaudible] back from his lunch break.

That's the power of [inaudible] right there.
    Somebody's looking out for you today. Next time

you might not—[inaudible]. Copy. Copy
    that. I'm going to place my fingers here & then

they need the room. [Inaudible]. Okay that's
    enough. I need to go & tell them what I've seen.

Elegy in Translation

Meg Day

I was trying to wave to you but you wouldn't wave back
—The Be Good Tanyas

Forgive me my deafness now for your name on others' lips:
each mouth gathers then opens & I search for the wave

the fluke of their tongues should make with the blow
of your name in that mild darkness I recognize but cannot

explain as the same oblivious blue of *Hold the conch to your ear*
& hearing the highway loud & clear. My hands are bloated

with the name signs of my kin who have waited for water
to reach their ears. Or oil; grease from a fox with the gall

of a hare, bear fat melted in hot piss, peach kernels fried
in hog lard & tucked along the cavum for a cure; a sharp stick

even, a jagged rock; anything to wedge down deep to the drum
inside that kept them walking away from wives—old

or otherwise—& the tales they tell about our being too broken
for their bearing, & yet they bear on. Down. Forgive me

my deafness for my own sound, how I mistook it for a wound
you could heal. Forgive me the places your wasted words

could have saved us from going had I heard you with my hands.
I saw Joni live & still thought *a gay pair of guys put up a parking lot.*

How could I have known *You are worthless* sounds like *Should we*
do this, even with the lights on. You let me say *Yes*. So what

if Johnny Nash *can see clearly now Lorraine is gone*—I only wanted
to hear the sea. The audiologist asks *Does it seem like you're under*

water? & I think only of your name. I thought it was *you*
after *I love,* but memory proves nothing save my certainty—

the chapped round of your mouth was the same shape while at rest
or in thought or blowing smoke, & all three make a similar sound:

10 A.M. Is When You Come to Me

Meg Day

Louise Bourgeois, 2006

In some other life, I can hear you
breathing: a pale sound like running
fingers through tangled hair. I dreamt
again of swimming in the quarry
& surfaced here when you called for me
in a voice only my sleeping self could
know. Now the dapple of the aspen
respires on the wall & the shades cut
its song a staff of light. Leave me—
that me—in bed with the woman
who said all the sounds for pleasure
were made with vowels I couldn't
hear. Keep me instead with this small sun
that sips at the sky blue hem of our sheets
then dips & reappears: a drowsy penny
in the belt of Venus, your aureole nodding
slow & copper as it bobs against cotton
in cornflower or clay. What a waste
the groan of the mattress must be
when you backstroke into me & pull
the night up over our heads. Your eyes
are two moons I float beneath & my lungs
fill with a wet hum your hips return.
It's Sunday—or so you say with both hands
on my chest—& hot breath is the only hymn
whose refrain we can recall. And then you
reach for me like I could've been another
man. You make me sing without a sound.

Stephen Lightbown

SEARCHING FOR DIGNITY

In January 2017 Anne Wafula Strike, a Paralympian and wheelchair user, described how she felt "completely robbed of her dignity" after a train she was traveling on did not provide a toilet that she could use and she was instead left to urinate on herself. In an interview with *The Guardian* she said, "I would like to ask the train company when will they give me my dignity back?"[1]

Four months later, in May of the same year, I read another interview in *The Guardian*. This time with Christopher Stapleton, also a wheelchair user, who like Anne described having to urinate on himself due to a broken toilet. In the article Christopher says, "I think it happens all the time, but many disabled travelers feel too embarrassed to speak out about it."[2]

My response on reading these articles was not to be shocked that it had happened but to recall the number of times this had also happened to me. I have lost count of the occasions where I have missed a train because prebooked assistance has not arrived, or where I have not been able to sit in a designated wheelchair space because it has been full of luggage, or where I have also had to urinate on myself due to the toilet being out of order. And each time I sit and think about how I left my dignity back at the train station.

Unfortunately, these sorts of instances are not limited to train travel. In 2016 I traveled to Thailand to be the best man at the wedding of one of my oldest school friends. I was traveling independently as my partner had traveled out a week earlier and I would follow later. I prefer to break long-haul flights up and so punctuated my trip with a stopover in Dubai.

Landing at Dubai I did what I always do on a plane and sat tight as the other passengers disembarked, waiting for my chair to be brought to me. I waited. Then I waited some more and then I carried on waiting. Apparently my chair had been sent to the baggage carousel and I was expected to have gone and collected it myself. Quite how I was meant to do that was not a question that had been thought through. So, instead, a wheelchair the size of an articulated lorry was brought for me and I was wheeled to the carousel to see my wheelchair looking bereft making its way around and around the luggage belt in among the suitcases.

I spent the night at a Dubai hotel that was horrendously inaccessible and then made my way to the airport to board my onward flight to Thailand. At the check-in desk I was told I would not be able to board the plane, as the airline policy was that disabled passengers had to have assistance with them. I pointed out that I had flown to Dubai on the same airline without assistance and that seemed to be OK. Around thirty minutes later I was taken into an interrogation room and told I was traveling illegally and had been in Dubai for three weeks. Again, I pointed out that I had arrived the day before. A further thirty minutes later and I was allowed to board the plane. I then had seven hours to once more question whether there was a more dignified way that I could travel independently as a wheelchair user.

I live in a city called Bristol in the southwest of the UK. I am sure there are many facts that I could share about Bristol but the one I tend to lead with is that Bristol is an old city with terrible pavements. Strange fact you might think, but as a wheelchair user this is an important point. Many of the pavements are made from old flagstones that over time have become displaced, leading to many raised edges.

These raised edges are a hazard when using a wheelchair, since the front wheels can become caught, which then propels the wheelchair user out of their chair and onto the ground. This has happened to me many times and on each occasion people run over and offer help. Some don't even offer, they just grab hold of me and lift me back into my chair.

It's often, as I'm sitting on the ground among cigarette stubs in a pool of my broken dignity, that I question if there is a better way to do this. What would help? If the Council showed this was an important issue and repaired the pavements. If people asked if I needed help before grabbing me. If people accepted that I said I was OK and could manage rather than helping anyway. If I just accept that people are mainly trying to be kind, and offering help to someone who has fallen out of a wheelchair is a perfectly normal thing to do.

I sometimes wonder if there was a perfect time to have a life-changing accident? Perhaps, if there was, I found it when I had mine at age sixteen. Sixteen, an age when I had not yet discovered what it was to desire respect from others or fully know my own worth. I think of the need to be treated with dignity, to feel of worth, as I reflect on my two poems, "After the Check-In" and "Grounded," both of which were inspired by the pavement and flying examples given earlier in this essay.

I was asked recently when I first realized I was disabled. It is an interesting question and one I have thought about before. And the word itself, "disabled," one I have at times embraced and at others sprinted away from.

Maybe surprisingly, it was not when I first returned home from hospital after my accident and needed to be lifted into the house, when the front room became my bedroom. Nor when I had to use a commode in the room where, weeks earlier, my mum had entertained friends—now she emptied the pan from the commode in the bathroom upstairs, walking as she left past walls with mirrors I could no longer see my face in. I don't think the idea that I was disabled came into my mind. The reason? Because I was treated with dignity, respect, and in the eyes of my family I was not worth any less than when I had left the home six months earlier, on the day of my accident.

Instead, I think it is a gradual realization that comes with every request for help, every offer of help that is unasked for, every form that is filled in to ask for support that is turned down because you might not need help enough. It takes a lot for someone to ask for help, to admit that they need assistance. I know personally it is something I have struggled with since my accident back in the '90s, when I was sixteen.

Asking for help can be hard enough: Understanding that you may have to bury your dignity or leave it at home in order to exist in society is even harder. I think of the experiences of Anne and Christopher, of my own examples given in this essay, of the many disabled people whose experiences have not been made public but who still crave the desire to be treated with dignity, with respect, and again I wonder if I could ever write enough poems to do those experiences justice.

Perhaps not, but poetry does provide an opportunity for me to interrogate these experiences and find a way for me to reclaim my dignity from a baggage carousel.

Notes

1. *The Guardian*, Jan. 2, 2017. https://www.theguardian.com/society/2017/jan/02/paralympian-anne-wafula-strike-wet-herself-train-no-accessible-toilet.

2. *The Guardian*, May 21, 2017. https://www.theguardian.com/society/2017/may/21/disabled-man-forced-wet-himself-virgin-trains-toilet-out-of-order.

After the Check-In

Stephen Lightbown

They take my DIGNITY
and I'm strapped to an aisle chair.

I realize I've lost my legs all over again.

I ask, *make sure my* DIGNITY
is by the door when we land,

not on the baggage belt.

I ask   again.

Out of the window,
I see my DIGNITY on the tarmac.

Hello, welcome aboard
thank you for flying with Generic Airlines.
Our priority is the safety of all
our passengers and crew, apart from you,
the DIGNITY user, you won't be able
to get to any of our eight exits.

I'll skip the scramble for the exit,
place on a life jacket, blow my whistle.

The plane will empty,
don't worry sir, your booked
assistance is on the way.

And I'll wait, as instructed,
DIGNITY in hold, legs not moving.

Please sit back and enjoy your flight.

Grounded

Stephen Lightbown

I flutter to the ground
like a falling kite.
Legs trail along the floor,
my fluorescent tail.

I lie with face in gravel
pray for a gust of wind
so I can return
from pavement
to wheelchair
before

a hundred strangers
try to release me back
into the air.

Lateef McLeod

HOW POETRY CAN EVOKE EMPATHY AND MEANING

My aim in writing poetry is to give the unique and wonderful experience of my life as a Black man with cerebral palsy the defining words to illustrate its importance. In my childhood, I found poetry to be the best vehicle to express my innermost thoughts and feelings. I also discovered in middle school that I enjoyed writing poems and people also enjoyed reading them, so it is then I started considering myself a poet. I try to reflect my vision of the world through my poetry and to highlight aspects of society that the mainstream dominant culture does not see. That is what I try to do in my poems that were selected in this anthology.

The poems that were selected for this anthology are "So Much" and "Absence of Routine." My goal with these poems is to make the sometimes unseen challenges and oppression of Black and disabled people in America both visible and prescient for the reader. In both poems I use tactile imagery to assist the reader in visualizing the scene that each poem describes and interpreting the meaning behind that description. In this way the experiences of having to consciously remember to swallow or being shot and murdered by a racist cop become visceral. The reader is more able to empathize with the experience in question and will have a little more understanding for the people who go through these experiences in their actual lives. Poetry can be a bridge of understanding in these situations.

The poem "So Much" was inspired by the murder of Trayvon Martin by George Zimmerman and the lives of other Black and brown men and women whom police and white vigilantes murdered. The words of the poem, "Bullets lurch out of guns" and "Eat away at our muscles and bones, / burrow through sinews and blood vessels," are made for the reader to have a mental picture of what it is like to be shot and to have a bullet burrow inside you. This sickening situation is to compel the reader to have empathy when they see police or vigilantes murdering people on the news or witness it in real life. The readers should relate to these victims, who had bodies and lives, just as the readers do, and should mourn them and be enraged that their lives were taken too soon. Not only should they be enraged, however, but they should also be moved into action to prevent these state-sanctioned murders from happening again.

Similarly, in my poem "Absence of Routine," I try to give the reader a vivid experience of what it is like to have to remember to swallow for every waking moment of the day. Within the verses I repeat the word "swallow" throughout the second half of the poem with an increased frequency to connote the number of times I must think about swallowing and how that task can become a little overbearing, especially when I am concentrating on other tasks. It is a message for those who take swallowing for granted, how laborious it can be when your body does not control your saliva automatically. The reader can have a little taste of what it is like to be in a body like mine, which functions differently than theirs. The poem centers a disabled experience that able-bodied people do not necessarily think about and raises awareness of another way of being outside the norm.

Both of my poems in this collection connect to what I see as disability poetics. My interpretation of disability poetics is to make the disability experience seen for the diverse and beautiful variety that people with disabilities experience every day. It makes visible aspects of life with disability that temporarily able-bodied people often ignore when thinking about disability. It clarifies that, although there may be challenges, the disabled life is also full of pleasure and joy as much as any other life. Disability poetics artfully expresses the principles of disability justice and the potential that they have to change society. Disability justice principles like intersectionality, leadership of the most impacted, and collective access aim to center the life experiences of people with disabilities in society and culture in a similar way that disability poetics does by highlighting the disability experience with the poetic form. The result is to illustrate that the disability experience is an integral part of the human experience and cannot be separated as marginal. As a result, the narrative of people with disabilities must be highlighted and studied like other narratives to get a full picture of what it is to be human.

I hope people enjoy my poems that are in this anthology. I hope my poems widen people's perspectives into understanding a little more the experiences of people of color and people with disabilities. At this time in history, we all need a little more empathy and understanding for human experiences that we are unfamiliar with and I hope my poetry will further that discussion.

Absence of routine

Lateef McLeod

Slender gray lines
on jacket sleeves
that musty smell on my clothes
drool is all over me
and you think it is disgusting

"Just swallow"
you say to me
and I really do try
catch and force down
pools of drool
from coming out of my mouth
cuz I be wearing tight fits
like Rocawear jeans, big Ekco

shirts, Gap hoodies
or fresh to def in tailor-made suits
and drool does not go
with tailor-made suits

you know I try to look suave

24/7
so at a party I can get my
grown man on

So there shouldn't be a problem with
me swallowing, right?
Well I have to remember to

swallow
every minute

every hour
every day

that means when I roll down the street
swallow
whenever I talk to someone
swallow
when I exercise
swallow
when I go to school
swallow
cuz I don't want anyone to see

me drool, especially you
you always say that
it makes me look gross
and it is not my intention
to disgust you
so I try to swallow
like a madman

(swallow)
try and
(swallow)
consciously do something
(swallow)
that everyone else
(swallow)
does unconsciously
(swallow)
and you still
(swallow)
can't understand
(swallow)
why
(swallow)
can't I
(swallow)
learn

(swallow)
to swallow all
(swallow)
the time
(swallow)

it is like
(swallow)
to toss you a tennis ball
(swallow)
telling you
(swallow)
to throw it
(swallow)
in the air and catch it
(swallow)
every fifteen seconds
(swallow)
and yell at you
(swallow)
when you drop the ball

swallow
just swallow
come on and swallow
you know you want to

So Much

Lateef McLeod

I hear their painful cries jut up from cracks on the street.
The block is a scorching frying pan,
frying my brothers on the pavement.
Our bodies are etched on the concrete,
blood drenched as permanent ink.
Chalk should not outline our deathbed
or a body bag be our first casket.

Bullets lurch out of guns,
slice the air, and
pierce the thin borders of our Black skin.
Eat away at our muscle and bones,
burrow through sinews and blood vessels,
until it reaches and stops our hearts.

It is not just the gang member on the corner
whose aim we have to dodge,
but also police on the beat
whose itchy trigger fingers
leave us with our brain matter
splattered on the concrete.

Now we have to watch out for
the neighborhood watchmen.
The wanna-be cops who think
we are foreign to our own neighborhood.
Trayvon had a hoodie on to protect him from the rain,
but it didn't protect him
from the bullet from Zimmerman's gun.
Old George just couldn't help
being a deadly Don Quixote,

and shoot at every Black boy,
claiming he was a hardened criminal.

My cocoa skin is not a target for your gun.
It is the sacred encasing of God's masterpiece
that gives warmth and joy to every loved one it touches.
No bullet will destroy what God has made immortal.
We will all rise again one day to walk under the sun.

Jill Khoury

UNIMAGINED POSSIBILITIES

The medical system that I use for my health care has made an upgrade in the past five years: When I schedule an appointment I am asked, "Do you have any special needs?" It's at this point that I disclose particular disabilities that may be relevant to the doctor's appointment. And I struggle to spit it out. "I'm blind." "I have low vision." "I'm visually impaired." "I can't see that well." But those descriptors don't really answer the question. Do I not know my needs? Or am I just overwhelmed by the concept of turning them over to the monolithic medical-industrial complex? What should I say exactly? "Please redesign your office/facility/hospital with better signage and point to where the signs are so that I know where to look for them. Personally escort me to all rooms and facilities. Please don't walk too fast. Don't get mad if my white cane bumps your shoes. Be kind and patient. Be very obvious about where you want me to sit/stand/lie when I get in the room. If you think you are being too obvious, that's probably about right. Tell me every time you are going to touch me, and never touch me without asking or announcing it first and waiting for my consent." I'm pretty sure I would then become "the difficult patient," and this causes my stomach to drop. I am an abuse survivor, and thus rings the ancient refrain: I have no power in this situation, better to just get it over with. "I have CPTSD. I don't trust you. Tell me everything you will do before you touch me." *Or don't. It's not like I can stop you.*

I was raised to minimize my own emotional needs and to work my remaining shred of vision like I had 20/20 in both eyes. I didn't even start using a white cane until I moved to Ohio for graduate school—my mind reels at all the unsafe situations I had put myself in without it. In the town where I was mainstreamed, and even after I went away for college, someone would often tell me "But you don't *look* blind," not knowing how many calculations of bodily choreography it took for me to pass as sighted. I kept trying and failing to appear normal. Failing and falling. As I enter middle age, my knees throb from all the times I've fallen and gotten back up with blood running down my legs, sauntering across the street and down the sidewalk like it was nothing. This militant denial of pain was something I could do that I considered normal, and it's ironic, or perhaps causational, that I developed fibromyalgia in my late twenties. My body of poetic work, which centers on blindness, mental illness, and chronic pain, is my way of carving a space in the world that is me-shaped.

In her short essay "Meat Life," which appeared in *Beauty is a Verb,* Danielle Pafunda writes, "Like the male gaze, the medical gaze doesn't exist discreetly in the human eye, but is a sort of collective eye. A cultural peeper."[1] My poems respond innately to this casual voyeurism of the disabled that society, both medical and civilian, deems permissible, in different ways.

"Cranial Nerve II" was brought into being when the editor of my first book, *Suites for the Modern Dancer,* told me that "this book needs the 'origin story' of your blindness." I thought about superheroes, those experts of the dramatic origin story.[2] I imagined an audience lasciviously licking lips, ready for a story about How I Overcame My Blindness and So Much More. Wanting danger, romance, a climax, and for it to all turn out okay in the end. Also the medical community, trying to tame and enhance my optic nerve hypoplasia into something more orderly. This led me to make my origin story a twisted, somewhat sarcastic fairy tale full of contradictions and multiple voices that ended in a question instead of a moral.

"An Object Approaches the I" is a poem from a chapbook-length series of erasures of a text called *Understanding Low Vision.*[3] Orientation and mobility (O&M) is a subject that many blind and low-vision people learn. It is a method of wayfinding and a group of strategies to more easily move in this world that wasn't built for us. I received most of my orientation and mobility training from the time I was five until I was eighteen years old and ready to depart for college. My earliest O&M instructor added to the trauma of home and school life, conducting object-finding and gait-training exercises in front of other elementary school children. In a small town, this kind of attention places a target on you for life, or for as long as you live there. This instructor never bothered to ask whether any particular exercise felt shameful or terrifying. It is this traumatic formative center that the manuscript, tentatively titled *UN VISION,* seeks to explore—ferreting out my truth from in between the words of lessons and case studies in this best practices textbook from 1983. I found my own voice, lurking in there among the words of the clinician / helper / oppressor, and felt a definite satisfaction as I tweezered words around the virtual page.

The poem "[rotary nystagmus]" celebrates the condition that constitutes part of my blindness, the eyes that were the target of so much childhood and adolescent bullying. As part of moving more wholly into my disability identity, I had decided to love what was mocked, and this poem was a reflection of that. In its formal aspect it took the shape of what I call "anagram poetry." That is, I created a title, and the rules were that any words in the poem were to contain only the letters in the title. "[rotary nystagmus]" is part of my chapbook *Chance Operations*, wherein many of the poems were formed by using this anagram form, n+7, cut-ups, and other methods of allowing luck, surprise, and play into my work.[4] The project of *Chance Operations* was twofold: to offer a personal response to the power imbalance and dehumanization created by the medical-industrial complex, and to explore a new language with which to talk about my particular relationship with pain, illness, and disability.

Before I knew I had mental illness, my brain was drawn to the poems of Anne Sexton like an insect to a beautiful flame of bleak light. Poems were my friends and role models before I ever met another blind person or another person with pain that never goes away. My hope is that, writing from my own amalgam of authentic experience, I can contribute to greater cultural understanding and, perhaps, connection.

In his poem "Touring Harvard, 1986," Johnson Cheu writes about inaccessible spaces: "you are just about to knock, hopeful; / your other hand reaching for the knob, for admittance, / until you realize that being an unimagined possibility / leaves you no space, no room to enter."[5] I think of these lines often, every time I must exist in a space that was clearly not conceived with blindness in mind, or the needs of someone with chronic pain. Depiction of disabled life by disabled people is paramount to expanding our societal imagination, and something disabled people still struggle for. In too many spaces, both terrestrial and of the mind, we still are a set of circumstances of which the majority of people cannot conceive.

Notes

1. Danielle Pafunda, "Meat Life," *Beauty is a Verb*, 313.
2. Jill Khoury, *Suites for the Modern Dancer* (Sundress Publications, 2016).
3. Jose, Randall T., ed. *Understanding Low Vision* (American Foundation for the Blind, 1983), 100–101.
4. Jill Khoury, *Chance Operations* (Paper Nautilus, 2016).
5. Johnson Cheu, "Touring Harvard, 1986," *Rattle Magazine* (August 4, 2019). https://www.rattle.com/touring-harvard-1986-by-johnson-cheu/.

Cranial Nerve II

Jill Khoury

the optic nerve

If the axon thicket
        does not flourish
the child will be IRREVERSIBLY BLIND.

        : and the kingdom weeps :

Say *lack of thread*

        : make it a romance :

Say *dead just dead*

        : moonless sky :

Say *hypoplasia*

        : In the coppice waits a deer   He rubs his antlers on a tree :

Say *usually correlated with other central nervous system defects*

        : Grew up near a river alongside the thalamus :

        : we are waiting for our :

Girl in a white robe with feathers
Girl with a knapsack stepping off a cliff
Girl with a picnic basket containing cake and wine
Girl with the face of a honey-colored dog
Girl on charity website who looks like me

Say *she was one of the lucky ones*
Say *she wasn't one of the lucky ones*

: the huntsman took scissors / cut open the mother's belly :

: girl wakes up in a spare circle of saplings :

Ask *can she see*

An Object Approaches the I

Jill Khoury

If the patient is monocular

rays of

light have a negative power

The eye

cannot accommodate it alters

proportion

focus

people

are useless unless they

adapt

a front

Source text for this erasure: *Understanding Low Vision*, edited by Randall T. Jose (American Foundation for the Blind, 1983), 220.

[rotary nystagmus]

Jill Khoury

Nystagmus is a term to describe fast, uncontrollable movements of the eyes. . . .
The term dancing eyes has been used to describe [it].–nih.gov

an oarsman army storms my aura

tango, tantrum song

taut-strung
gnat-stung

turns us
turns us
turns us

Kay Ulanday Barrett

WE WILL BUOY EACH OTHER

Excerpted and lightly edited from an interview by Alice Wong with Kay Ulanday Barrett that appeared on the Disability Visibility Project website in March 2020.

What kinds of change would you like to see in the publishing industry that would uplift and center Brown, Trans, Queer, and Disabled poets and writers?

I think it is very rare that I even see BIPOC (Black, Indigenous, and people of color) and Disabled Queer, Non-Binary, and Trans editors in poetry. The folio collaboration I edited with Nat.Brut, *Beyond Resilience,* was one of the few where I feel Trans and BIPOC curation occurred. I find that white editors and mostly straight cis people dominate literary space for Disabled mainstream publication. I was asked to be on a panel where I was a last-minute addition and so many of the white poets spoke about Disabled and Sick life separate from the institutional trappings of racism, poverty, xenophobia, and queer/transphobia. I realized at the moment how oftentimes I can move back as someone who acquired physical Disability as a young adult and not someone born physically Disabled. I also learned how the extent of what gets play in CripLit is very white, straight, and cis.

It is crucial to note that white and BIPOC Abled and/or Abled perceived poets and literary leaders rarely want to make events accessible, rarely have a Disabled Poet included in their rosters, or worse, even tokenize where there's this white Disabled person, so that is the check box met. I'm frequently the only Transgender and/or Disabled person on a panel or featured event. Is there this unsaid rule that there can't be more of us, that we are to compete even with each other? Interestingly enough, I have seen poets who didn't identify with Disability, Disabled culture, and community, now co-opting "spoons" yet make little to no effort to make basic accommodations at their readings or events, have no sense of Disabled poetry, arts, and activism that paved the way for that word to even enter their mouths.

Privileged people want to steal language and yet do little to shift the cultural landscape to center BIPOC Disabled, Sick, Neurodivergent, and Mad poets. We notice this now with COVID 19, how so many readings and events would apparently "suffer" if contributors or readers were online reading remotely, however as soon as Abled people are in fear, accommodations are now viable and streamlined. Again, about a year ago, it was frowned upon and deemed lazy, undedicated, *what do you mean this reading/event/conference isn't accessible?* Well, too bad for *you!* The onus is on *you,* **not** the general literary culture invested in Abled productivity and labor.

The key point is, reimagine the landscape. Make applications accessible and fees optional. So many fellowships, residencies, contests, and events are financially out of reach for many Disabled, Sick, and working class/Poor people. This isn't by accident. So many places that dub they have accessibility, actually don't, have highly scented areas or no alternatives for stairs, no active captioning or caption descriptions, have climates entrenched in a limited assumption of what Disability even is. I applied once to a writing retreat that deemed itself "accessible" and it was a nightmare, beds on the ground, crowded rooms, food meal times being pushed out of schedule. There was no acknowledgment of the inaccessibility. Instead I was told, "I'm so sorry this experience is not working for you. I am so sorry that you're having a hard time." The space's flagrant inaccessibility somehow became my fault for not bootstrapping it, for knowing my own access needs, for not being able to assimilate to Abled standards.

I want to say that many Disabled and Sick, Neurodivergent, Deaf, and Mad BIPOC have been doing the writing, the community work. Our communities create concrete strategy on a day-to-day basis due to the erasure and the institutionalized oppression we face on multiple levels. If literary space doesn't open up these avenues of accessibility, then dance, theater, and performance arts have filled that gap. Lastly, I receive many rejection letters. The criticisms are in this vein:

> Dear Poet,
>
> We thought your submission of XYZ poems were beautiful, strong, and engaging reads. We did feel however, that we had a problem connecting with the subject matter. Our concern was that there would be a disconnect with our readers.
>
> Signed,
> Likely Abled, White, Cis Straight Editorial Team

This isn't to say that every poem deserves a home, that there isn't revision or big edits I need to do. I am curious: What if my audience isn't the intended audience and therefore [I am] not publishable? What if people in power make assumptions of audience long before [work] even gets the option of being published? What if Disabled and Sick poets wrote for each other, that was our standard? What if in our stanzas, we longed for a new world we kept creating, line by line, spoon by spoon, the same $10 Venmo back and forth? Dear Disabled & Sick Poets, I will read you, we make space for each other on the page the way we do in real life, in Skype calls, in chat threads, in neighborhood mutual aid collectives. I don't think people will make room for us, we must take it, spasm in it, cough, and mask in it. We will write, read, and buoy each other.

Sick 4 Sick

Kay Ulanday Barrett

Her body patched, swollen skin,
hair flecks gone rogue, mismatch
knees, ache knits quilt throughout.
Curvature, a soft thing.

She said that if we hum close,
close enough that our chests touch,
shared breath comes from belly up,
—that, that is *not* platonic.

Now breathe same air, nostril kinetic
by way of brow cleft in migraine.
Syllables chop temples. Strain is
something to lull here, together.

When nerves are ablaze, I'm told
to be blanket. Lay my torso on theirs,
abdomen to abdomen, core to core,
is this what a field does to a hill,

spill it with poppies? I wait on
their skill. How she will sigh.
The human body is heating pad.
Limbs bonfire, flip sheets, you can't
reverse sick. Chests pulse softest lake.

Come spring we never do this again.
There's only memory of it,
how their lungs cathedral. How I prayed
there, on the ledge of inhale,

sternum sacred, coughed hymn, spasm
luminescence.

Syllables stretched, muscled
                sacrament more than splay,
                us petals in overlap, us
an ampersand
on fire.

I use the word Disabled

Kay Ulanday Barrett

because every doctor thinks—they know more about the cavity echo—of my feet
[than I do] because it's dirty word—where every stranger—self-discloses their arms—
skin—fevers like [family secret] because bodies aren't meant—to live—in whisper—
because whole events still [rampless]—how clipboards are—biggest fear—[monger]

because everyone can name one [token] Disabled or Deaf—poet who is usually white—
[and always] straight—because after speaking—as an expert [for a whole hour] in a
packed auditorium—during any Q&A—someone [eventually] doesn't ask a question
but says *You're not that.—You'll get better soon*—as though I haven't measured—

my sternum into—a city of MRIs—gazed at comet splatters—of X-rays—hospital
gown high hat ultrasounds—my season's [best]—as though my soundtrack isn't—
bass of prescription—bottles gone empty—every lost friend—every abled grimace
like a death—[somewhere] joy in crook of toes—equals some cold—nobody

wants to catch—about colds—every January some people—conflate their—dalliance
with cough syrup—with [my] blacking out—at laundromats—subways—a new partner's
bedroom—how the concave of chest—is altar where [friends] stopped checking in—
forgot to invite—candlelit rib for—every time someone in new pain—says *I get it now*—

an [incantation] for every time—you forever pang—in your skull—& a friend says—
[yeah] *I get headaches when I'm hung over too*—for if you don't make—a potluck—
meeting—twitter hour—you might be the dog [taken] out back—your work silenced—
for its own misery—together [we] pass lidocaine &—salonpas the way—our aunties

shared adobo recipe—we inherit collective—[care] because we—swap how-tos—on
advocacy with nurse—specialist—to oncologolost & [again]—to access-a-ride—our
texts from scratch—to survive spasm song—because another date—asked you about
your leg—& you know that you'll never [see]—them again & nobody understands

rejection like a sick—crip who brings you weed—& a casserole—tells you to not move a muscle—they'll get the tea—hope still twined on their—[throats] we have been a movement—all of us—an inhale—at the closest—sunset [windowsill]—as somebody tries to text—fried—but autocorrect anticipates—grief [same thing]

In which your white doctor informs you that he was in the Navy & based in the Philippines

Kay Ulanday Barrett

after Bao Phi

(Misgendered by Nurse. Puts on hospital robe. Doctor enters the room, shakes your hand to greet you. Misgenders you, again. Swings feet on the exam table. Kicks the air. Kicks the air. Kicks the air.) *

---

* feels like calling an older sister *Baby* / feels like *Baby* is now a first name for hundreds of women because that is what soldiers called women in my country, which means getting women ready for something / feels like wanting to fuck a grown woman with a payment of an American candy bar / feels like war town is misspelled and actually needs more letters, like R&R / feels like white men like this doctor say *maganda* to you, in the lobby, in the street, walking to the grocery store with a tank top on and you are only twelve yrs. old / feels like the notion of Spam as nostalgia doesn't apply when it is protein in a can when you are fleeing military checkpoints because it is light and easy to carry / feels like nanny carrying other people's children / feels like nanny means someone to fuck with when the wife and kids are away on day trips / feels like you are lucky we even let you live here / feels like nose to tail eating isn't as savage when white people sit at communal tables in candlelight / feels like their nurse is a hand job / feels like their massage therapist is a hand job / their care aid is a hand job / feels like they are devoutly Catholic, fear God, so essentially fear white people / feels like my outer layer open, exposed, and my medical treatment relies on this moment / feels like hipdeep dank dysphoria / feels like too many emotions hanging on the laundry line / feels like when the doctor tells you about the ocean, in turn, you are parched / feels thirsty, please give me water to get a moment alone / feels like another white man at some reading who talks to you about water torture when you were talking about tanka poems / feels like tanks again, in your dreams, dreams of your lola, inheritance / feels like stethoscope, clipboard, MRI / feels like you are seen right through and invisible / feels like you get why mama carried the rosary at all times / feels like if there weren't a needle taking my blood, I would tell you / feels like hunt and cleaver even before the knife is mentioned / feels like they are stealing me out of my body / feels like this not just about blood samples / feels like this theft is killing me.

consider the gender spectrum

Kay Ulanday Barrett

"I know what it is to be broken and be bold
Tell you that my silver is gold"
—Moses Sumney

when all your skin / reads trespass / reads not worth a piss /
literally / reads not even worth excrement / reads good enough to not be
dead / maybe if she sleeps with me / i am trained to think / pity

once / a man spat in my face / kicked / my cane / touched his
dick like a small itch / i erased into words like / dyke she-man die die /
you're never going to be / real / he says / i cannot tell you what that

does / to a person / as i was saying / another dude pushed me / stalked
me for blocks until i turned the corner / and faked a call on my / cell phone
that guy said / you don't have any friends / and he wasn't wrong exactly

i am not a real man / this doesn't happen to / everybody right
to be real / doesn't mean a war to meet someone's / parents or
to wear a shirt at the mall / because what is your love / but shame / worthy

this world / makes me feel that way / no matter the / constellation of well-
intentioned quotes / or rainbow like buttons / there are so many buttons /
no words can be barrier / for night terrors so i make / like a flicker / smile

at parties / which is a lie really for wanting / to be here / which is the scapegoat /
of something larger / says my therapist / and he quotes me throwing fire /
back to my heart / when all I want is to be melted / not almost ashes /

another dark poem / says another editor / and i think this is nothing /
i have a therapist at least / picture an alley / where your legs are tangled to
/ dumpster groans / and if actually reported on the news / they jam you

between a funny bird story / and a partly sunny forecast / and for fifteen
seconds the anchor / doesn't blink and bet you / they get your name
wrong / again / hashtag here

Raymond Antrobus

IS THERE A RIGHT WAY TO ACT DEAF [CAPTIONED]

Recently I had a conversation with a family member, who, after some small talk made a remark about my deafness that seemed to come out of nowhere. "You're about as deaf as I am blind." He said this without any malice in his voice (he is short sighted). It surprised me. I laughed it off, but it lingered.

[sound of sharp sensitivity]

A teacher I had at school once made a similar remark after I told him I need to sit at the front of class: "But you're not really deaf." Both these comments came from hearing abled-bodied (men with deep voices that I find it easier to hear). They seemed to rely on the stereotypes of what deafness looks like. I know these are narrow, flippant remarks, but there is something that interests me in them. How do people who don't engage with deaf people have such a fixed idea of what deafness is?

[sound of lost instructions]

In the 1989 film *Hear No Evil, See No Evil,* Gene Wilder plays David "Dave" Lyons (a non-signing, lipreading deaf man) alongside Richard Pryor, who plays a blind man (Wallace "Wally" Karew).[1] Wilder's performance fits the usual stereotype of deafness, aloof and buffoonish. He becomes a guide for Wally, while Wally fills in what is said behind David's back meaning the blind-deaf duo build a friendship. David appears to hear no sound. In one scene a gun is fired while David waits outside a shop. He doesn't flinch. This scene appears early in the film and affirms David's (stereotypical) deafness.

[sound of anomaly]

I have sometimes felt relief when I have to turn up my hearing aids or use my external microphone, or meet a deaf person I can sign with, because it asserts (to the hearing world) their expectation of deafness. In 2019, after being announced as the winner of the Ted Hughes Award, I was ushered into a back room to take a phone call from a BBC journalist. "Congratulations, Mr. Antrobus!" The voice was male, very English, strongly pronounced. The kind of voice I'm used to hearing on the radio. I could make out every other word said. This is how lip-reading works for me, I gather the words I can hear and guess at the context, the same is true for any conversation, but because the man had a clear voice and I had connected the phone to my Bluetooth hearing aids I could navigate the conversation efficiently. The first question he asked was, "It's my understanding that you're deaf, so how are you able to talk to me now?" It felt like an indictment, if it came from any kindness or deaf awareness he would have thought about this before the interview to assure I was properly prepared. I explained myself but the journalist sounded skeptical or disappointed that I wasn't the kind of deaf person that he expected.

[sound of more media consumption]

In the 2021 podcast episode of *The Daily* titled "Is There a Right Way to Act Blind," blind journalist Andrew Leland explains the phenomenon of coming up against people's expectation of blindness when you're not completely blind.[2] At an airport checkpoint he has his plane ticket in his hand, and he had been seen checking his phone, so when Leland tells the border agent that he is a journalist, the agents eyes suspiciously drift toward Leland's cane. He goes on to explain his type of blindness (a regenerative disease) and that he feels a sense of affirmation when he missteps on a pavement or bumps into a lamppost. In these moments his identity is (safely) affirmed.

[sound of spiral]

When *The Guardian* announced that I had won the Ted Hughes award, the article read "Deaf Poet Wins Award."[3] My sister had screenshot it and sent it to me, erasing the word "Deaf."

I had been educated in a deaf school in London and struggled in the hearing world after I left the school. I lost many day jobs because of pretending I could hear rather than affirming my deafness and asking for instructions to be repeated, or explaining that I wasn't ignoring the phone ringing at the reception desk or the customers greeting me.

[quietly burning]

I don't think my sister wanted me to claim my deafness. I'm used to her voice, I lipread her seamlessly, she forgets that I'm deaf. She seems uncomfortable when I'm referred to as a deaf person. I think it embarrasses her. But growing up I seemed quirky and aloof to her and her friends. I remember when I was twelve the 1999 film *The Matrix* came to prominence.[4] Friends everywhere had an opinion on the film. I pretended that I had seen it before I did. What I gathered from people's opinions was that the film was about something that people pretend to understand. So when I couldn't hear what someone said I would randomly blurt, "The Matrix!" and this made people laugh at the strange boy's (deaf) logic.

[sound of labour]

In David Lodge's 2008 semi-autobiographical novel, *A Deaf Sentence*, the protagonist, retired professor Desmond Bates, loses his hearing and struggles to come to terms as a late-deafened man.[5] He weighs the hierarchy of disability and how it is represented in "great art" (i.e., mainstream imaginations). He gloats, "blindness is tragic" because it has been examined and lived through by the greats (Milton and Shakespeare's King Lear, etc.); he concludes, "deafness is comedic."

[sound of flat light]

Recently I've got so tangled up in other people's assumptions, stereotypes, and confusions that I've gone back to calling myself "hard of hearing" rather than deaf. It doesn't require any follow-up questions from hearing people. Hard of hearing is generally a label for non-signing late-deafened people; however, I was born deaf. It's all I've ever known.

[sound of gold in head]

Paralympic archery champion Matt Stutzman was asked in an interview with astrophysicist Neil deGrasse Tyson whether he believes he has an advantage in archery as someone born without arms, rather than an athlete who lost their arms later in life. "Absolutely!" says Stutzman, not missing a beat. "It's all I know, I've never had to grieve or make any kind of readjustment—this is just who I am."[6]

[sound of living on a continuum]

I have found affirmation through poetry. On the page I get to navigate, interrogate, and investigate sound. I get to measure it against the assumptions of a hearing-centric culture, I get to write back to it, but more importantly I get to write with and to fellow deafies and non-able-bodied people who share this kind of lateral-non-abled language, knowledge, and logic.

[sound of soft reporting]

The day after the *Guardian* article appeared, a teacher of the deaf reached out and invited me to address an assembly at her school for Deaf Role Model Day. I stood in front of fifty deaf young people. I said something like "I am not interested in what we have lost as deaf people, I am interested in what we have gained." I read my (deaf) poems and I'll never forget the silence we sat in afterwards.

During the student Q&A, the first question came from a twelve-year-old boy, who sat at the back with a cut lip and brown hearing aids. He asked, "If you're a poet, does that mean I can be a poet?" "Yes!" I said, and the boy, under his breath, in a voice that was a whispery yell, said "Yes!"

[sound of conducting]

There isn't one way to be deaf and there isn't one way to write a "deaf poem." The poems selected here prove that you can engage with a news article (as was the case with "Two Guns In the Sky for Daniel Harris"). I had read a short article about the incident while visiting New York and knew it was a story I wanted to give volume to. You can engage with an existing text from a harmful document and erase it (as was the case with the erasure of Alexander Graham Bell's speech in "The Mechanism of Speech"). And you can assert your deaf myths as Oshun, my Deaf Goddess of music (who appears in "The Acceptance"). The poems have done their living and their thinking. They have navigated multiple modes of communication, they know they are more than poems, they are documents, affirmations, experiments, experiences, and a deaf poet has crafted each of them.

Welcome.

Notes

1. Arthur Hiller, *See No Evil, Hear No Evil* (Tristar, 1989).

2. Andrew Leland, "Is There a Right Way to Act Blind," *The New York Times*, July 1, 2021, https://www.nytimes.com/2021/07/01/magazine/in-the-dark-blindness.html.

3. *The Guardian*, March 27, 2019, https://www.theguardian.com/books/2019/mar/27/deaf-poet-raymond-antrobus-wins-ted-hughes-prize.

4. The Wachowskis, *The Matrix* (Warner Bros., 1999).

5. David Lodge, *Deaf Sentence* (New York: Penguin. 2009).

6. "Earth, Wind, and Water with Dr. Skateboard, the Armless Archer, and Jud Ready," August 6, 2021, https://startalkmedia.com/show/earth-wind-and-water-with-dr-skateboard-the-armless-archer-and-jud-ready/.

Two Guns in the Sky for Daniel Harris

Raymond Antrobus

When Daniel Harris stepped out of his car
the policeman was waiting. Gun raised.

I use the past tense though this is irrelevant
in Daniel's language, which is sign.

Sign has no future or past; it is a present language.
You are never more present than when a gun

is pointed at you. What language says this
if not sign? But the police officer saw hands

waving in the air, fired, and Daniel dropped
his hands, his chest bleeding out onto concrete

meters from his home. I am in Breukelen Coffee House
in New York, reading this news on my phone,

when a Black policewoman walks in, two guns
on her hips, my friend next to me reading

the comments section: *Black Lives Matter.*
Now what could we sign or say out loud

when the last word I learned in ASL was *alive*?
Alive—both thumbs pointing at your lower abdominal,

index fingers pointing up like two guns in the sky.

The Mechanism of Speech

Raymond Antrobus

His tongue was too far forward

His tongue further back

His tongue too high, too low

His incorrect instrument

his difficult power

to muscle

meaning

Lectures delivered before the American Association to Promote the Teaching of Speech to the Deaf by Alexander Graham Bell. An erasure.

The Acceptance

Raymond Antrobus

Dad's house stands again, four years
after being demolished. I walk in.
He lies in bed, licks his rolling paper,
and when I ask *Where have you been?*
We buried you. He says *I know,*

I know. I lean into his smoke, tell him
I went back to Jamaica, I met your brothers,
losing you made me need them. He says
something I don't hear. *What?* Moving lips,
no sound. I shake my head. He frowns.

Disappears. I wake in the hotel room,
heart pounding. I get up slowly, the floor
is wet. I wade into the bathroom,
my father stands by the sink, all the taps
running. He laughs. I ask him *Are you*

back? He takes my hand, squeezes,
his ring digs into my flesh. I open my eyes.
I'm by a river, a shimmering sheet
of green marble. Red ants crawl up
an oak tree's flaking bark. My hands

are cold mud. I follow the tall grass
by the riverbank, the song. The Orisha,
Oshun in gold bracelets and earrings, scrubs
her yellow dress in the river. I wave, *Hey!*
She keeps singing. The dress turns the river

gold and there's my father surfacing.
He holds a white and green drum. I watch him
climb out the water, drip toward Oshun.
They embrace. My father beats his drum.
With shining hands, she signs: *Welcome.*

4

MEDICALIZATION

Stephanie Helt

DISABILITY AS A CREATIVE PRACTICE

Do I begin this essay with pen on paper, for the feel of cursive curves in my body and the visceral contact of my left hand dragging over ink? Or do I tap it out on the computer keyboard with its seductive delete key? These questions of medium and form direct my writing process. The poems in this anthology are part of *Psych Murders* (Wayne State University Press, 2022). When I'd begun writing this book about my experiences of shock treatment, memory loss, psych hospitalizations, and bipolar extreme mind states, I wasn't sure about the form the work would take. For me, usually content comes before form. I write by hand in an unlined journal and later—days, months, sometimes years, or not at all—I transfer the words to the computer and then revise. The next step is to listen to the material and figure out the form on the page. What shape or feeling does the poem wish to take? Where on the page? How does it breathe? What are its edges? Soft parts? Textures? What are its movement qualities?

This choreography on paper, of how the words move and dance in the white space, is a result of my first language, movement. I trained to become a professional dancer from a young age, focusing on modern dance, improvisation, and choreography. This career trajectory was interrupted when depression, which had been a frequent childhood visitor, grounded me from my eight-hour training days as a college dance major. I couldn't walk a block, much less dance. I'd always been a writer too, often combining words and movement in my performances. Poetry entered more strongly in my life as a creative outlet when my beloved medium, dance, wasn't available. Instead, I played with words, considering the choreographic principles of space, time, and energy, only this time on the page instead of the stage. Poetry became another way to make dances.

This fluidity between disciplines and forms is one I value and need to thrive. Disability has required me to be extra creative and adaptable—to come up with adjustments and new forms to accommodate my own changing capacities. As someone who identifies around mental health difference, and more specifically, bipolar, my moods and capacities shift: levels of energy, focus, concentration, interest, ability to read and write, ability to move. I don't necessarily have a ground or baseline I can take for granted. Sometimes I need/want/have to change things up.

Years ago, I started thinking about bipolar as its own discipline, alongside writing and movement. Indeed, it is something I've trained in and studied for the majority of my life. It is a discipline I know intimately. And it demands that I pay attention, notice shifts, alter my lifestyle and pace based on the current constraints of bipolar energies. This attunement means that my art practice doesn't stay the same and often has an unpredictable timeline and production schedule.

In the process of writing *Psych Murders*, another factor that worked as a creative constraint was my closeness to the material. I was writing about lived experience whose trauma still left (and leaves) its traces on my bodymind. Also, these events were barely in the rearview mirror when I started writing about them. But I needed to write these poems. Like the anesthesia used to put me under during the shock treatments, so many of my experiences were blurry and surreal. It had taken so much out of me to make it through those five-plus years of intense suicidal ideation and over a dozen psych inpatient stays. I wanted to explore how time and sequence work when memory is disrupted, in my case due to traumatic brain injury. I needed to document and reclaim my own sensorium. To take back the language used by medical people to write their version of my story. To write my own narration.

The shock poems came to life in a new way: content followed form. I created three sections based on how the hospital basement was organized for electroconvulsive therapy or shock: waiting bay, treatment room, recovery bay. These became the framework for the material, and their physical geography informed where individual pieces lived on the page. In revision, some of these initial details changed, but this spatial arrangement gave me an entry into difficult material. I was able to narrow my focus into specific moments of before, during, and after the shock sessions. The placement on the page gave the material a strong container that made it more manageable and a little less raw; all those sharp and swirling feelings had a home outside of me that I could revise and hone.

Another crucial aspect to my art practice, and definitely to the creation of these poems, is collaboration. I like to mix up writing and dance, and I like to do that with other people. My main collaborator is my wife, the community performance artist and disability culture activist Petra Kuppers. We engage in regular somatic investigations, often outdoors, where we move together and tune our senses to our inner and outer surroundings. Then we write. This touching in, literally, with another human as I worked on *Psych Murders* offered me a way to stay connected and not get caught in any painful memory loops, or at the very least, offered me a safety mechanism to return to the present moment and my bodymind when I did get stuck.

Bipolar is a creative practice for me. It is integral to who I am (as is being a poet and dancer), how I move through the world, what I notice, and to what intensity. I spent many years wanting to get rid of bipolar; it certainly comes with a lot of painful and difficult aspects. Eventually, I realized bipolar wasn't going anywhere without me, so I began to figure out how to honor and harness all those energies and ways of being. Now I embrace being a disabled poet and dancer, and I do my best to live my life as a creative practice—in community, in care, in joy.

Electrical Work Index Series

Stephanie Heit

"Index Series" is the term used in electroconvulsive therapy (ECT) to describe the initial six to twelve shocks that generally do the trick. Then there are "continuation" and "maintenance." My course (or their course, depending) was approximately thirty sessions from October 2011 through March 2012.

Treatment Room

Drive-thru fast. Curtain pulled. Bed head hinged horizontal. Doctor in the corner in white. Anesthesiologist out of sight behind my head. I interrupt the oxygen mask, ask for names. Before I am ready they push sleep,

push their batons

on both my temples, hit on.

Recovery Bay

I investigate what my body did. See a program on ECT with a scene at the university with one of the Whitecoats. I can't look away. Whitecoat places his hand on her foot while she is seizing (notice the pronouns, they rarely change). My cells rally screaming, *Don't touch her.* I want to know what happened to my body while I was away. Who touched me. What pressure. Where. During the seizure what did my face do. *Homeland* Claire Danes ECT scene. I look away. But glance at the TV before it is over. I replace my face with her squinched one, arched neck.

Dear Brain

I'm sorry.

I remember when Whitecoat told me I'd have a new brain after this, like it was a present. I felt sadness even in my apathetic stupor. I liked my original brain. This new one fails me, betrays its injuries daily as I navigate my city only with Siri's aid. It acts more colander than container.

Emilia Nielsen

A NOTE ON THE POETRY AND POETICS OF DISSONANT DISABILITIES

In their introduction to *Dissonant Disabilities: Women with Chronic Illnesses Explore Their Lives*, Diane Driedger and Michelle Owen ask: "Can women with chronic illnesses identify as people with disabilities all the time or only sometimes?"[1] This is a complex question because while chronic illness can be a source of disability for some, for others it is unpredictably so. In fact, if I am not currently experiencing unmanageable symptoms, what is my relationship to chronic illness? What is my identity in relation to disability?

What I wish to explore is engendered by fierce love and fueled by curiosity. I am querying what the poetry and poetics of disability might offer, as a mode of writing, theorizing, and community making, for those of us who identify as chronically ill. Uncomfortably, my poetic exploration is self-referential, for I'm obliquely curious as to why *I* decided to write to my experience of life-altering illness, and the protracted nature of chronic illness, through the genre of poetry. While my second book of poetry, *Body Work*, seeks to do so, this predicament is not, in fact, straightforwardly resolvable because at one time if there was anything in my life that I most wanted to keep private it was my struggle with chronic illness.[2]

In those first years of living with autoimmune disease, I first refused and then reluctantly came to terms with the fact that illness, for me, was not only too often distressing, it was too often distinctly disabling. My new role of "patient" was profoundly uncomfortable, especially as I had constructed a rather narrow identity complicit in tacitly espousing "compulsory able-bodiedness."[3] In living with chronic illness, I came to understand my own dialogue of self-worth—my own self-conception—as unwittingly ableist. But I do not believe such a disproportionate investment in able-bodiedness is an inevitability of living much of one's life as normatively nondisabled. The reality of chronic illness is that it is disruptive and too often persistently so. It defies traditional biomedical understandings of disease because "chronic illness is about being both sick and healthy—at the same time."[4] Such a reconceptualization suggests that the protracted nature of chronic illness must be examined in relation to dominant discourses that continue to understand disease most often as acute, but not ongoing. Given that I was living in dissonance, simultaneously well and unwell, I had a new awareness that I had as much to unlearn about disease as I did to rethink how illness and disability were now an ongoing part of my life.

If crip theory can bring concepts such as "compulsory able-bodiedness" and "compulsory heterosexuality" together, I was seeking to understand not only what this might say about my own identity but about how to understand chronic illness through such a mode of theorizing.[5] When I had first needed it, queer theory provided me with a useful frame to understand my experience of desire, and thus to destabilize categorical notions of "heterosexual" and "homosexual." I have long understood "queer" to function as so much more than a synonym for "lesbian" or "gay," and the subversive potential of queering sexuality remains. Eve Sedgwick's 1993 assertion that "what it takes—all it takes—to make the description 'queer' a true one is the impulsion to use it in the first person."[6] With this knowledge, why was claiming "crip" proving so difficult? Then, it was much more complicated than a diagnosis of chronic illness might suggest.

At that time, during active autoimmune disease, unlike many people with disabilities, I was sick and unsure if I would ever be well again. I lived with enormous uncertainty where the future was concerned. In those early years of truly struggling, ironically, others did not recognize me as ill, and I certainly was not understood to be a person with a disability. Because my illness was seemingly "invisible," although I experienced both physical and cognitive impairments, I felt written out of disability culture because I did not see my experience reflected in the images and words with which I was engaging. When I happened upon the term "dissonant disabilities" to describe chronic illnesses I became further convinced that chronic illness requires study not only from disability frameworks but demands articulations about the lived experience of ongoing pain and fatigue. Often, this research and writing takes place in the context of being rendered invisible as a person with a disability. Overwhelmingly, I also came to understand that the best people to do this scholarship are those living with chronic illnesses, not because other researchers are unable to uncover the realities of dissonant disabilities, but because I came to value reading work that was as disruptive, unpredictable, and unruly as the bodies and minds from which the work emerged.

I am reminded now, as I was stunned to learn back then, how little writing about women with chronic illnesses exists within the academic literature. Importantly, Pamela Moss and Isabel Dyck's 2002 book, *Women, Body, Illness: Space and Identity in the Everyday Lives of Women with Chronic Illness*, makes a substantial contribution to the discourse. Here they propose a "radical body politics" to better understand how women with chronic illnesses negotiate identity formation and daily spaces in everyday life.[7] This theorizing emerged out of Moss and Dyck's qualitative study where they sought to reembody—"spatially, materially, discursively, politically"—chronically ill women "as ill bodies in a healthy society."[8] Moreover, I want to suggest that any "radical body politic" of chronic illness demands an examination of how gender, sexual orientation, race, ethnicity, socioeconomic status, and age influence the diagnosis and treatment of disease; therefore, the difficulty of living with complex diagnoses. More importantly, this frame of "radical body politics" illuminates how biomedical definitions of chronic illness do not adequately give voice to the intensity of living with an unrelenting state of bodily uncertainty, nor how this affects identity formation. Here, then, is where I see the role of poetry, because as a genre it provides a space for the deeply subjective articulation of experiential knowledge. Poetry, too, is radical in that it often defies the very genre that is supposed to lend it definitional stability.

Body Work explicitly undertakes to write the undoing of the body via a crip poetics. This is poetry written out of crip experience in the mode of a poetics that explicitly engages with innovative or experimental techniques. Here the footnote functions as another poetic voice, as this "found poetry" is made up of lines of prose taken from Anita G. Jablonski's *Skin: A Natural History*.[9] While it is my intention to crip chronic illness in the long poem "Symptomatic," in the end, I also understand that meaning making is co-created with you, reader, as you distill these words through a crip perspective or as someone willing to be nudged, winced even, into another way of understanding the world. In these poems, language play is brought to the fore, as there is pleasure too in evoking playfulness, in claiming what might otherwise be understood as a personal tragedy as a site of unexpected whimsicality.

Notes

1. Diane Driedger and Michelle Owen, eds., *Dissonant Disabilities: Women with Chronic Illnesses Explore Their Lives* (Women's Press, 2008), 8.

2. Emilia Nielsen, *Body Work* (Signature Editions, 2018).

3. Robert McRuer, "Compulsory Able-Bodiedness and Queer/Disabled Existence," in *Disability Studies: Enabling the Humanities*, ed. Rosemarie Garland-Thomson, Brenda Jo Brueggemann, and Sharon L. Snyder (MLA Publications), 2002.

4. Pamela Moss and Isabel Dyck, *Women, Body, Illness: Space and Identity in the Everyday Lives of Women with Chronic Illness* (Rowman & Littlefield, 2002), 14.

5. Adrienne Rich, "Compulsory Heterosexuality and Lesbian Existence," *Signs: Journal of Women in Culture and Society* 5 no.4 (1980): 631–60.

6. Eve Kosofsky Sedgwick, *Tendencies* (Routledge, 1994), 9.

7. Moss and Dyck, 9.

8. Moss and Dyck, 10.

9. Anita G. Jablonski, *Skin: A Natural History* (University of California Press, 2006).

From "Symptomatic"

Emilia Nielsen

Tremors

First morning, thought: atmospheric. Unpredictable
uproar, external. Jackhammer roadwork—
too much caffeine? Thought fault line
                                        this quaking;
geologic, tumult; thought semi-trailer and traffic.
Thunder, galvanic.[1] Waited, felt chemical.

[1] Our skin, a compromise worried over the table of evolution.

Emotional Lability

Indifferently, indefinitely smashing
plates. Bull in glass house. Gauche,
tactless. Pressed between pages: clinical,
capricious. Performance unremarkable,
unexceptional. Predictable.°

°Skin is a complex layering of both physical and chemical properties. This laminar construction gives the skin its resistance to abrasions and punctures.

Polyphagia

Full: illusive.[p] Bright idea refusing
illumination—conjecture at best—
a failed twenty minute rule; theory
absenting practice, phenomena not
of this appetite, this stomach that begins
and ends, day in and day out—empty
as most questions.

[p]It shields us from the environment, resists water, stains, microbes, and many chemicals. This outermost layer, the epidermis, is smart stuff.

Hypertensive

Ask leapfrog heart to put down
roots, stay put.[t] Roost: seize
time to settle. Settle down, sapper-
ticker. Animal, mineral, vegetable,
blood pumping organ grinder. Heart
on the brain, percussive in throat.

[t]Our expressive faces convey subtle nuances in relation to what we are feeling. Through these expressions, we not only have compensated for a lack of tactility via body hair that can fluff and bristle, some of us can even smile, grimace, or cry on demand.

Travis Chi Wing Lau

THE CRIP POETICS OF PAIN

Does pain's nature change just because I can now name it?

Despite having shared most of my life with pain, I only recently learned the formal name of my disability: *kyphoscoliosis.* A combination of two spinal deformities—kyphosis (from the Greek *kyphos,* meaning "bent," referring to the rounding of the upper back that can create a severe curve colloquially referred to as a "hunchback") and scoliosis (the curvature of the spine left or right into an "S" or "C" shape)—kyphoscoliosis often manifests in childhood and usually gets identified through routine screenings done in grade school. If diagnosed early enough, physical therapy or bracing can prevent further curvature or even correct it. Yet for many, including myself, the curvature can develop late and without cause—what medical professionals describe as *idiopathic.* While kyphoscoliosis is referred to as a singular diagnostic entity, it is also a conflation of two separate spinal deformities. Accompanying this complex condition is a host of other conditions related to its effects on my musculoskeletal system, from shortness of breath due to the contortion of my rib cage, to brain fog, anxiety, and irritable bowel syndrome, closely linked with my chronic pain.[1] Interconnectedness, even if painfully so.

Without the certainty of origins, a younger me found it easy to speculate wildly, to blame genes and the follies of nurture, to blame my own ignorant self. *Why this set of conditions? Why this pain? And if I found out why, what then?* I spent years writing toward these origins that I slowly sensed were illusory, if not irrelevant. While I remained fixated on the past, the health care providers I met were busy looking ahead: They all see a future where my pain will worsen, whether or not I discover the cause. Some more fatalistic than others, these prognostications resemble the fatalistic definitions from Molly McCully Brown's poem "Dictionary of Hereditary Defects": they seem to imagine nothing else in my future but pain and only pain—a blanketing totality that permits no escape.[2] Admittedly, this future is not entirely exaggeration: I have witnessed so many of my family members with spines that curve and fingers that gnarl. *The writing is on the wall,* my primary care physician recently warned me. But is what is written only incapacity and dread of its inevitable coming?

Crip poetry has taught me how to imagine futures with bodies like mine thriving. Alongside the disabled writers I have come to admire, I find myself returning again and again to works of speculative fiction and poetry, which Margaret Ronda valorizes for aesthetics that "play on the tense, shifting, unstable relationship between what was, is, and could be, offering other imaginative possibilities that recast present historical tendencies in new light."[3] Despite speculative fiction's "predominantly narrative modality," speculative poetry's "capacities for paratactic leap and temporal play, its nonlinear logics and modes of expansion and condensation" have made it a particularly exciting site for crip intervention.[4] Or as I have tried to show, crip poetics has been doing this work all along. I have come to understand crip poetics as engaging in its own capacious project of speculation into more inclusive and accessible futures. Disability poetics is hopeful world-making, and understanding how my chronic pain and scoliosis-related disability contribute to that larger project involves an ongoing process of ethical reflection about what it is that chronic pain has taught me. Emma Sheppard remarks that "chronic pain does not require constant remaking of the world and of the self because it creates a new state of being: one becomes a person who lives *with* pain rather than a person or body *in* pain."[5] For me, this cripistemological process of learning how to live beside and with my pain has been the work of poetry.

In recent years, my mother has taken to placing a hand on my shoulder when we take walks together during my visits home. Despite her fatigue and sharp pains after about fifteen minutes of slow walking, we make the effort because we appreciate the fact that we can still share this pained experience together. I used to feel like we were taking steps closer and closer to our inevitable loss of mobility—a bedridden end that she has seen happen generation after generation in her family. My mom herself laments what she sees as her increasing dependence on others to do "something as simple as walking." This is what compulsory ablebodiedness does: It makes us mourn the loss of something mythical—our independence. But I finally appreciate the interdependence made possible by our shared experiences of scoliosis-related disability across generational lines. Our two bodies connected by her arm on mine, our mutual balancing in careful motion. We teeter, we limp, we backtrack, we stop to rest. This, too, is crip poetry.

While I may never fully know my mother's pain and she may never fully know mine, this is not the unbridgeable chasm of difference that Elaine Scarry imagines in the encounter between two bodies in pain.[6] In fact, if I have learned anything from my own pained poetics, it is precisely an appreciation of the pain of others that opens up new crip models of care that can truly cater to pain's queer forms. This appreciation is a relinquishing of perfect knowing, a cripistemology that remains vulnerably open to being unable to fully access one another's pain but still honoring it. In Javier Moscoso's cultural history of pain, he alludes to Ludwig Wittgenstein's relational theory of pain as a rejoinder to Scarry's theory of pain's unsharability: "Scarry's great intuition, that pain has to do with meaning, weakened when we accept that meaning should always be referential (which is obviously not the case) and when we miss its collective nature."[7] Wittgenstein's claim is simple: that we only know pain and the pain of others through language, which constitutes communities of pain as an interdependent, interrelational set of experiences. We may approach pain's event horizons through language, but the point is not to achieve perfect understanding of each individual experience of pain—this is futile work that gets us no closer to the solidarities we need to achieve the accessible futures we desire.

What remains at stake is a collective project of imagining what living with pain together can look and feel like rather than working to imagine painless worlds or a world of private pains. Such a pluralistic vision was what David Morris, five years after Scarry's thesis, speculated would be the future of pain: "a pain that has recovered or discovered its multiple voices," that "promises not so much a chaos or babel of competing tongues as the possibility that we may learn how to enrich our knowledge of pain by listening to more than one voice."[8]

Notes

This essay has been excerpted from "The Crip Poetics of Pain," *Amodern* 10 (2020), https://amodern.net/article/the-crip-poetics-of-pain/.

1. I am indebted to Susan Sontag in *AIDS and Its Metaphors* (Farrar, Strauss, and Giroux, 1989) and Paula Treichler in "AIDS, Homophobia, and Biomedical Discourse: An Epidemic of Signification," *AIDS: Cultural Analysis/Cultural Activism* 43 (1987): 31–70, for their reminder that AIDS is not only carelessly conflated with HIV but also flattens what is actually a series of different illnesses and opportunistic infections that affect immunocompromised individuals.

2. Molly McCully Brown, *The Virginia State Colony for Epileptics and Feebleminded* (Persea Books, 2017), 56.

3. Margaret Ronda, "The Social Forms of Speculative Poetics," *Poetry's Social Forms,*

ed. Margaret Ronda and Lindsay Turner, *Post45: Contemporaries* (April 8, 2019).

4. Ronda, "The Social Forms of Speculative Poetics."

5. Emma Sheppard, "using pain, living with pain," *Feminist Review* 120 (2018): 65.

6. Elaine Scarry, *The Body in Pain: The Making and Unmaking of the World* (Oxford University Press, 1985).

7. Javier Moscoso, *Pain: A Cultural History* (Palgrave Macmillan, 2012), 5.

8. David Morris, *The Culture of Pain* (University of California Press, 1993), 283.

Treatment

Travis Chi Wing Lau

after the verdict
begins a series of acts
in the name of correction
for nature's error cannot be
left to its own machinations so
you martial your own mechanics
into a hard solution of gear and gravity
really a tissue of theories stretched like my
body on the rack that at first feels something
like pleasure when the spaces between the vertebrae
expand against the ill will of time whose years are
compressed into minutes but the relief slips like
the discs back into an inaccessible place
indexed only by a species of cry that
permits no escape other than in
viced gasps that remind you
reluctantly when to stop

On the Anniversary of an X-Ray

Travis Chi Wing Lau

the technicians peace offering is layered
neatly into quarters
to be drawn with string

a gown to cover what will be
exposed
to the light of truth
sharp cold

how it makes
an opening of me

to an augur hiding behind
screen and oath
when verdict reduces flesh to word

spare and sanitary
without the traces of filth
that separates me from a
number

a call
a value
peals strip away skin
two bells to reassure her
it is safe
safe from dangerous
truth

Brain Fog

Travis Chi Wing Lau

after Charles Dickens

implacable
as much mud in the streets
as if the waters
had but newly retired
from the face of the earth
waddling like an elephantine lizard

smoke lowering down
a soft black drizzle
with flakes of soot
gone into mourning
for the death of the sun
undistinguishable in mire

a general infection of ill temper,
losing foot-hold since the day broke
(if this day ever broke)

adding new deposits to the crust
upon crust of mud,
sticking at those points
tenaciously

fog everywhere
fog up the river,
fog down the river
where it rolls deified
great (and dirty)
fog creeping
fog lying
fog drooping
fog in the eyes and throats

fog in the stem and bowl
fog cruelly pinching the toes and fingers
shivering
a nether sky of fog

the raw afternoon is rawest
and the dense fog is densest
obstruction
at the very heart of the fog

the groping and floundering condition
most pestilent
holds this day in the sight of heaven and earth.

Pithy

Travis Chi Wing Lau

All day, all night the body intervenes.

—Virginia Woolf

1. I shrug off my messenger onto the floor and forget to kiss you when I walk through the door.
Pith: the pain has its steel hoop around my lumbar.

2. I catch myself tottering—a deformation of my walk.
Pith: a family resemblance: the curvature progresses faster than any other before me. I am not yet thirty.

3. I take a tumble after I miss the curb.
Pith: had you not caught me by the arm, I would have finally broken my first bone.

4. I switch positions before I even alight.
Pith: I never thought pain would claim intimacy for its own.

5. I crack three different places. It annoys you. It worries you.
Pith: they said it would make my knuckles bigger, but it is one of my most futile of pleasures.

6. I submerge myself in an epsom bath.
Pith: smelling like eucalyptus and lavender is the closest to relief because you can fool at least one of your senses.

7. I lay against you as we watch the ship go into warp.
Pith: I laid this way while doing homework all through high school, and my case silently went from light to moderate.

8. I cannot form sentences. Non sequitur, organic hesitancy.
Pith: I would never wish upon anyone a life in the thickness of fog. The shame of being lost in it.

9. I can't make it up the stairs while cradling the box.
Pith: I hate admitting that I will have to depend on you more and more. That you will have to lie to me that it's okay.

10. I am cold and distant.
Pith: pain is subterranean, a geography to which you will forever be foreign. To be present is to also be far away.

11. I will myself to take deeper breaths. You think something is wrong.
Pith: the shallowest part of me is my breath. Some days feel breathless in all the wrong ways.

12. I look perpetually exhausted.
Pith: pain redefines what labor means.

13. I look unhappy.
Pith: joy so often feels remote, but you are teaching me that it never left me.

14. I wish it were otherwise.
Pith: magical thinking can really be cruel optimism.

15. I choose not to operate.
Pith: why should a boy ever have to choose between a life in motion or recumbence?

Kelly Davio

A LITTLE POCKET FOR RAGE

Two things in my mortal existence were meant to ennoble me and failed: First among them is living in a disabled body, and the second is doing something literary about it.

No one can pinpoint where this trope came from, can they? But it's long been with us: the idea that a person is morally improved by the experience of a less-than-normal body. The physically bent, busted, or broken breeds patience, generosity, empathy, rectitude, and so forth—this litany of good traits is bound up in the notion of overcoming. Long-suffering. Generic-brand asceticism and sainthood.

Wherever the idea came from, the person who piloted the archetype should earn a royalty, because it's really got lift. Whether it's a novel, a college admissions essay, a human-interest news story, or a dating show on prime time, a triumph over the "challenges" of the body is a narrative that won't let us go. And the owner of the challenging body has a role to play—a script to satisfy, a sense of moral edification to deliver.

Unfortunately, I haven't risen to the occasion.

My neuromuscular disease and everything that's come with it have not put me on the path of quiet personal growth. I am told that I should have developed patience and that I should have learned (among other things) to seize the day, but a fairly quick personal inventory does not reveal much that's reassuring.

Have I developed patience? If that's what we want to call waiting years for medical appointments that our state health system cancels again and again, then I have developed patience. Do I live every day as if it were my last? I certainly live with that fear now that we live in a slow-moving viral apocalypse that harrows bodies like mine. Have I grown an extra whole chamber of my heart to house all of the empathy that my experience has given me?

Empathy—now that is a word that we literary types like to throw around, don't we? For some years, it was hard to sit through an author's Q&A after a reading without having to hear about "a study" (methodology unspecified) that demonstrated that people who read a certain Chekhov story were more empathetic after their half-hour or so of reading than they were before. The takeaway, more than a few people suggested, was that we writers were Big Empathy Generators, capable of improving other people, even.

By extension, if we disabled writers had the courage to tell our stories, bare our pain to the world, or (to handle Hemingway roughly) sit down at our typewriters, open a vein, and bleed, we could Do Something about the human condition.

Unfortunately, I've failed here, too.

There have been times in my writing efforts that I've attempted to write for the abled gaze—tried to unpick the stitches on my existence so that people unlike me could get a good look at the inner workings. I explained what it's like to live in a body like mine and to heave it around town with me, how it feels to be carved upon like a Christmas goose, what it is to be viewed by medical students who are excited to a get a look at a living, breathing rarity. I did it so that—maybe—others would understand and possibly even care.

But that effort at firing up the empathy machine in my writing left me with an email inbox full of people I'd never met telling me about the different attitudes that I should take. Telling me what I should do differently with my life. Telling me that I am wrong to feel, think, and know what I do. They delivered all of this as if I were a bin for their worst fears: their terror that "mindfulness," positive thinking, and a diet of vegetables won't really stave off the reaper. Their fear that, if they were in a body like mine, they wouldn't want to stay tethered to it.

So I'm not making myself better, nor am I improving anybody else with this life or with the things that I write about it. What's it all about, then?

Sometimes I think about my disabled poetry like it's that little jeans pocket that nobody's ever known what to do with. You know the one I mean—the tiny bit of your trousers that's not big enough to cart around much of any bulk, but not small enough to escape notice, either. And I think about that pocket—small, nonfunctional, and inessential as a poem—as a place to carry my anger.

I do not need to list for you the sources of disabled rage. If this volume of poetry is in your possession, it's probably because you know as well as I know the ways that the world was never made for us, and that it is, year after year, increasingly hostile to our existence. If you, like me, have made it this far during a global pandemic (and I hold the possibly silly hope that maybe one day we'll have made it beyond), I know what you've had to do—what you've had to give up—to stay alive.

And if you, like me, are incandescent with anger, that's what my poems are for. They are little pockets for rage—yours and mine. Places where it's safe to let our anger burn. A few stanzas where I—and you are invited—don't have to improve myself or anyone else to be allowed to put words to our experience. A place where we can imagine, anyway, that we can burn it all down.

I May Appear Drunk

Kelly Davio

When the dog tag arrives by mail,
it is too small. An inch long at best,
the front surface is all but covered
by a medic alert symbol, a staff

twined by two snakes in shadow.
On the back, carved warnings crowd
the metal plate. They leave no margin,
no space around the Latin term

that slurs a diagnosis, each word
brushing the next. It cautions that I
will have trouble breathing. My eyes
will lack focus. I won't form words

that sound like speech. I'll try to stand
and fail. Check my purse for pills, it says,
and for emergency phone numbers.
No room to say the rest, to explain

that where bones anchor my cloudy
film of a soul, I contain mysteries.
I want to say that if my pupils swing
from side to side, they aren't unlike

the eyes of God, pendulous on a thread.
That they're coiled tight in the hum
of the planet's whirling. If I smack my face
to the soil, knocking myself senseless,

then I have learned the ecstasies just
as Saint Theresa knew them, my body

so still you'll never see me rise, never
notice me levitate. My breath crackles

with all Saint Julian learned as paralysis
filched her toes, then knees. What remained
was her knowledge beyond all telling:
We must both fall and be aware of falling.

He Died After a Long Illness

Kelly Davio

That's how the obituaries phrase it. He had
an *underlying condition*, they assure us.
We shake the newspaper free of its creases
and are comforted, somehow, by the conditions
of death. We are invited to imagine it as a pebble,
flung by chance or wedged by a bystander
into the long-grinding gears of pain. A mercy,
we say to one another. A kindness, really.
We assure ourselves that nothing underlies us;
no pathogenic beasts rumble under mattresses
while we lie open-eyed in the dark, unable to sleep
for the shadows that loom on our walls. We
don't need mercy. We laugh at kindness.
Our gears rotate freely on, greased by luck,
by good and careful programming of genes.

Etymological Note

Kelly Davio

Before the seventeenth century,
the English language had no noun
for *comfort.* No way to describe

that state of better-off-ness
for sleeping on a bed of hay
than on a bare plank. No word

to express how much that hay's
texture might be improved
without the creep of insect

or midnight scuttle of mouse.
Comfort was only a verb—to solace,
to strengthen, to give what aid

or blessing one could against
a hemorrhagic wound or lung
splitting with rot. To be

comfortable meant nothing beyond
able to bear someone else's idea
of help: the smoke of censer

at prayer, the crumbling wafer
of last rites—bodily gestures
that lead a spirit into the dark.

When the nurse cracks the door,
the thin wedge of light raking
at my eyes, reminding my body

that it is body still, she asks if I
am comfortable. I say yes, reach out
my silent hand for touch.

Camisha L. Jones

POETRY, SELF-ADVOCACY, AND SURVIVAL

I am sitting in the waiting room of a hospital after checking in for surgery. My spouse is with me. On the car ride up, I've talked him through my plan. The hospital staff have told me they will "assess" whether he needs to come back with me when I arrive. Just a few months earlier, the hospital altered its COVID visitor restrictions after receiving complaints from disabled patients who'd been denied the accommodation of having someone accompany them while in the hospital. I've mentioned that I'm hard of hearing to every person involved in the presurgical registration process—the person who calls me to find out what medicines I'm taking and advises me on what to do and not do prior to the surgery, the person at the check-in desk who takes my insurance card and payment, the person I'm sent to after making my payment. Each tells me the same thing: "they'll assess" prior to surgery. One does so with a tinge of attitude.

I've shown up more prepared than I've ever been to visit a medical facility. I've had years of bad experiences at this point, compounded by the pandemic. There have been numerous virtual doctors' appointments for which I've asked about captioning service for video platforms and repeated cluelessness in response to my questions. There's been the dehumanizing standoff at the rehabilitation doctor's office—a staff member on one side speaking incomprehensibly and me on the other asking her repeatedly to speak to me not my spouse, talk louder, and come closer, to no avail. There have been an infinite number of times I've asked people to speak slower, face me, write things down, or pause between words, that got completely dismissed. Too many times I've been startled and alarmed by medical personnel lowering their masks instead of doing the small things I've requested of them.

This time, I've reached out for help. I've leaned on my community for support. One person suggested I write down all the accommodations I needed so I could be sure to name them all prior to the surgery. Another person suggested I take a magic marker with me and write “hard of hearing” on my patient wristband or arm. I have been reminded that my needs aren’t “requests” but “requirements” that make it possible for me to access information I have a right to know. Inspired by this encouragement, I’ve created a document that lists all my accommodation needs and I’ve emailed it to my doctors’ assistants, asking that it be put in my chart and shared with all the people who will have a role in my surgery. Why hadn’t I ever thought of that before?! I quickly make another version that can be sent to my other doctors’ offices so they too can put it in my chart.

The person who comes to get me from the waiting room clearly has no knowledge of my document. I was prepared. I was not going back without my spouse being present to take in information in case I missed something important and to help translate what’s being said. He needed to be there because he doesn’t resist writing things down or repeating things in ways that are clearer for me to understand as others are prone to do, and he’d been prepped on how to help me advocate for myself.

Most medical facilities have little if anything in place to support people like me—people with hearing loss who don’t know ASL, depend on captioning for calls and a transcription app for in-person interaction, and don’t fit the ridiculously inaccurate stereotypes of what someone looks like who requires accommodation. The pandemic brought new challenges, more necessary labor to communicate my needs and insist they get covered. Masks—which are absolutely necessary—mean sound is muffled and I’m unable to view people’s lips while they are speaking. While lipreading only adds a small degree of support, it is helpful and missed nonetheless. I have not yet encountered any medical personnel who made it a priority to have or use masks with clear windows—not even at the offices of audiologists or ear nose and throat doctors. Wouldn’t everyone have it a little easier navigating the pandemic if society didn’t hold such a strong allegiance to verbal communication?

For all these reasons, I’ve come to the hospital prepared. I’ve got several copies of my accommodation needs list, a copy of my most recent audiology report, the contact info for the hospital’s patient advocate department, a notebook and pen to insist things be written down, my transcription app, a marker, and I’m channeling every Black woman I know who’s ever had to emphatically respond with a firm “no” to unacceptable conditions. When it’s time for me to come to the back, I’m told my spouse has to stay in the waiting room. I reply firmly, “I am hard of hearing and I’m not comfortable being put in a position of potentially not being able to understand what’s being communicated with me." I don't move from my seat. Others in the room notice the interaction.

The nurse leaves and returns saying it's okay for him to come back. I hand her a copy of my accommodation needs list and it's put in the folder everyone refers to when they enter my room. All but one very soft-spoken anesthesiologist is respectful of my needs from then on. They check in with me when they enter to find out if I can understand them, tell me to just let them know if they need to slow down or repeat anything. Everyone knows that they need to share all vital information with me before they get to the moment where I have to take out my hearing aids, pack away my phone, and say goodbye to my spouse. I'm lucky. My elders would say "blessed," and while I carry gratitude to a Higher Being always, I choose "lucky" intentionally. Faith hasn't changed the harsh reality of how often people (including myself) aren't having the kind of experience I did that day. Having the energy and resources to advocate so ardently for yourself isn't always possible, especially when needing medical care. This degree of labor shouldn't be necessary for quality and equitable care.

My poetry is a way I try to interrupt a train of oppression that wants to run us all over. I share the story of my surgery because my lived experience and my writing life are intertwined and inseparable. I am writing for my life—to make plain that the status quo must change and our conditioned ableism must be interrupted. I write to interrupt my own internalized ableism and give the conditions of my life new names. There is no poetry in me without the prompting of lived experience. My poems are my truths, shared as loudly as I know how to express them. And they are what has connected me to crip kin who've taught me what I deserve and how to advocate for myself. For me, disability poetics has been a way to find each other, a way to survive, an act of faith rooted in the power that vulnerability has to change things.

Accommodation

Camisha L. Jones

The law wants my body reasonable
My body won't fence in its demands
Expects the world to stop
Whenever it wants to lay down
Throws up its middle finger
At deadlines, task lists,
Long awaited meetings
It ain't open to negotiation
Wants you to stop telling it to
Calm down
It has three settings: rest, spark, flare
All that talk about your inconvenience & your hardship
It calls that *Bullshit*
It will not wait in line
It will not be polite
It will not use its inside voice
It wants all the space
In every room of the house
The entire sky & the full lawn of grass
It wants to set it all aflame
My body is a fire starter
My body is the art
Of Angela Bassett's right hand
Letting reason go up in smoke

Ménière's Flare

Camisha L. Jones

and just like that
a light goes out
a bulb blows
sound becomes shadow
each sentence a gang in a dark alley
at the wrong time of night

the doctors
document the decline in angles
flat terrain and steep slopes
a landslide of loss

silence   swallows   everything
enjoys the taste of my pride
keeps me on a strict diet of asking for help
of needing accommodation

the blare of the tv
becomes whisper to me
a foreshadowing of the silent movie

my life becomes

spectacle
a 3-ringed circus
too many eyes on me
as each act unfolds

i become

"special" and suspicious
a dim light
flickering

In/Ability

Camisha L. Jones

in the shower
the sound of water
is crisp as a
head of lettuce
split in two

then fading
in the morning
when the running sink
becomes a whisper
in someone else's ear

daily I enter and exit
this turnstile of
here/hear and not here/hear

press my way through
a downpour of sound
divorced from meaning

I stand between the words
a mediator
and sometimes a barrier

sometimes
there is sweet song
birds chirping
a tune with no lyrics
keeping me company
in the silence

which isn't really silent
or quiet
but static
& loud

coupling & uncoupling
with comprehension

the mouth of each syllable muffled

language is an ocean
of murky water

words sinking
into buried grains of sand

a tide coming
and going

calling me the shore
calling me thousands of particles
stretched wide

receiving what the waves bring
surviving what they take away

My Hearing Loss Interrogates the World

Camisha L. Jones

Why so loud?
Why the mob of noise?
Why the clatter of simultaneous speech?

Why your words such rapid fire?
Such hurtling train?
You wanna run me over?
Wanna leave me in your tracks?

Do you know how to slow?
How to E-Nun-Ci-aTe?
How to repeat-repeat-repeat?
How to write it all down?
How to say it to my face?

Why so much "nevermind"?
Why you blow me off?
Why you walk away?
You think me helpless? Hopeless?
You comfortable with distance between us?

Jesse Rice-Evans

I WANT TO FEEL LIKE HOME

Content notes: medical neglect, misdiagnosis/diagnostic language, anti-fatness, ableism

It would be easier, I think, to make some sense of my bodymind, if I were able to neatly fit my experiences under the banner of "chronic illness" or "disability," but for me and many other sick and disabled people, inhabiting a bodymind that mandates medicalization remains messy, contradictory, and tenuous. I cannot stay well without medical intervention, but my disability justice politics mean I struggle to keep my professionalism intact for medical appointments. My body is a mashup of privileges and fears: fatness, neurodivergence, queerness and genderqueerness, whiteness, class and education privilege, and—to a certain degree—an ability to disguise my disabledness. I can dress up some of my pain and fatigue, but my body itself remains, marking me as noncompliant because I won't/can't lose weight and I am not obedient, nor am I in thrall to the godliness of health care workers.

I have been working on a sequel to "Pills" (titled "More Pills"). Many sick and disabled people can relate to the experience of trying new meds and experiencing side effects in an effort to minimize damaging symptoms. In my case, neurological impacts from my still-undiagnosed illnesses have been the most intense to manage and difficult to access medical care for. I'm at a difficult spot where I rely upon both the medical and social models of disability to explain my experiences: I am disabled by inaccessible infrastructure and public divestment from mass transit and comfortable public spaces, but I also am chronically ill with underfunded and under-researched medical conditions (hypermobility and related conditions and myalgic encephalomyelitis/chronic fatigue syndrome symptoms, specifically).

Much of my work hovers around the knowledge that if I struggle to access medical care/"accommodations"/support structures, the reality for many sick and disabled/MMINDS and multiply-marginalized disabled people is much worse. I'm a white femme pursuing a doctoral degree in writing and communication; I can navigate the administrative burden of medicalized disability moderately well, but I *should not have to be the only person invested in my medical care.*

Disabled poetics is flux: Language arrives or it doesn't; sense makes itself or doesn't. Rejecting sense, rejecting logic and aesthetics for aesthetics' sake, rejecting crumbs from the nondisabled literary "community" that tokenizes our work and practices creative parasitism of our brilliance, our refusal to over-explain for ableds who have never listened to us anyway. My work is for other sick and disabled people, especially femmes, especially fat queer femmes. Leah Lakshmi Piepzna-Samarasinha says in "I know crips live here": "Welcome / You are home." I wanna feel like home for other disabled femmes.

"All I'm looking for is a ceremony" captures the fleeting nature of theorizing and writing with chronic pain and fatigue. The final phrase remains unpunctuated because this is when my brain stopped creating language, and this piece, alongside much of my other work, captures the bursts of language that appear and then rapidly depart. Language and neurological illness are fickle companions. Memory loss has complicated everything further: *What has been written about? What have I missed? How many weeks went by between submissions? Did I miss the accessible housing deadline?*

Disabled people—especially Black and brown, poor and working-class, medically fragile, and intellectually disabled people—remain the most impacted by the global COVID-19 pandemic: Many of us are still at home and exhausted from begging our nondisabled communities to mask, get vaccinated (if possible), and make efforts to minimize risk so we can get medical care, pick up medications, go grocery shopping. Disabled writers are underpaid and under-published while nondisabled writers get glowing NYT reviews of their books about disabled people's resilience. I'm tired of it.

In my work, I want to reflect my lived experience of being embodied as fat, femme, crip, queer, in-pain-all-the-time, self-diagnosed autistic, white, and in tune with and continuously learning the complexities of these conflicting positionalities. I want to highlight that I am still alive because of sick and disabled communities online, that my needs don't get met by luck, but I am able to survive alongside other sick and disabled people by learning and by using every position of power I hold to demand better and more for us, especially for the most marginalized of us. Disability justice is not a trend, and I intend to take up (ample) space to make room for all of us.

Pills

Jesse Rice-Evans

1. duloxetine

I go from 30mg to 60mg—I bloom and run outside into the rain—to 90mg—I can do anything—to 120mg and finally I stabilize. I start to take so many other meds that I forget about these. I gain close to seventy-five pounds and feel great abt it

2. gabapentin

I barely remember what these are for; something about neuropathic pain—which sounds to me like "fake pain," because if something exists only in the brain, it isn't "real" in the sense that it is intangible, like "love," like "pain."

3. clonazepam

This one: self-explanatory.

4. cyclobenzaprine

For three months, I avoid these.

I am prescribed up to three a day "as needed,"
but I grow groggy to the point where my eyes cross, the world blurs.

When I take them at night, I thrash
in nightmares

5. lion's mane

nootropic—it is for my brain
for when everything   trickles   away

6. propranolol

I am supposed to anticipate triggers:
Things I know will send me spiraling,
negotiate male aggression before
I even show up. I learn to expect this

all the time, and the jittery goal of
beta blockers empties weekly.

7. brahmi

This is recommended by my acupuncturist after I tell her I am taking a tincture made by her friend, a punk herbalist. It "eases the fuzz" behind my eyes, the thrum of hearing my spine crinkle as I climb the stairs, when words blur into something illegible, the books I am required to study matter less and less.

8. tramadol

I learn to take these irregularly, for mild, controllable, pain: how can I read pain as tolerable, negotiable? When I know it is endless, timeless, infinite? Languageless?

9. Tylenol PM

I can't sleep at all.

My crip PhD-student friend takes three ibuprofen PM
at 8 p.m. to sleep a full eight hours, nomadic between
their cushy couch and their expansive king bed;

I try two one night, three the next.
My brain turns off; I sleep until 12:30 the next afternoon.

I feel invincible until I don't.

10. l-theanine

stress eats away at soft tissue

11. oxycodone

This one is prescribed in an emergency: I am desperate at the pain doctor.

They want scans: X-rays, MRI w/o contrast—I am allergic to iodine.

That's fine, that's valuable, that's covered by my state employee insurance;
I am unable to stand any more of feeling knifed between my ribs,
how when my bodyworker slides her fingers under my top two ribs
and bows them back into their hull,
I gasp for air like I've been punctured.

12. lorazepam

When my partner's dad dies, he leaves behind a half dozen bottles half-empty of Ativan, the benzodiazepine I was prescribed and sold for $3 a pill to pay for food in undergrad. This time, my anxiety is worse. I pocket several dozen.

13. diphenhydramine

This one takes me down, as if I am a submarine from conscious to unconscious, sluggish insomniac hauntings, how I haunt the pullout couch like a spirit.

All I'm looking for is a ceremony

Jesse Rice-Evans

A miracle isn't a miracle without sacrifice
Paige Lewis[1]

A disability aesthetic, you ask. The temporarily-abled (TA) attempt to delineate one for us, where life in pain is unsustainable, that self-selecting eugenics is a private eugenics. There is no reproductive justice that does not center how to live cared for, by the state, by a network of interdependence and monies allocated for caretaking, the feminized labor of paying attention to needs, anticipating pain or hunger or the need for a bath.

I want my grief to be transcendent: somehow worse than yours, more of a shredding sensation, the sharper form of pain than I am willing to admit, and that this almost invisible wrenching bracketed sawhorse that I strap to my back and do not loose for anything,

Between desire and the edge of motion, the crimp of arousal, the slip that I allow, an urgence, the note I leave behind.

1. "I've Been Trying to Feel Bad for Everyone," *Colorado Review* 43, no. 3 (2016): 131.

5

JOURNEYS AND BECOMINGS

Andy Jackson

BROKEN LINES AND BELONGING

As a boy, I never felt the desire to disappear. Sure, I was always a daydreamer and a reader, so a part of me was always elsewhere. But that wasn't anything other than curiosity, my child-mind keen to grow, question, and explore. I was still in the world, and my place in it felt unquestionable. Until puberty, when my growth spurt, sudden and dramatic, started contorting the lines of my frame. I developed scoliosis, kyphosis, and a kink at my knee, as if the bones and joints were becoming confused under all that pressure. I was lanky, elongated, and increasingly awkward, a cross between a baby giraffe and an ill-designed tripod.

As a twelve-year-old, I was admitted to the Royal Children's Hospital in Melbourne for orthopedic surgery. I went in again, a few years later, when my doctors realized my spine was determined not to be straightened. That second surgery stopped the curvature getting worse, but it was no use, in a way. I had already been admitted into that harsh spotlight of the wider world, a culture in thrall of the normal. I had done nothing to deserve what felt like punishment, but I had been made into Sisyphus, my load not a boulder but this stareable body, each day carrying myself into a world intent on staring at deformity, pushing it away while examining it, as if the world were not built out of bent and broken lines.

Poetry, for me, has never been anything but a necessity. I come to the page, every time, with a curious mix of hunger and dread, a compulsion to knead formless and painful things into language. I say "things," but I should say it more clearly: Shame. Resentment. Melancholy. Anger. Ambivalence. And what's the word for feeling the need for solidarity? Faced with all this, silence isn't an option. Slowly but surely, silence removes the oxygen from a room, poisons the soil of a life and a community. And straight prose just can't cut it either. What cuts through are the cuts, the interruptions that poems are composed of, each line break acting as a puncturing of the proper, or a necessary coming up for air.

I never wanted to write "Quasimodo," really. But the Hunchback figure was "teased into me" long ago, and it would have been worse to pretend otherwise. The unwritten poem—which takes literally the idea of Quasimodo being inside me—kept whispering in my ear, and it hurt. Writing it hurt, too. A labor of spleen and grit, purging and containment, inching forward (backward and forward) in the dark, not knowing what my fingers might touch next. Even just speaking his name was a kind of catharsis, albeit limited, as all precious things are.

At the poem's end—not that it's an end, more a pause before the larger work begins—I embrace him. And this is not about pride or self-love or anything else liable to become a hollow aspiration. Ableism can't be just exorcised or disowned. To wake, I think anyway, is a process, fitful and endless. No, this is about breaking the hold of the shame, the unsayable.

"Double Helix" came out of a different kind of grappling. In my mid-thirties, I found myself for the first time in an intimate relationship, intoxicated and disoriented by love. In this unfamiliar, bright light, old questions I thought I had settled suddenly seemed stark again, and new questions emerged that I hadn't even dreamed of. Yes, I'd inherited a genetic disorder, so you could say the line(age) was already broken, but what does it mean to be broken? Would you choose to share that "brokenness," to pass it on? What's it like to suddenly feel a sense of belonging in the world, to no longer be alone? How do you affirm the past as well as the future?

In response, I could only write in short phrases and with other questions—poised and enigmatic, distressed and confessional, always searching, mired in paradox. Early on in the writing of the poem, the pantoum form presented itself as a way of succumbing to (even reveling in) what Keats called "negative capability," or what I'd call an honoring of impaired knowledge. Once I'd arranged them, each line seemed to interrupt the feeling of the one before, to break it. The poem gave me a kind of answer, loving and contradictory, that I'd never have been able to find by myself. Aloneness just doesn't cut it, either.

So far, I've had five collections of poetry published, and while I think my sense of craft has evolved, my approach and my preoccupations haven't. I write to break the silences imposed by ableism, and to honor the woundedness hidden there. I write to pry open the cracks in stigma, so that exposure to the world might not feel so fraught. I write autobiographical and biographical poetry, out of my own life and into other lives, which includes the readers', in the hope that affinity might bloom into solidarity.

Decades since I started writing, I am still not done with this discomfort in being visible. To grow up deformed, to have strangers' overt attention remind you of that continually, plants a seed of shame and unbelonging deep in your chest. And no matter how much effort you put into eradicating this weed, there is always someone, or some experience, that fertilizes and waters the damn thing. To put it another way, the world is still disabling. I still need—*we* still need—a poetry that is not afraid of broken lines, of misshapen and beautiful forms, of bodies that cannot be fixed or entirely understood. This kind of poetry might help us belong to each other, and to this world.

Quasimodo

Andy Jackson

I am twelve when they tease you into me, name-first.
With your fist around my spine as I try to grow up
into my own upright self, I am quiet, think you small,
like you might climb out while I yawn or piss or sleep.

Your nest of collected sticks grows in this belfry chest.
Afraid and facing away, I blur mirrors with spit and hide
behind excuses to not take off my shirt at the beach.
The thin white frames of schoolgirls rise like lighthouses.

They call out my name in voices I have thrown.
No one is saved. Through my eyes, the flickering
fires you fuel are signs. Men begin to close in,
waving their torches of word and fist. I fix a rope

to my mouth and lower myself down inside.
These bones enclose a flapping of echoes, what darkness
can't silence. Tendrils reach for my legs, memories
begging to be fed. But at last I clutch your throat

and haul you out. Your face is white and wet,
your bottom lip trembling with the weight of our shape.
You smell of the filth and luck of cul-de-sacs, your home,
my flesh. My arms reach around your swollen bulk

before I can think or flinch. We are two halves
of a heart stitched together with myth. Over my shoulder
you stare out to where the sun reenacts its death.
Against your hump, my soft skin sweats and breathes.

Double Helix

Andy Jackson

a disorder of connective tissue sewn into who I am
a gift of frailty in a world of continuous improvement
          what looks like a pattern is composed of chaos
the universe an infinite reflecting web

a gift of frailty in a world of continuous improvement
          I didn't think of having children until I met you
the universe an infinite reflecting web
no self exists, but who said that?

          I didn't think of having children until I met you
genetic screening is not an anagram for suicide
no self exists, but who said that?
          try to put my finger on it and it disappears

genetic screening is not an anagram for suicide
you can be so lonely you don't want to be touched
          try to put my finger on it and it disappears
things fall apart or hold for now

you can be so lonely you don't want to be touched
          what looks like a pattern is composed of chaos
things fall apart or hold for now
a disorder of connective tissue sewn into who I am

Rigoberto González

THE MAN WITH THE CANE

I've been dealing with a neurological condition for the past fifteen years of my adult life. For half of those years, I could walk only with the use of a cane. To say this was a life-changing development is an understatement. I was a New Yorker during that period, and NYC is not adequately ADA-compliant. Since I had to commute from Queens to New Jersey using public transportation, my daily grind was a nightmare upon a nightmare. During those years, subway commuters offered me their seat only five times. Mostly women. One of them visibly pregnant. For all the others, I was made invisible. I was easier to deal with that way.

Eventually, after years of medication and therapy, I regained my mobility, but there's a catch: There is no telling when I will lose it again. Maybe in a month. Maybe in a year. Maybe in a decade. But by the time that happens, it will not be a cane that will sustain me, but a wheelchair. Suddenly, that cane didn't seem as bad as all that. The shame and embarrassment I experienced when I entered a room lost its gravity. The real challenges, emotional and physical, were yet to come. The only preparation I have at the moment are those memories of my time on a cane, which I wanted to forget. Now they are what will guide me through the next phase.

Therefore, I began to write about that experience, finally, in poetry. I did mention my medical struggles in my last two memoirs, but they were not the focus of the narrative. They were marginalized details, incidental to the story I was telling. Poetry was going to ask that I write from the charged center of my experience. Perhaps that's why I avoided doing so all these years.

Once I reached the age of fifty, I had run out of excuses not to face The Man with the Cane. I had wronged him all these years. I had tried to outpace him, hoping to leave him behind. I closed the doors behind me, praying he wouldn't get through. I had blamed him for my rage each time I was wheeled through airports, or each time I remembered that once I was a dancer. How graceful I used to be. During one performance, I had exited to the wrong side of the stage. In order to correct my error, I cartwheeled my way across in rhythm to the other dancers still performing. This delighted the audience, who thought it was part of the show. With The Man with the Cane standing in front of those memories, those memories drifted farther away. I accused him of sullying the joy of recalling my dancer past.

When I wrote "The Trees Keep Weeping Long After the Rain Has Ended" and "To the Man Who Walks with a Cane," I wanted to make amends with The Man with the Cane. I implicated myself—The Man with the Cane did not bring me those insecurities, anxieties, and sense of denial, they were in me all along. I know because I had accessed them long before my diagnosis. If anything, The Man with the Cane taught me a few valuable lessons: how not to take my body for granted, how to take better care of my body, how to love my body. But most important, that it is I who needs to be first to accept who I am; the commuters on the subway don't matter. These two poems are only the initial step. And I'm looking forward to the rest, wherever they lead to.

The doctors tell me there will be indicators. Gradually, I will have difficulty with balance, the pain in my legs will intensify, and my motor skills with be compromised. I was horrified when I was informed of this. The more I engage with that likelihood, the less frightening it becomes. Because now I don't feel so alone. When my affliction first manifested itself, I felt so abandoned in it, and the terrible ableist public life underscored that loneliness each time I felt ignored or pitied. I became antisocial. I declined invitations to dinner or to public readings or to parties, imagining that I was doing the world a favor by not inconveniencing anyone. Today, like I do every day, I invoke The Man with the Cane for strength. The Man with the Cane places his hand on my shoulder—a most comforting gesture—and then he leans in to whisper in my ear, "Don't worry, I'll be right there with you."

The Trees Keep Weeping Long After the Rain Has Ended

Rigoberto González

just as I keep moving long after my body stops
at the door. The sidewalk turns the corner and there
I go, smooth as the sailboats of Puerto Rico

that drift into quiet thought on the horizon.
The boats float over the sun's reflection, leaving it
behind to shudder on the cold surface, alone. My body

knows such abandonment whenever I'm four steps
ahead of it. Some mornings I catch the train
just before the doors close. On the platform,

my body slumps over its cane, looking betrayed
and forlorn. When the train zooms into the tunnel,
for a minute or two I deceive myself into thinking

that my body will never find me again, that I'm
free, finally free of that slowpoke who takes away
my dignity at the airport, where I'm forced to board

on a wheelchair even though I can do so on my own.
Is it really gone? Where are the NYC subway acrobats
with their loud music and peddler hats? I want to

spin around the pole with them, jutting my feet
in the air. My backflip will not be as spectacular
as theirs, but give me time, fellas, to get used

to this. I too was young, I too could dance
without affliction once, a very long time ago.
But just before I get lost in daydream entirely

I notice my body looking back at me
from the mirror of the window. Weary yet intact,
it made it to the train after all. And I'm ashamed

to have misjudged its capability. How stupid. It is I
who needs to catch up to this body, its persistence
and grace—how it makes itself so public, defying

stares and second looks, how it's unafraid to be
the center of attention, like that sailboat at sunset
that doesn't drift away as I once believed. It shows

the way. *Here, timid sun on the water,* the boat
says. *I'm clearing a path for you. Not so you can
follow; so you can travel right beside me. Let's go.*

I get it now. Just as the trees weep long after the rain
has ended, so too the heart beats while the body's
not in motion. And while it rests. And while it sleeps.

To the Man Who Walks with a Cane

Rigoberto González

Welcome back, old friend, the stairs
didn't miss you though they've waited
at the same spot, in the same pose,

loyal as a dog and just as patient.
The doors are as arrogant as always
and will refuse to step aside as you

come through. You pause on the NYC
sidewalk. The current of bodies curves
around yours. You, the steadfast stone

at the center of the creek. If a story
took place at this corner between Macy's
and Madison Square Garden, you'd be

the last one asked to tell it,
though you are today's most reliable
witness. There's a woman in an orange

dress who spills like yolk into the crowd.
A double-decker bus rushes in to lap her
up. A tall man walks hand in hand with

a seven-year-old version of himself—same
pale legs, same baseball cap. They both
turn when the ambulance sneaks up

behind them. They look nothing alike.
A young man holds a pretzel as if he's
looking at a galaxy. How lovingly he eats

star after star. When you hobble forward
the city street is unresponsive because
it wants you no less or no more than any

other anonymous pedestrian exchanging
one view of the skyline for another.
When a man with the same cane

crosses paths with you, you wonder
if your canes recognized each other
or if they refused to see the fleeting

truth of this encounter. You and that
man pulled the canes and yourselves
apart. A tear so slow and so painful

it's still hurting when you lie back
in bed and shut your eyes. In that
twilight before sleep, you revise

the moment of the meeting: no, you
didn't simply pass each other by,
you stopped mid-street and stopped

traffic too. Every person froze in place,
as did all noise, except for you and this
man who blink in unison. The evening

so still your eyelashes are a band of cymbals
clapping. You keep your hands to yourself
because eye contact is evidence enough

of human warmth in this place and time.
Now everything's aware of the matching
canes, their holders face to face, fusing

two stories into one great kiss that turns
blue holding its breath until you both
agree to let the restless world move on.

Cath Nichols

IT'S A BIT LIKE THIS

1977. I make friends with a boy called Darren. We sit on the bench at playtime and watch a game of kiss chase. I don't understand why the girls squeal and run. I do not feel this urge to squeal.

"Why?" I say to the running children.

I get Darren to lean over and touch my face-skin with his lips. It is soft-dry.

"See?" I say to them. "There's nothing to scream about."

I think myself wise, explaining this to them.

1979. I can't stand socks. Putting them on is painful-ticklish. School mornings are bad. My parents try everything: They warm socks on the radiator; make sure my socks are cotton or wool mix, not polyester; they stretch socks fully between both hands, then try to surprise my feet. They are very patient. Still, I twist and squeal.

I am over-sensitive.

Or am I over-sensitized? Now, I see the words have different weights.

I just find socks really difficult.

Hot sun. Massive field and white lines. Despite my long legs, I'm only good at the obstacle race or egg-and-spoon. I sit on the grass and hug my knees.

"What you doing?!" Someone points at me. "Eurgh!"

I have licked my knees and sniffed them. Am I weird or are they weird for not admitting they do this too?

I used to suck the ends of my plaits at primary school too—but doesn't every girl do that? I made the quill ends brushes and painted endless nothings on my cheeks.

Stimming, I guess.

1979. There is a new version of kiss chase with no kissing. The boys chase us and try to pull up our skirts to see our knickers. Huh? There's nothing interesting about knickers.

I decide to hold my skirt in the air and show off my pants so they can't take me by surprise. My best friend Fiona does the same, and we walk about the playground as if to say, "Nothing to see here, what's all the fuss?"

What saves me from everything is knowing I am right. This is useful, it keeps my ego strong. I know I'm right, and they are wrong and silly, and my parents are kind, and we have a cat, and I go for walks to the woods on my own, and school . . . School is good. I like gym and dance. I can do all the reading and writing and maths. I'm very clever!

I get called names and pretend I don't care.

Yet my self-esteem is good, and I am mostly happy. As an adult, this has worked against obtaining certain forms of help. I didn't realize I was neurodiverse till this year, and I didn't realize I was highly anxious till a few years back, because when you're physically very ill and there's no obvious cause, after negative test results, your doctor only asks questions about depression. But I am not depressed! I do not fit their criteria.

> I bite off split-ends,
> mesmerised by the way each flaring shaft
> catches the sun, fern fronds
> transfixing in low spring light.
> I rationalize: biting lets me avoid the hairdresser,
> biting saves money.

Years later: "Alopecia," says a hairdresser. "Have you been stressed lately?"

I think: "Tearing her hair out with grief?" No, it's more an idle twiddling, done when watching TV! For years, I'd caused sores to appear on my scalp but didn't know I was causing them. I'd been using sulphur shampoos to control what I thought was an itchy scalp but it was caused by me all along. Trichotillomania—you can look it up.

Sometimes we misidentify what we are doing, or experiencing, because the language around it is the wrong language.

As a result of having some stressful years in my forties plus an early, heat-drenched menopause, I lost sleep and slowed down. I started mild hormone replacement therapy, which stopped the sweats. Then I injured my back and became seriously cold, wore mittens, socks, and three duvets in bed in summer. It was like living in a permanent state of shock. Later came the same diagnosis as my Mum, two cousins, and three cousins' children: myalgic encephalomyelitis /chronic fatigue syndrome (ME/CFS).

Everything has an environmental and a genetic component, says the rheumatologist.

I was involved with literary disability studies at Liverpool Hope University prior to this, so had good role models both in friends and in literature. Disability is fine, it's "other people (and spaces) that are the problem." Apparently, this is "the social model"; it was already my worldview!

I didn't drive and I liked to walk, bus, or train everywhere. Now, I couldn't even walk our neighbor's dog, Ruby. I had difficulty walking from room to room and lay on the floor a lot. Pain relief was a hot bath, then eighteen months later, ice packs. I was only offered pain meds several years later, after the CFS clinic referred me back to my doctor for "having too much pain to work with." I should have been offered a pain clinic in 2017. Whatever, the pain meds didn't work.

When I self-diagnosed anxiety with atypical reactions in 2020, anti-anxiety meds helped with my abdominal pain, but not the pain in my arms, wrists, fingers, shins, and ankles. From 2016, I was off work for six months. I applied for benefits and was refused; returned to work on reduced hours. I bought a power wheelchair for use outside the house, but mostly I stayed indoors because of pain. I applied for benefits again with support, was refused, but got them on appeal. Then: pandemic. Lockdowns changed little, but I returned to work teaching online and that helped me manage my pain better.

"Tender spots" came from a particularly bleak time. In 2017 I set up a rest area on our landing as the CFS clinic recommended to my patient group that we take day-rest away from the bedroom. Using our beds in the day might compromise our ability to sleep properly at night! I gave it a go: laid a mat and pillow on the floor, had a quilt draped over the banisters to drag down for warmth.

To answer the "Where's Wally?" question in the poem, Wally was usually there or in the living room, but when my body failed between spaces I would lie down wherever: on a train's manky carpet after work, on a bench, in a teaching room, or in our hallway.

I am still ill, but I have packed away these temporary shelters. Forget the advice. When I rest, I use my bed—it makes no difference to my night-time sleep!

Now my dad is reaching the end stages of Parkinson's, spending more time at Accident & Emergency after falls, and my partner's mother has lost sight in her working eye this very week. We are all falling apart, I think. But there is still love, so it is not all doom and gloom.

I spend time teaching students how to write essays, but in writing this, I've broken some rules. No introduction, no conclusion. It's fragmented, confessional, and sometimes sharp and vibrant. Life can be like that. As Robert Frost said, "No surprise in the writer, no surprise in the reader."

In real life, I don't like surprises, but in poetry—bring it on!

Tender spots

Cath Nichols

You say I've become Where's Wally?—
prone to disappear about the house.
Am I hiding on the landing, at the bottom
of the stairs . . . in cushions on the sofa?
Sometimes there's a blanket or pillow,
but mostly I rough it, take what's given.
You find Wally on the landing. I have cold feet.
"Press your hands on my feet," I say.
You kneel down, shins over my slippers,
palms on my propped-up knees. Standing up
for you is tricky—mustn't press too hard.
Then you leave. We kiss
through banisters, me rolled sideways,
you turned halfway down the stairs.

Eli Clare

TURNING TOWARD EACH OTHER

1980. The summer before my seventeenth birthday, I spent a weekend in Portland, Oregon. A girl from the backwoods, I had no skills yet to navigate the cacophony of a city—even one as slow and small as Portland. And still I fell in love with Saturday Market, the arts and crafts fair tucked underneath the Burnside Bridge. Amid the concrete pilings, I encountered tie-dyed T-shirts and honey-gold cutting boards. Several months earlier Mount St. Helens had erupted seventy-five miles to the north, volcanic ash filling the gutters; everything I touched felt gritty. I remember watching a power chair–using poet selling his wares. I knew that he, like me, had cerebral palsy.

I had no disability politics or community, no analysis of ableism. I didn't even know that word. I believed all the bullying, staring, invasive touch, invisibility, and lack of access I faced was my fault. I hated the sound and cadence of my slurring voice. I tried hard to hide and failed.

Yet at a distance, I stood watching this poet, yearning toward him, recognizing myself. I couldn't even bear to say hello. This encounter sparked my first disability poem.

We turn to the old stories and the new, poems to cradle our aching bones and poems to tuck beneath our pillows.

Watching a Cerebral-Palsied Writer at Saturday Market

(written in 1981)

Arthur, I am Elizabeth,
let us shake
spastic right hands,
we face the same ocean
inside our heads,

if you write and I run,
if I write and you sit
at Saturday Market,
we are courageous cripples.
I cringe beneath careful hugs,
careful as though I am
one of those glass ships
that were for sale
in the booth next to yours,
ships that would break in
your strong spastic hands.

I imagine what you see:
you listen to them quietly stare,
and then walk away whispering
or they ask you about
work, writing, CP,
your hands grab the air
while your tongue
struggles to grab the answer
caught in your skull.
But we do everything we do
as only we know how,
as we run and write and sit
at Saturday Market.

We creak, groan, shiver our way toward beauty.

In 1981, the words, metaphors, stories with which I name myself here and now didn't even exist as glimmers in my heart. Nor did my literal name—Eli. Instead I lived with a name my parents chose; a name attached to the gender assigned to me at birth; a name that, as a trans person, feels utterly private and personal. But I've decided not to change a single word of my forty-year-old poem. Rather, I want to crack open the shifting unsteady work of naming ourselves and each other into existence.[1]

Turning, turning, we need the rhythms of stim and stutter, spasm and seizure, flutter of aspen.

2020. Out of the depths of my filing cabinets, I pull "Watching a Cerebral-Palsied Writer at Saturday Market." It fills me with quiet tenderness: this bare-boned poem, a birch tree in the middle of winter. I can feel my younger self—that lonely disabled girl on the cusp of coming out as queer—her words leaning into an imagined encounter that she wasn't actually ready to have in real life.

Remembering blurry fragments of that long ago afternoon, I decide to re-vision the poem, turn again toward the image of delicate glass ships and strong spastic hands. To this process, I bring the disability communities that have saved my life over the last four decades, the home I've built with queer and trans disabled people.

Together we fine tune the art of noncompliance and snarky answers. Unfold the maps. Learn the histories. Fashion the pry bars.[2]

You at Saturday Market

(written in 2020, re-visioning my 1981 poem
"Watching a Cerebral Palsied Writer at Saturday Market")

1
We shake spastic
right hands, grin lopsided
at each other, your tremors
reaching into mine. I sit
on a creaky wooden chair
and we talk slow,
a rhythm of stop
and go, knee to knee,
hands flying. What
we say and what we don't:
songbirds and ghosts.

2

you know, you know:
how they pat my head,
kiss my cheek,
sometimes cry,
sometimes whisper,
sometimes stink
of perfume and sweat, but always
they are careful as if
I were one of those glass ships
for sale two booths down, crystal
spired and thin that would shatter
in your strong sexy hands,
careful, careful until
their pity withers:
you know every word
of this damn story

3

They interrupt us with vacant
inquiries about your poetry
zines, zany broadsides, never
pausing for your replies
that arrive in bursts
of uneven words—the first
daffodils of spring. They turn
to me, ask if you have this
diagnosis or that, surprised
by my slurred refusal.
It is better when they leave, except
you need their five-dollar bills
for coffee and rent. I linger,
forget you're a stranger,
ignore the spitting rain.

Knee to knee, hip to hip, we gather the bare bones of mid-winter, the quivering leaves of late summer, dreams so tender we can barely conjure them.[3]

Notes

1. As I think about naming and writing ourselves into existence, I turn to Audre Lorde. She tells us: "[Poetry] is a vital necessity of our existence. It forms the quality of the light within which we predicate our hopes and dreams toward survival and change, first made into language, then into idea, then into more tangible action. Poetry is the way we help give name to the nameless so it can be thought." Audre Lorde, *Sister Outsider: Essays and Speeches* (Crossing Press, 1984), 37.

2. As I think of transforming ourselves, each other, and the world—using poems as pry bars—I turn to Laura Hershey. She tells us: "Poetry aims for the thing itself, not just to name the thing. Poetry draws a straight line connecting the desire, the request, the fulfillment. Poetry is power of words to effect change, to move people." Laura Hershey, "Getting Comfortable," in *Beauty is a Verb: The New Poetry of Disability*, edited by Jennifer Bartlett, Sheila Black, and Michael Northen (Cinco Puntos Press, 2011), 132.

3. As I think of the work of turning toward each other, of gathering, I turn to Leah Lakshmi Piepzna-Samarasinha. They tell us: "Prefigurative politics is a fancy term for the idea of imagining and building the world we want to see now. It's waking up and acting as if the revolution has happened. . . . As a performer and curator/producer, I believe that how you do it and who is there to see it is as important as what is on the stage. My favorite performance spaces . . . become temporary, two-hour communities . . . autonomous zones that feel like freedom." Leah Lakshmi Piepzna-Samarasinha, *Care Work: Dreaming Disability Justice* (Arsenal Pulp Press, 2018), 149–50.

A Survivor's Wail

Eli Clare

1

He was neither the first nor
the last drunk to beat me—a child unsure

of their gender, hair tangled with hay
and feathers—the gold

tips of his cowboy boots
became shrapnel lodged

in rib and hip,
untouched for decades.

2

When he died, I wailed,
prayers gusting into the cosmos:

let every cell, platelet,
molecule of oxygen

settle anew. And no,
I did not go to his funeral.

whoever wrote his obituary
forgot the word *rapist.*

3

Tender, tender—that hinge where hip
meets spine: My bones radiate

heat ’til those golden tips
come flying out—twirl

and shimmer, gold never meant
as weapon or wound, they become

meteorites streaking across
the sky, stars hanging in the ether.

Confluence

Eli Clare

I lay out syringe, alcohol pad, vial: a ritual
connecting me to junkies. Draw the testosterone,
and push needle deep through skin into muscle.

And yet, I would have chosen hermit, storm-high river, heron flying upstream.

Open the windows, forsythia spills its dense yellow.

North on Baldwin Road, I walk my everyday walk.
Bottom of the hill, a dog barks, boy yells, "Hey mister.
Hey mister. Hey mister." We've traded names a dozen times.

Then "Hey retard. Retard. Retard."
Schoolyard to street corner: words
slung by the pocketful.

Crip skin marked,
white skin not.

Open the doors, daffodils rear their bright heads.

Cypionate suspended in cottonseed oil,
a shapeshifter's drug the color of pale sunlight:

Voice cracks.
Stubble glints.

Open the cellar. Soon, soon the maples will unfurl their green fists.

And yet, girl arrived first, bones set to the current.

In the mirror I wait,
the difference a simple ritual—
verb, skin, muscle, hormone.

Body begins.

Split the stone open, then the lilacs' deep purple.

In another time, at another place, I might have relied upon
insistent dreams; gods, goddesses, spirits all;
an herbalist stepping out back, nettle or ginseng.

Jaw squares.
Hips and ass slim.

> *And yet, had I been given a choice, they would have demanded clay or granite, saltwater or fresh, as if the confluence could never be home.*

Open, palms stretched wide, apple orchard still bare boned.

But today I have Pfizer, Upjohn, Watson,
doctors saying yes, saying no, judging
the very stretch of skin over bone.

Crip skin,
white skin:
which stories
do I tell the best,
and which
rarely begin—
turn, flutter,
settle?

Open to the peepers, coyotes, faint crescent moon.

This drug I shoot in careful fractions:
I step into its exam rooms,
pay its bills, increase its profits.

Pecs bulk.
Skin roughens.

Body begins to settle.

Let them draw my blood, check
liver, kidney, cholesterol, hematocrit,
track the numbers, write the script.

Open, orchard soon to be enveloped in blossom.

Round the next bend, other boys want my name,
hand me theirs, ask as only five-year-olds can,
"Why don't you talk so good?" I shrug, keep moving.

> *And yet, here at the confluence, river and ocean collide—current rushing headlong, waves pushing back—stones tumble, logs roll. Tell me: Where in this hiss and froth might I lay myself down?*

L. Lamar Wilson

"I WOULDN'T HELP IT EVEN IF I COULD"

The Thursday afternoon Michael Jackson died, I sat on a chartered bus with other artists handpicked by Toi Derricotte and Cornelius Eady, the Cave Canem Foundation's founders. We were headed from our University of Pittsburgh-Greensburg dorms to the big city nearby with only two days remaining in our weeklong retreat, which had been a temporary panacea for my then-undiagnosed anxiety and depressive disorders. From the moment I'd awakened before dawn to write, as I do almost daily, to this late-afternoon ride through the Laurel Highlands' breathtaking landscape, something had felt askew. Certainly, it was no surprise that I was unhappy with the poem I'd submitted for that day's workshop, set to be led by Eady once we arrived in the City of Asylum, a haven for persecuted artists on Pittsburgh's near North Side. Each day of the summer retreat at Cave Canem, affectionately "CC" among fellows, we were expected to craft new lines, and I rarely appreciate my first drafts' potential. Anticipating a set of disquieting, if empathetic, critiques, I shifted in my window seat, my eyes darting between email at *The Washington Post*, where I worked as a copy editor, and all the verdancy this June day offered to lift my ambivalent spirit.

Then, flashing on my cell's screen, I saw it: The embattled King of Pop was being rushed to the hospital; he wasn't responsive, and it didn't look good. We'd need an all-hands-on-deck newsroom to prepare to report the worst. Around me, the din of fellow poets' banter and laughter continued unchecked, so I didn't say a word. I didn't want to kill the good vibes that so often eluded me. Maybe it was a hoax. The rumor mill had killed Whitney Houston prematurely only a few years before. Since I wasn't at the *Post* to sift between fact and Hollywood embellishment, I let out a long sigh, slipped my phone in my pocket, and made small talk with my artistic kin. During workshop, Eady and my CC colleagues were kinder than I deserved about a poem declaiming my disdain for a popular shorthand for the black phallus, a work that I hope never sees a printed page, but all I could hear in my head was the soundtrack of my childhood, every Michael Jackson masterpiece I knew by heart.

"Are you OK? It wasn't *that* bad," one fellow who knew of my propensity for worry and melancholy said as we left the eatery where we'd chatted about our group's works. "What's *really* going on? I saw you peeking at your phone. Is something wrong at work?"

I demurred and dismissed her concern. I didn't want the terrifying newsroom updates I'd been reading, which would go live across the globe by dinnertime, to be true. Subconsciously, as we made the short journey to a nearby museum where Eady and other retreat faculty would read new poems, I began humming the chorus of my favorite MJ song, a tender ballad sculpted from a timeless Stevie Wonder poem. "I can't help it if I wanted to / I wouldn't help it even if I could." No one thought it strange. Song, like breath, comes easy. After years of therapy, I understand that singing is my Kevlar vest, an antidote for moments like this one, when I'd rather climb in bed, curl fetal, and succumb to the ever-looming gloom and dread. Even when I decide it shouldn't outshine a piece's conceit and intellectual heft, song suffuses every piece I craft. As I hummed, the part of my neurodivergent brain that atomizes song, imagery, juxtaposition, anaphora, and irony into poetry began to remix this B-side gem from MJ's 1979 hit solo debut *Off the Wall* into the twenty lines that would spill out of me like a torrential rain, like tears, in one predawn sitting the next morning, after hours of dancing and crying to every hit from every Jackson Five and MJ album we could cobble into a looping, proto-streaming-era playlist. Then, as Eady stepped up to share poems about the sculptural church hat Aretha Franklin donned at President Barack Obama's historic inauguration and other Black American wonders, everyone's phones began to light up, and the litany of gasping, sulking, and muffled weeping ensued. Before the next faculty member's reading, what I'd refused to acknowledge all day was announced.

Our King was dead.

Thus, "I Can't Help It" was born. The first poem in my bildungsroman *Sacrilegion* (Carolina Wren Press/Blair, 2013), it aims to honor MJ's well-documented daddy issues and my own. Like him, I owe my beloved father and mother—and the Southern Black Baptist church doctrine they reared me to revere—not only for my unwavering faith in my capacity to accomplish any goal I set but also for my struggle with depression and anxiety, exacerbated by a dangerous brew of ableism, chauvinism, and homophobia that went unquestioned in my formative years. The poem confesses my tendency to fall into the arms of other men scarred by Christianity and ends with a prediction that I'll "die thrashing telling any body all my secrets." Mid-book, "Legion: Human Immunodeficiency Virus," inspired by the titular graveyard wanderer Jesus allegedly exorcized, cements this elegiac thesis. Even as a small child who'd not yet learned about the vast spectrum of mental illnesses, I felt unsettled by the pathologies Matthew, Mark, and Luke, the latter dubbed "the beloved physician" by the apostle Paul in his letter to the Colossians, mapped onto this man's narrative, the implicit lack of empathy for and banishment of the so-called "demon-possessed" and others that only Jesus's holy touch healed.

As *Sacrilegion* was going through its final edits in the months after MJ's passing, I lost three friends in succession to complications of the virus that causes AIDS, and I witnessed all but those of us closest to them disappear as they became "untouchable." Legion's story, then, seemed the perfect vehicle for a new song for MJ and my dearly departed. I opened a villanelle that felt too saccharine to live on the page alone and began to surround it with a body of language I gathered in an hours-long fever dream—"& him & her & you & him & . . ." the poem's never-ending refrain. I had to literally implicate you, Dear Reader, and "any body" I could divine. Breathless, that villanelle now literally gutting it, I opened a file with a failed Petrarchan sonnet's closing sestet. Thus, "Nothing's ever dead in a graveyard" seemed the ideal opening for "Legion," a poem that, like my friends' memory, aims to haunt us forevermore.

"I talk too much," I confess as "I Can't Help It" (and *Sacrilegion*) begins, and those remain the truest words to capture how my physical disabilities and neurodivergence galvanize my art—and often repel those who can't stand to look in the sublime mirror that my wondrously complex embodiment offers. I rise every morning, especially now as I add post-long Covid brain fog and attention deficit hyperactivity disorder into the mix with my other special gifts, to exorcize every morsel of shame that could so easily beset and silence me if I don't. It gives me some resolve that in 2026—fifty-seven years after Robert Rayford, a sixteen-year-old Black child studied in St. Louis–area hospitals for fifteen months, became the first soul to succumb to AIDS complications, which disproportionately kill Black men, women, and children—we're finally disentangling our lives from stigma. May this volume and my poems be a beacon that inspires others to join us in raising the world's love quotients with our unapologetic truths.

I Can't Help It

L. Lamar Wilson

I talk too much. I cannot tell a liar
from a preacher, so I tell you
what you want: I'm saved & sick
of this world, safe in God's arms. God,
give me this world in an honest man's
arms. An ego is hard to stroke. Or easy if
you know how to quiet it, let a man feel
his burn in your throat. I talk too much.
I'm sorry I'm not sorry enough. I'll dance
all over you. O liar. Preacher. Daddy-
o, your tongue lashing is never hard
or fast enough. When you lie still,
stroking your chalice, the quiet makes me
retch. I am a lone dandelion in a field,
waiting. Come. Blow me to bits.   Still.
You'll die this way, saved by the lies
that burn like the ice water & alcohol
Mama sits me in to break the fevers
our silences brought. I'll die thrashing,
telling any body all my secrets.

Legion: Human Immunodeficiency Virus

L. Lamar Wilson

Return to thine own house, and shew how great things
God hath done unto thee.
—Luke 8:39

Nothing's ever dead in a graveyard.
When you cry out for God, for touch,
our father who is not in heaven
or hell but in every body will send me.
When I'm with you, I'm only with you.
When I'm with her, I'm only with her
& you. When you're with him, I'm only with you & him & her & him
& him & her & him & you & her & him & her & him & you & her & him & her & him & you &
him & her & him & you & her & him & her & him & him & her & him & her & her & him & her &
him & your mama & him & her daddy & her & you & him & him & him & her & you & her barber
& him & her & her & him & her & your neighbor & you & her & him & his professor & her & her
twin brother & him & your stylist & him & her & her favorite teacher & him & her & him & her &
him & her last date & him & him & her & him & you & her & his best friend & him & her & him &
you & her husband's boyfriend & him &
him & her & him & her girlfriend & him &
her & his brother & him & him & her &
her grandmother & you & her & him &
her & her & him & her & her & you &
him & your cousin & her sister & her & &

When you are alone & cannot be stilled
I will never leave: my hands, your hands:
your blood's taint coursing; your high-
yellow heart's flesh hunger for bodies bruised
blue: who can hide what yours cannot

his nail tech & him & her & him & you & her & him & you & her & her & him & him & her pastor
& him & her uncle & her & him & you & her & her & her plumber & you & her godfather & him &
her & him & you & her & his stepdad & her & her boss & her & her & him & you & her & him &
her & him & him & your dentist & him & her & him & you & him & her & him & how could you?
you didn't even know his name & him & her & him & her & him & you & you'll spend the rest of
your life wondering why & him & her & him & her & him & her & him & we are still dying in
shame & you are numb & her & him & you & her & him & her & him & a cold Saturday morning
& you were bored & him & her & him & him & her & him & her & how could you? you didn't even
know his name & him & him & her & him & her & in your mama's house you swept & washed
Saturdays away & you & her & him & her & him & while ReRe wailed if you won't let me & her &
him & her & him & him & her & you & her & we are dying shamed are you numb & her & him &
him & her & him & her & him & her & him & enough to tell her this man didn't even come & her
& him & her & him & you & her & him & with flowers or tales of a desire to kiss the groom & you
& her & him & her & him & you & her & how could you? you didn't even know his name & him &
her & him & her & him & her & you closed your eyes when he eased inside & wandered & him &
you & her & him & her & him & wondered what D.J. stood for soaked through & him & you & her
& him & her & him & you & we are still a shame to him & her & numbed to fear & her & him &
you & her & him & her & him & you were open & you break easily when cold & her & him & her
& her & him & you & & her & him & come Saturday he'll find you walled in & you & her & him &
her & him & you & there ain't no way for you to love you & him & her & him & her & him & him
& her & him & how could you? you don't even know your name now & her & you & him & him &
him & you & we are dying ah this shame we are numb & him & her & you & you & you & you &

Emily K. Michael

THE BLOOD AND CANDOR OF CRAFT

I stand at the register, ready to swipe my credit card. My groceries are being collected into crinkling paper bags. Because my guide dog can sense my preoccupation, he sniffs for derelict crumbs under the counter. I ask him to sit, so I can use both hands to finish paying.

"Your total is $57.50," the cashier says. She leans over the low counter. "Your dog is so handsome!"

I feel for the chip on my credit card and insert it into the machine. "Thank you, he's a good boy."

The machine chirps, and she retrieves my receipt. "So, how exactly does he help you?"

"He's a guide dog." I stretch out my hand for the receipt. "I'm blind, and he helps me travel safely."

"But, you can't be completely blind," she protests. "You're looking right at me. So you must have some vision."

I slide my wallet into my purse. "You know I can hear you, right?"

Behind me, another customer chuckles. The cashier, still uncomprehending, sputters, "Well, yes, but—"

I deliver my parting shot with a big smile: "It's not hard to figure out where you are, unless you can throw your voice."

She has to laugh. Everyone else is laughing. Even the bagger is cracking up. But I walk out of the store, wondering if my response actually taught her anything.

Maybe I should not expect her to understand and accept my blindness in this five-minute encounter, but I can't help resenting her disbelief. Strangers often say, "You can't really be blind," as the preamble to something they think blind people can't do:

"You can't really be blind. You dress so well!"

"You can't really be blind. You walk so confidently!"

"You must have some vision. Your résumé is so organized!"

The cashier touched a nerve, a tender spot she may know nothing about. And my irritation grows when I think of all the enjoyable conversations we might have had. Instead of focusing on the part of my blindness that didn't make sense, she could have taken me at my word and asked more about how my dog guides me safely. She could have guessed what I was planning to cook with fresh kale and ground turkey. We could have compared notes on almond milk and Icelandic yogurt. But we got stalled in a conversation about the nuts and bolts of my vision.

This exchange with the cashier is an exhibit at the Disability Museum, my label for interactions with intrusive or persistent strangers. At the Disability Museum, I am called upon to explain how a blind person shops, cooks, puts on makeup, or loads the dishwasher. Rather than occasions of gentle wondering, these meetings are shaped by an insatiable fascination that disregards my need to safely cross a street, carry a hot coffee, or get my restless dog outside.

The Disability Museum is frequented by strangers who have not earned the right to personal details about me. Here are some questions they like to ask:

"How much vision do you have? Can you see me?"

"Has your vision gotten worse? Is that why you use a dog?"

"How do you match your outfits?"

"What are your dreams like?"

"Is your condition genetic? Was it a birth defect?"

Usually I give these conversations a chance to turn productive, especially if the stranger is earnest and respectful. When someone opens with, "I'd really like to ask you a question, but I don't want to be rude," I am more willing to listen and answer. But I try to impress upon these strangers that sometimes I need to finish ordering my coffee before explaining how I manage. I have learned to say, "If you'll give me a minute to complete this task, I can answer your question." Genuinely interested people take the hint and step back, allowing me to pay for my latte and move to the pickup counter. Disability Museum patrons march huffily away, grumbling about my bad attitude: "What's her problem? I just wanted to ask one question!"

I have no hope of escaping the Disability Museum. I wear dark glasses and walk beside a big black Labrador. In most rooms, I am the only blind woman, and my pup is the only service dog. For many people, I am the first blind person they have ever met. So the need for education is real, and the curiosities are valid. But the heedless fascination is exhausting, because knowing my visual circumstances does not bring others any closer to knowing me.

Encounters in the Disability Museum are one-sided: The disabled person is bombarded with questions and expected to discuss only their disability. Nondisabled people receive a genuine shock when I try to turn the conversation in another direction. The whole process feels like an interview with a pushy reporter, where I am pressed for confessional details about my physical experiences. I want to overrule this pressure and set it aside, because it coopts not only these chance meetings but the deliberate depictions of disabled people.

I have worked as a poetry editor for *Wordgathering* for three years. As a journal dedicated to disability literature, *Wordgathering* publishes poetry by disabled writers and poetry about disabilities. And it's no secret that estimable journals often reject at least two thirds of the submissions they receive. What troubles me is not the quality of the submissions we receive but the angle they choose.

As I review submissions, I notice how often poets write about the medical aspects of their lives. Blood, bones, gore, surgeries, insensitive doctors, unraveling bandages, scars, invasive treatments. Many writers orbit the doctors' offices, emergency rooms, gurneys—as if only a medical context can illuminate what it means to be disabled. They are willingly entering the Disability Museum, finding places on a stage created by curious outsiders.

For some of us, disability is a highly medical experience, where hospital stays and medical treatments are more common than the nonmedical aspects of daily life. But a catalogue of medical circumstances is not necessarily a good poem. A description of surgery doesn't take readers into a surgical experience.

For me, being blind isn't about what my retinas are doing or what my eye doctor tells me. It's about the feel of my guide dog's harness or the smell of coffee. I can talk about blindness. But I can also talk about birds, butterflies, salted caramel, chemistry, and new crochet patterns. My blindness is not the most interesting thing about me.

When I published my first book, the journalists who interviewed me often tried to use this angle: "She writes about more than her disability." This approach seems like a plausible literary profile only because the Disability Museum haunts my steps, demanding medical answers from many publicly disabled artists. I can be tempted to honor the urgency of this demand, to think that if I supply a little of what they want, they will stop roaring for more.

But when I give in, I render myself as a patient conveniently charted, not a woman living a significant life.

Blood alone is not enough. The scalpel is not sufficient. Even medical trauma does not equal poetry. It is how I transform these experiences that makes me a poet.

Faith

Emily K. Michael

Dan and I lounged under an olive tree and laughed
    as the blindfolded do-gooders tried to pour dried beans
into red plastic cups without spilling. "This is hard!"
    came the wail over tuneful pinging—
cold beans against the card table.

Dan and I lounged under an olive tree and sighed
    as the loud man rushed toward us with the promise
of sight—"Just believe!" And all our blind sorrows would wipe clean.
He had a briefcase stuffed with tiny Bibles. Nothing
    in braille or large print—

Dan and I lounged under an olive tree and remembered
    that first time two like us waited by the road
to call for a good man. Others tell that story
    for the sleeping vision that broke bud—
    the restored sense that always takes precedence.
We tell it because the man hushed the crowd
    and asked what was needed.

Among the Blind

Emily K. Michael

I insist that blindness doesn't separate me from sighted people
  when I'm the only blind woman in the room—
a novelty with something to prove.

But loveliness blankets a coffee shop filled with blind people.
  Someone asks, *Mary, is that you?* or *Is Joan here yet?* without a trace
of self-consciousness. Amid the click of unfolding canes and the jingle

of guide dog harnesses, no one apologizes for blindness.
  It's our shortcut for getting each other. We bring
to the table the old jokes, the same hang-ups. Elsie ties a napkin around her teacup

handle, so she won't drink Mary's coffee by mistake. Lydia can't read
  my name tag, and I can't read hers, so we shout over the din:
Where are you sitting? I'll sit beside you.

We wear tags only for the waitress who threads
  through a dozen conversations with practiced ease.
We trust her not to trip on dog paws and folded canes—

and she's learned to say, *Your coffee cup is to the right*
  the sugar's on your left. She can even be prevailed upon
to announce newcomers and direct them to vacant seats.

The waitress tells Eliza that fifteen years haven't changed her one bit,
  and Eliza, totally blind, says, *Well you look the same to me, too.*
My dog sniffs toward the black Labrador curled decorously beneath a nearby table,

and as the server takes our orders, Anna sings out, *Remember Rosie can't have dairy.*
  Someone asks, *Oh is Rosie here?* Eliza says no. *But she's coming.*
Wonderful, we say. We'd love to see her.

Deficiencies

Emily K. Michael

Under the table my guide dog lies nose-to-nose
    with a red-gold retriever named Conrad
their bodies poised in fragile silence
    that spotlights the rhythm of swaying tails.

I reach down to find muzzles close—
    unflinching at my touch. Two dogs
absorbed in each other. I wrestle

the sudden urge to tumble
my untailed body from this chair

to lie down and measure my worth
against their intimacy. But hesitation

comforts me. Delay eases the truth:
I'm only one kind of companion.

Natalie E. Illum

IF YOU ARE DISABLED, AND THERE IS AN [INSERT], YOU [???].

On February 29, 2020, I was discharged from a short-term nursing home after having a foot correction. A surgery I had had before as both a child and an adult due to the spastic cerebral palsy I have had since birth. So I knew about being pulled out of your own life. I knew about not being able to walk (according to them) and not being able to walk (meaning no weight bearing). Meaning: no crutches, no braces, no crawling, no weight through the limbs that others have decided are too disabled to recognize as good enough.

The daily life skills you have as a disabled person, regardless of what they are, are a significant part of your world. They are a marker, and when those shrink, it's noticed. And on your worst days, they evaporate.

I was bed-bound when Washington, DC, shut down due to COVID-19. Friends couldn't visit. I couldn't access my kitchen or bathroom—in-home nonurgent "health care" was suspended. I tried not to see it as a foreshadowing of a (disabled) culling.

I wasn't trying to write or document the suffering within the pandemic. I wasn't trying to elevate my experience in it, even when I contracted the virus in early March 2020. In what became the poem "Some of us travelers" (published in *Passengers*, August 2021), I started with the line *my body is not a small town.* And then I had to support the tiny universe contained and contaminated by a vast isolation. I think of poems as scaffolding. What am I grabbing onto as a writer, and what do I literally grab? I hold myself up metaphorically through writing. I lean into the world I know so that the reader knows it too. And, whatever type of reader they are, in whatever type of body, they can't pull that structure down.

> *My body is not a small town. I've seen the Pacific Ocean. I am not mad at the sunlight I can see—the aloe plant someone else will water. I could stare long enough so the curve of the bedrail becomes a mountain. We could say*

I am in training for a marathon—the bathroom is the 5K mark. The grab bars form a highway from east to west, just in case I can get out of bed

. . . .

I have been in this room for 231 days. Both of my feet are the work of Frankenstein's doctor.

For me, at first, the pandemic was about staying home. Then about feeling isolated; trapped. What comes out of an "abundance of caution"? The first level is we stay alive. The next, some of us work from home. The next, we feel hopeless; unmoored. I've written three poems that mention the early pandemic (before variants). This is an excerpt from the second poem, when I was able to write beyond just my own isolation.

Out of an Abundance

I woke up. An un-Olympic feat.
I thought I was late for work. But the laptop hummed—
the emails beckoned like a new type of fresh air.
Ironic, the jackhammer I hear at the intersection has more to accomplish—
a gold medal in crushing something.
I woke up, neck tugging at a nightmare—no calendar—
not the time to Tinder a happy hour; risk losing
a phone number; risk seeing our mothers. Just hit send instead.
Your desktop is truly a window now.

A poem can travel us anywhere; into anyone. I need the reader to get to the most accessible (and/or inaccessible) corners of a poem and sit with any dissonance and discomfort it brings. Balance on the edge of that yucky platform.

Who feels free and who does not? Regardless of disability, that dichotomy is cyclical. Winter is coming. COVID is here, and it can kill you. And what is worse—the danger that inclement weather or disease can cause, or the entrapment of ableism? I tried to strengthen both ideas in a third poem that mentions disability and the pandemic:

We left some without inhalers, like we always do. What did you learn here?
        The National Guard protected everything but the ventilators.
How do you fill the indoor hours alone?

My best friend learned how to roller-skate and blackout. So I
YouTubed how to become a cardio expert from a wheelchair.
This is what isolation is for. You should still produce even inside an ICU.

I think giving strength to disabled voices and their experiences is its own justice; the agency of a poem fighting the privilege of a more "normative" body is what I'm building on when I write.

What the brain hemorrhage says

Natalie E. Illum

Pretty blackout. Soft, simple
cortex. I cannot guarantee
you will be cerebral. So focus
on all those beautiful black
holes. You might have nothing but
ether and wish to stand on.

So don't focus on all those other
people with their lightbox brains,
their neurons firing like a symphony.
All that brilliant cartography is nothing

but chaos. Maybe you're lucky.
Better a still room than an anxious
house. Better no ballet lessons
than the choreographer's rage.

Look at what I've spared you!
I'll stop bleeding now if you
give in to crooked feet; these crutches.
Maybe I'll be nice and leave you

Broca's area, intact and nestled
above your left ear. Look
at all that pretty activity.
Your own supernova
inside a dead tundra.

There's no need to cry
into either hemisphere.
No need to resist
what is spastic.

I know I made it hard for you
to relax, but *relax baby.*
I gave you all the verbs
you'll ever need.
Be grateful I left
your tongue alone.

If you are disabled and there is a bomb cyclone, you

Natalie E. Illum

don't relish snow days.
Don't sled down the unplowed streets.

Maybe you don't eat anything
other than panic attacks.

If you are disabled and there is a blizzard, or

two inches, the snow berm will block
the curb cuts. The curb cuts are yours,
but the refreeze unfreeze refreeze doesn't

care about the width of your wheelchair,
about how even the slush and salt
can crash you.

You know cyclones, how the lack
in pressure and consciousness
drops and spins you

from elevator to alternative route
to broken lift to abandon.
Regardless of the season.

Look out the window.
See their joy crystallize
as they spin around
and throw things

without caring if you're warm.

Liz Whiteacre

PLAYING POETIC TELEPHONE TO EXPLORE PAIN IN POEMS

In 2011, Michael Northen invited me to write an essay about my poetry for *Wordgathering* (vol. 5, no. 1). The magazine had published poems that focused on my experiences with spinal injury and chronic pain the previous year, and I was new to the disability studies community and writing about pain. At the time I wrote, "The vocabulary of pain, the stereotypes associated with it, and the comparisons we choose to describe unique moments of pain must meet to forge a relationship that the audience can not only recognize but also welcome into their own realm of experience, so they have something to give back—hopefully, something that spurs the conversation forward." A decade later, as a poet and educator who works with emerging poets, I'm still exploring the thesis of that essay, titled "Extending Conversations of Pain."

One of my spinal injuries, after which it took two years of therapy before I could walk again without aid, was a catalyst for my exploration of figurative language that could create bridges between a poet's and an audience's shared perceptions and experiences of abstract pain. My first audience in 2000, medical professionals, would comment on my "creative" responses when explaining nerve pain during examinations or therapy sessions. A scale of 1–10 was inadequate, and I learned quickly that paying attention to my body and naming specific pain sensations helped my treatment. It was an easy transition, then, to poetry—experimentation with craft has helped me communicate my pain and how it's influenced me.

I started off writing narrative poems in first person, which led to third person poems where I could be a witness. Living with daily pain for decades has shaped who I am, not unlike my family, and I discovered that creating the character Pain, whom I could talk to and about as I would a person, presented opportunities to characterize the unique pain I live with, build upon readers' understanding of pain as a stock character, and, in some ways, give Pain a voice. "Pain Pouts" is part of this sequence that personifies pain, following a timeline of spinal injuries. In this poem, Pain and I are at my wedding—even on the most celebrated days, as we know, pain doesn't take the day off.

"Pain Pouts" highlights the consistency and pervasiveness of pain. I also chose to use second person point of view, which I hope makes the poem feel both like an internal monologue and a direct address. Cataloging the speaker's management of her tethered relationship with Pain in this form invites readers to connect personally to it. (They might have a pushy ex in their lives?) When we can connect shared experiences and emotions to abstractions, as Robert Bly would say, "leap" to them, we can extend conversations: The reader might say, *oh, I know a little about what that's like, here's my story* . . . and a back-and-forth using the tools of figurative language helps us explore each other's lives with greater empathy and curiosity.

This exploration of craft prepared me for the opportunity to work with Ball State University researchers Darolyn "Lyn" Jones, Roger D. Wessel, Christina L. Blanch, and Larry Markle. I was invited to review transcripts of interviews conducted for an academic study with students who used wheelchairs. The study focused on these people's transitions from high school to college, and I was encouraged to develop poems prompted from the data to extend the academic conversation initiated by the study to a more general audience. For this project, I shifted from personification to persona—developing ten speakers with distinct voices, perspectives, dictions, etc., working from anonymous interview transcripts and a focus group discussion transcript, research on the disabilities represented, and personal experiences with wheelchairs, disability, and working with first-year college students. "The Stoic's Universe" is from the point of view of a person with osteogenesis imperfecta (OI) or brittle bone disease.

I wrote this persona sequence after completing six other characters and felt pressure to develop something distinct (they all answered the same set of questions); fortunately, the personality and interests of the person in the transcript made me leap right to stoicism, which became a touchstone for this character. This person described a very confined life in high school and noted the intense feeling of freedom once the accessibility afforded by campus buildings and transportation and the ability to manage care and time themselves occurred—it was a transformative experience. Stoicism and frustration of confinement during injuries myself connected me to this person, and I felt that the structure of the persona poems should reflect those intense moments (prose for confinement/outside control; caesura for freedom/self-choice). "The Stoic's Universe" comes at the end of this character's sequence of poems. It begins with a swirl of transformative transitions the person observed during an interview and ends in centered prose that reflects the character's new sense of self-control and ownership of their future (the form's established "rule" has been repurposed). The challenges of developing authentic moments and voices in poems for characters prompted by other people taught me a lot about extending conversations about pain, and more widely, disability. First, I had to form my own connections and bridges as a reader to the anonymous testimonies as these people answered academic research questions; then develop characters through my own research; and then create narrative vignettes for characters in persona poems that would help other readers explore and engage with different perspectives. It's a little like playing poetic telephone, but I hope it encourages readers to ask questions, share back, and continue important discussions.

Using figurative language—simile, personification, or leaps—to offer readers opportunities to connect and engage with abstractions like pain, love, or identity can be a successful way to engage people in conversation. As I've worked with emerging poets in college classrooms, I've noticed that after I share my poem "Trashcan, Unmoved" in an Intro to Creative Writing lecture that presents Bly's concept of poetic leaps (because I can walk students through my choices when I was an emerging poet experimenting with leaps during revision for the first time), students start writing about unique, vulnerable topics, many of which explore pain. Understanding the power of *it's like . . .* to help a reader *get* feelings about unique experiences offers emerging poets a starting point. A way into conversations. And while most of these introductory students will not pursue poetry, they will use these skills to help them communicate more effectively moving forward. That's ultimately what motivates me—not just talking about pain in poetic ways, but in poetic ways that are accessible. On the page, in a doctor's waiting room, or in a grocery line. Ways that prompt *oh, I get it* during an exchange. That's the beauty of disability poetry: the intimate invitation to share and understand in a safe space.

Pain Pouts

Liz Whiteacre

You push Pain's digs away like
ghost voices of middle school boys.
You've picked this man and these
subtly orthopedic pumps and a dress
kind to your torso—easy to pee in.
Its straps won't slip, if you stand straight.
The woman who murdered your hair
with a hot iron, you've forgiven.
Your mangled-haired matron of honor
says this will be what you laugh about
later, and Pain mopes at the suite's minibar.
You've practiced this walk on cotton,
down an aisle straight as the treadmill,
your dad surefooted, strong beside you.
Banished to a corner, without a place setting,
Pain pouts. You ignore its bites and whimpers,
a dismissed suitor who whines about what
could have been. This is your day. You will not
slouch on this dance floor, jazz jumping
hot down your spine as your husband holds you.

The Stoic's Universe

Liz Whiteacre

face

avoid \—confrontation—|

stranger

|—roommate—/ friend

tradition

\—religion—/

exploration

open

\—doors—/

closed

In my islandic universe, transitions pulsate.

cramped

\—bedroom—|

spacious

disciplined

/—school—|

apathetic

Interconnected, each part of my whole, like my hand to my wrist, my patella to my femur, my atlas vertebrae to my skull, works in harmony, in dissonance, in response to conflagrations and tranquilities. The sweet hum of stardust weaves a path through this void I choose to explore. What happens to one part of me, affects another, and I brace for inevitable pain and pleasure as I trust. Trust more each day that I am made up of all that has happened to me, and I

am stronger for it.

Kobus Moolman

THE POETICS OF FALLING: AN OVERVIEW

At the time of writing the earliest of these three poems, "The Shoulder," in 2010, I did not know that I was a disabled writer. I know that must sound odd. But the fact is, it took me a long time to put the two words, "disabled" and "writer," together and to come up with a third idea.

Of course I knew I was disabled. I had known that since birth. I knew that my life had started off incomplete. Split open at the back toward the bottom, with some of the raw and vital parts missing. Properly known as spina bifida with a myelomeningocele.

I knew too, then, that I was a writer. At that point I had been writing for some time. I had published three collections of poetry and some plays, and won some South African and international awards. (Though little of that really matters, I know now, except the actual writing; the squiggly black ink in the old notebook.)

But I had not thought of myself—I know now that I did not *want* to think myself—as a disabled writer. That was an apology in my mind, then. It was some sort of excuse. A way of propping up the writing with pity. After all, the twisted, broken, incontinent body was something I was writing against, or trying to write past.

It took a long time for me to become me, you see. Because my body did not know how to stay the same in one place all the time. It kept on becoming. Now it would crawl over the wooden bedroom floor. Now it would roll under the kitchen table. Or drag itself across the cold bathroom tiles. Or collapse. Just like that. Dropping like a sack of potatoes, as my mother always used to say. Or my body would stumble. And not fall. And almost fall. And jerk and twist, then come up like a heavy bird out of water. A heavy bird in big black boots and iron callipers up to the knees. And a lifelong soft spot for straps and buckles and Velcro. And pain.

I did not know the language that would enable me to join and close and heal the holes, you see. I still do not know. But it was poems like the three published here that helped me conceptualize what I was as a disabled writer.

The poem "The Shoulder" is a particular case. It is part of a short series of poems entitled "Anatomy." There are six parts in total: the hand, the foot, the other one, the shoulder, the foot revisited, and the wrist. (I have a private joke with myself here, because there was in fact another section, the lower back, but I removed it!)

Aptly, the hand—the right one—came first. It was written around six months before the other parts of the body, late in 2009. And it sat in my black book, looking at me. I looked back in puzzlement. I read it at a festival. And it seemed to make sense to people. But it made me itchy. It made me want to scratch my flesh.

It had come out of nowhere. Out of my inner dryness. My restlessness with myself and with my thin dry white voice. I could sense that just below the surface of the words there was a shark of hungry potential lurking; something I desperately needed in order to make my words raw and open and vital again. But the poem, ultimately, was knocking up against something for which I did not yet have a language and therefore had no way of representing. It was reaching into a territory that was unknown to me at that stage.

Then early in 2010 I went on a local ten-day creative residency. The aim was to bring writers and visual artists from South Africa and the United States together, and to see what conventions and boundaries in our respective fields we could push past by collaborating on a series of lithographs (with text and image—I worked with the American artist Fahamu Pecou) and the production of handmade chapbooks.

And there something profound happened.

The parts of my body that previously had been important, but mute, suddenly could talk, and they were talking back to me in a strong and fluid voice. In a voice that sounded like home. With parts like my left foot with its pressure ulcers. My right wrist that bore all the weight and the twist of me walking with my wooden cane. And my right shoulder that burned day and night as a result of the surgery into the top of my neck in order to insert a shunt to drain the hydrocephalus that had developed in my early twenties.

I had been searching for a new language to express the parts of me that my old and tired words could not. How does pain talk, for example? What words can I put in its clenched mouth? Or shame? Standing there in its short, wet, gray school trousers. How can the body be given words to speak its indissolubly unique truth? To give word to the wordless. Up until that residency I had only glimpsed the possibility.

And I discovered that it was not about searching for comparisons for my body. Or equivalents for its being-in-itself. By working alongside a visual artist, experiencing his art that could speak without uttering a single word, merely using shape and form the way music does, I began to understand the possibilities of language differently. How the language in a poem is the poem before it is the thing that the poem is about; the same way that color and gesture are their own things before they become a subject.

And this self-consciousness in language created the possibilities for the images in a line to operate with greater responsibility, with greater weight, but also with greater risk and daring. The way that the boots in "Three Views of a Pair of Orthopedic Boots" immediately, without any set-up or situation, swap angles and pose in a range of different startling friezes.

And this gives rise to a sense of language hearing and seeing and tasting itself. For indeed the tongue is rooted. It is radicalized, by being returned to its root. And its root is of the flesh. Its root is of bone. And nerves and muscles. So that when the bone speaks, this is not a figure of speech. The shoulder is not a symbol. There is no ventriloquism involved. It is instead raw and naked authorship of the actual. It is self-identity identifying itself. Being. Becoming. By being and because of being broken. Ultimately.

A language, then, not of any absence. No. Nor even incompleteness. But a language nevertheless, that draws its breath from its very breathlessness. A language that stands its sack of skin unbalanced and toppling on unbalance itself. On the beauty of falling. And knowing how to.

The Shoulder

Kobus Moolman

Fire most times.
And ice the others.
Fire when the ice has melted,
and standing is impossible.

Fire when the wind blows the night over,
when the invisible river running through the night
runs out of breath.

Fire most times.

And others a blade
like a butcher's,
a hammer, a chisel: bone and tissue
separating every day and returning
with every step.

Three Views of a Pair of Orthopedic Boots

Kobus Moolman

1

Tired boot
twists on the
rope of the body.

2

Dry boot
squeaks like a
rusted guillotine.

3

Brown boot
longs to be
ash-black again.

In the Bathroom

Kobus Moolman

Something happened, all those years ago, in the small bathroom silent as the steam on the rectangular mirror, after he had taken off his boots, first the right and then the left, and he was standing there, still dressed, waiting for the water to cool, the rest of the house holding its breath on the other side of the yellow door. To be precise, it was more of a feeling, hard to describe, even harder to remember, rather than something concrete that happened. An aloneness that was preparing itself for something. A quiet that had been separated from the clamor of the house in order for something to be done to it. The same as when, after the pre-med injection, he lay white and still on a trolley in a side room dizzy with light, waiting for his turn to be operated upon. A kind of surrender to the ambiguities of water, the inevitability of heat and habit. And standing there, still dressed, holding on to the washbasin, holding him up, he felt always the presence of something, close as his skin and yet disinterested, something that just watched him, the way the surgeon used to when he asked him to walk up and down the carpeted consulting room, heel–toe, heel–toe. And the feeling always made him remember that there was not just a front and a back to himself, but, more importantly, an outside. That he was standing up inside a sack of skin that went with him wherever he went, and this was what the rest of the house saw. That even when he was alone, as then in the slowly steaming bathroom, he was truly not so. Because something was always there with him, watching and listening, through the keyholes of his skin. And reporting on him to God.

ACKNOWLEDGMENTS

The editors would like to thank Parneshia Jones, Marisa Siegel, Courtney Smotherman, and Northwestern University Press for believing in this project and helping us bring it into the world. We would also like to thank Adrean Clark for the beautiful cover art in ASL urging us to continue onward.

All possible care has been taken to trace ownership and secure permission for the poems and other material quoted from and reproduced in this book. The editors, authors, and publisher would like to thank the following organizations and individuals, including the editors of periodicals where some of these poems first appeared, for permission to reprint copyrighted material. Any poems, essays, or other contributions appearing in print for the first time are by permission of the author. (This page constitutes a continuation of the copyright page.)

Ekiwah Adler Beléndez. An earlier version of the essay "On Writing 'I Bargained for This Wheelchair'" and the poems "The Speed of Sound: Skydiving from one life to another" and "Falling into Truth" first appeared in a self-published collection, *Amor sobre ruedas* (*Love on Wheels*), that was subsequently republished by *17, Editorial* in 2021. "The Speed of Sound" and "Falling into Truth" were translated from English to Spanish by Ekiwah Adler-Belendez and Kenia Cano as "La velocidad del sonido" and "En verdad caer."

Shahd Alshammari. "Public Disgrace," from *On Love and Loss* (2015). Reprinted by permission of the author and publisher, Strategic Book Publishing & Rights Agency, LLC, 2015.

Raymond Antrobus. "Two Guns in the Sky for Daniel Harris" and "The Mechanism of Speech," from *The Perseverance* (Penned in the Margins, 2018), and "The Acceptance," from *All the Names Given* (Picador, 2021). Copyright © 2018, 2021 by Raymond Antrobus. Reprinted with the permission of David Higham Associates.

Oli Barrett. The image "Two Guns in the Sky for Daniel Harris" appeared in Raymond Antrobus's *The Perseverance* (Penned in the Margins, 2018). Reprinted by permission of the artist.

Kay Ulanday Barrett. The essay "We Will Buoy Each Other" is an excerpt from a published interview with Alice Wong that appeared on the *Disability Visibility Project* website in March 2020, https://disabilityvisibilityproject.com/2020/03/29/qa-with-kay-ulanday-barrett/. "Sick 4 Sick" appeared in *Zoeglossia Poem of the Week Series* (April 2021); "I use the word Disabled" appeared in *The Rumpus* (November 24, 2020); "In which your white doctor informs you that he was in the Navy & based in the Philippines," from *More Than Organs* (Sibling Rivalry Press, 2020); and "consider the gender spectrum," from *Disabled People: The Voice of Many* (Shades of Noir UK, 2020). Reprinted by permission of the author.

Roxanna Bennett. "What do you do for a living?" and "Wherever You Go, There You Are," from *The Untranslatable I* (Gordon Hill Press, 2021). Reprinted by permission of the publisher.

Molly McCully Brown and Susannah Nevison. Collaborative poems from *In the Field Between Us* (Persea Books, 2020). Copyright © 2020 by Molly McCully Brown and Susannah Nevison. Reprinted by permission of Persea Books, Inc., New York. All rights reserved.

Eli Clare. "Turning Toward Each Other" and "A Survivor's Wail" [previously published under the title "Fifty Years After He Beat Me"] from *Unfurl: Survivals, Sorrows, and Dreaming* (Duke University Press, 2025). Copyright © 2025 by Eli Clare. Reprinted by permission of the copyright holder and the publisher. All rights reserved. "Confluence" was previously published under the title "And Yet" in *Self-Organizing Men: Conscious Masculinities in Time and Space*, edited by Jay Sennett (Homofactus Press, 2006) and also appeared in *The Marrow's Telling* (Homofactus Press, 2007) and *Troubling the Line: Trans and Genderqueer Poetry and Poetics*, edited by TC Tolbert and Trace Peterson (nightboat books, 2013). Reprinted by permission of the publisher.

Kelly Davio. "I May Appear Drunk," from *The Burden of Light* (Short Fuse Publishing, 2014). Reprinted by permission of Foreword Literary, Inc. "He Died After a Long Illness" was previously published in *Southern Indiana Review* (Fall 2014). Reprinted by permission of the publisher. "Etymological Note" appeared in *The New York Times* (May 19, 2019). Reprinted by permission of the publisher.

Meg Day. "Deaf Erasure of the Gospel According to the TSA Agent at Atlanta Airport" originally published in *The New York Times* (May 19, 2019). Reprinted by permission of the publisher. "Elegy in Translation" originally published in *TYPO Magazine* 25 (2016), republished in the Academy of American Poets Poem-a-Day series on March 18, 2018. "10 A.M. Is When You Come to Me" published in the Academy of American Poets Poem-a-Day series on July 1, 2019. Reprinted by permission of the publisher and author.

torrin a. greathouse. The essay "Poems with Bodies Like Mine," and the poems "Weeds," "Abecedarian Requiring Further Examination Before a Diagnosis Can Be Determined," "*That's So Lame*," and "Essay Fragment: Economic Model of Disability," from *Wound from the Mouth of a Wound* by torrin a. greathouse (Minneapolis: Milkweed Editions, 2020). Copyright © 2020 by torrin a. greathouse. Reprinted by permission from Milkweed Editions.

Stephanie Heit. The essay "Disability as a Creative Practice" originally appeared online at *Mad in America* (March 17, 2023). Reprinted by permission of the publisher. "Treatment Room," "Recovery Bay" and "Dear Brain," from *Psych Murders* (Wayne State University Press, 2022). Reprinted by permission of the publisher and author. "Treatment Room" is also included in *We Are Not Your Metaphor: A Disability Poetry Anthology*, edited by Zoeglossia Fellows (Squares and Rebels, 2019).

Natalie E. Illum. "What the brain hemorrhage says," first published in *Riggwelter* (March 1, 2018). Reprinted by permission of the publisher and author. "If you are disabled and there is a bomb cyclone, you," first published in *Former People* (January 10, 2018).

Andy Jackson. "Quasimodo," from *Among the Regulars* (Papertiger Media, 2010); "Double Helix," from *the thin bridge* (Whitmore Press, 2014). Reprinted by permission from the publisher and author.

Camisha L. Jones. "Accommodation," "Ménière's Flare," and "In/Ability," from *Flare* (Finishing Line Press, 2017). Copyright © 2017 by Camisha L. Jones. Reprinted by permission of The Permissions Company LLC on behalf of Finishing Line Press. "My Hearing Loss Interrogates the World" previously appeared online as part of *Zoeglossia Poem of the Week Series* (May 31, 2021).

Ilya Kaminsky. Parts of the essay "Reading Celan in Ukraine" previously appeared in *Poetry* magazine in a different version, titled "Of Strangeness That Wakes Us" (January 2, 2013). "That Map of Bone and Opened Valves" and "In a Time of Peace," from *Deaf Republic* (Graywolf, 2019). Copyright © 2018 by Ilya Kaminsky. Reprinted by permission of Faber and Faber Ltd. and The Permissions Company, LLC, on behalf of Graywolf Press, Minneapolis, Minnesota.

Jill Khoury. "Cranial Nerve II," from *Suites for the Modern Dancer* (Sundress Publications, 2016). "[rotary nystagmus]" previously appeared in *Paper Nautilus.* Reprinted by permission of the publisher and author.

Travis Chi Wing Lau. The essay "The Crip Poetics of Pain" previously appeared in *Amodern* 10 (special issue on Disability Poetics, edited by Orchid Tierney and Davy Knittle, 2020). "Treatment," from *The Bone Setter* (Damaged Goods Press, 2019). "On the Anniversary of an X-Ray" previously appeared in *Barren Magazine* (October 2019) and "Brain Fog" previously appeared in *Tupelo Quarterly* (Disability Poetry Folio, August 2022). "Pithy," from *Paring* (Finishing Line Press, 2020). Copyright © 2020 by Travis Chi Wing Lau. Reprinted by permission of The Permissions Company LLC on behalf of Finishing Line Press.

Aurora Levins Morales. "Asher Yatzar," from *Rimonim: Ritual Poetry of Jewish Liberation* (Ayin Press, 2024). Reprinted by permission of the publisher and author.

Liv Mammone. "Surgery Psalm" previously appeared in *Brooklyn Poets* (May 16, 2016). "A Crip Is," from *Stoked Words: An Anthology of Queer Poetry from the Capturing Fire Slam & Submit* (Capturing Fire Press, 2018); it was previously published in *Monstering Magazine,* 2017. Reprinted by permission of the publisher and author.

Lateef McLeod. "Absence of routine," from *A Declaration of A Body of Love Poetry* (Atahualpa Press, 2008), and in an earlier version in *Something Close to Beautiful* (Inglis House Poetry Workshop, 2005). "So Much," from *Whispers of Krip Love, Shouts of Krip* (Poetic Matrix Press, 2020). Reprinted by permission of the publisher and author.

Constance Merritt. The essay "Some Notes on a (Dis)/Embodied Poetics" previously appeared in *Poetry International.* "Jay-Walkin Blues," "Revelation Blues," and "Less Than Greater Than Blues," from *Blind Girl Grunt* (Headmistress Press, 2017). Reprinted by permission of the publisher and author.

Emily K. Michael. The essay "The Blood and Candor of Craft" previously appeared in *Wordgathering* 14, no. 1 (March 2020). Reprinted by permission of the publisher and author. "Faith" previously appeared in *Nine Mile Magazine* (September 2019). "Deficiencies," from *Neoteny: Poems* (Finishing Line Press, 2019). Copyright © 2019 by Emily K. Michael. Reprinted by permission of The Permissions Company LLC on behalf of Finishing Line Press.

Kobus Moolman. "The Shoulder" and "Three Views of a Pair of Orthopaedic Boots," from *Light and After* (Deep South Books, 2010); "In the Bathroom," from *Left Over* (Dye Hard Press, 2013). Reprinted by permission of the publisher and author.

Cath Nichols. "Tender spots," from *The Brown Envelope Book* (Caparison, 2021). Reprinted by permission of the publisher and author.

Emilia Nielsen. An earlier version of the essay "A Note on the Poetry and Poetics of Dissonant Disabilities," under the title "Chronically Ill, Critically Crip? Poetry, Poetics and Dissonant Disabilities," was published in *Disability Studies Quarterly* 30, no. 4. Poems from the Symptomatic series, "Tremors," "Emotional Lability," "Polyphagia," and "Hypertensive," from *Body Work* (Signature Editions, 2018). Reprinted by permission of the publisher and author.

Naomi Ortiz. The essay "To Reclaim Power" previously appeared in *Poetry* magazine in a different version, titled "Crip Ecologies: Complicate the Conversation to Reclaim Power" (February 1, 2022). "Benefaction," from *Rituals for Climate Change: A Crip Struggle for Ecojustice* (Punctum Books, 2023), was originally published in *The Texas Review.* "Shelter Is a Privilege (one & two)" previously appeared in *Tending Survivorship,* 2024. "To the Non-Disabled White Grrrl with the Frida Kahlo Altar in the Living Room" previously appeared in *Zoeglossia Poem of the Week Series* (Nov. 9, 2020). Reprinted by permission of the publisher and author.

Leah Lakshmi Piepzna-Samarasinha. Parts of the essay "Why We Do This Thing Called Disability Justice Writing" appeared in different form in *The Future Is Disabled: Prophecies, Love Notes and Mourning Songs* (Arsenal Pulp Press, 2022). "I know crips live here," "Bad road," and "Adaptive device," from *Tonguebreaker: Poems and Performance Texts* by Leah Lakshmi Piepzna-Samarasinha (Arsenal Pulp Press, 2019). Reprinted by permission of the publisher and author.

Jesse Rice-Evans. "Pills" previously appeared in *Honey & Lime* (2019). "All I'm looking for is a ceremony" previously appeared in *Peculiars Magazine* (2019). Reprinted by permission of the author.

David James "DJ" Savarese. "The Librarian in the Trees," "Swoon," and "Tongue," from *Swoon* (Nine Mile Books, 2022). Reprinted by permission of the publisher and author. "The Librarian in the Trees" was originally published in *A Doorknob for the Eye* (Unrestricted Interest 2017). "Swoon" and "Tongue" were originally published in *Seneca Review* 27, no. 1 (Spring 2017); "Swoon" also appeared in *The Quarry: A Social Justice Poetry Database* at Split This Rock (2022) and the documentary film *Deej: Inclusion Shouldn't Be a Lottery* (Rooy Media LLC, 2017).

Daniel Sluman. "my love is sponsored by the warmth of opiates" and "& this is love," from *the terrible* (Nine Arches Press, 2015). Copyright © Daniel Sluman. Reprinted by permission of the publisher. The poem "& this is love" also appeared in *Wordgathering: A Journal of Disability Poetry and Literature* 9, no. 2 (2015).

Liz Whiteacre. "The Stoic's Universe" previously appeared in *Wordgathering: A Journal of Disability Poetry and Literature* 13, no. 3 (2019). Reprinted by permission of the author.

L. Lamar Wilson. "I Can't Help It" and "Legion: Human Immunodeficiency Virus," from *Sacrilegion* (Blair, 2013). Reprinted by permission of the publisher and author.

CONTRIBUTORS

Ekiwah Adler Beléndez is a bilingual and bicultural poet, speaker, and teacher born in Amatlán, Morelos. He is the author of several books of poetry, *including Amor sobre ruedas (Love on Wheels)* and *The Coyote's Trace* (with a preface by Mary Oliver). He won the George Garrett Literary Teaching Award in 2019. His work has been presented in Mexico, the United States, Germany, Hungary, and Canada. He is passionate about reading poetry in spaces where poetry and love for literature usually have no voice, such as Mexican prisons, rehab centers, and low income schools. He is the proud father of Lucio Valentin.

Shahd Alshammari is a Kuwaiti professor of literature whose works include *Notes on the Flesh, Head Above Water: Reflections on Illness,* and *Confetti and Ashes: Reflections on Wellness.*

Raymond Antrobus is the author of the poetry collections *The Perseverance, All The Names Given,* and *Signs, Music,* as well as two picture books for children, *Can Bears Ski?* and *Terrible Horses.* His accolades include the Ted Hughes Award, the Lucille Clifton Legacy Award, and the Sunday Times Young Writer of the Year Award, as well as the Geoffrey Dearmer Prize (judged by Ocean Vuong).

Kay Ulanday Barrett is a 2024 Disability Futures Fellow and 2022 winner of the Cy Twombly Award for Poetry from the Foundation for Contemporary Arts. They have received support from Baldwin For The Arts, Millay Arts, and MacDowell. His contributions have appeared in *The New York Times, Academy of American Poets, Literary Hub, Poetry Unbound, The Advocate, The Rumpus, Al Jazeera,* and elsewhere. Their second book, *More Than Organs,* received a Stonewall Honor Book Award from the American Library Association and was a Lambda Literary Award Finalist.

Roxanna Bennett is the author of numerous books, including *Uncomfortability, Unmeaningable, The Untranslatable I, The Suspect We* (with Shane Neilson), and *Unbecoming Prophecy* (with Khashayar Mohammadi).

Jay Besemer is the author of numerous poetry collections, including *Your Tongue is as Long as a Tuesday, Men & Sleep, Wounded Buildings/Simple Machines,* and *Theories of Performance,* which was a 2021 Lambda Literary Award Finalist in the category of Transgender Poetry. Besemer's book *Chelate* was a finalist for the 2017 Leslie Feinberg Award for Trans and Gender-Variant Literature.

Sheila Black is the author of five poetry collections, most recently *Radium Dream.* She was a coeditor of *Beauty is a Verb: The New Poetry of Disability* and a cofounder of Zoeglossia, a nonprofit to support disabled poets. She lives in Tempe, Arizona, where she is the assistant director of the Virginia G. Piper Center for Creative Writing at Arizona State University.

Molly McCully Brown is the author of the poetry collection *The Virginia State Colony for Epileptics and Feebleminded,* which won the 2016 Lexi Rudnitsky First Book Prize, and the essay collection *Places I've Taken My Body.* With Susannah Nevison, she is the coauthor of *In the Field Between Us.* A recipient of the United States Artist Fellowship, the Civitella Ranieri Foundation Fellowship, and the Amy Lowell Poetry Traveling Scholarship, she directs the creative writing program at the University of Wyoming.

Eli Clare—white, disabled, and genderqueer—lives near Lake Champlain in unceded Abenaki territory, where he writes and claims a penchant for rabble-rousing. He is the author of *Unfurl: Survivals, Sorrows, and Dreaming,* the award-winning *Brilliant Imperfection: Grappling with Cure*; and *Exile and Pride: Disability, Queerness, and Liberation.* Clare works as a traveling poet, storyteller, and social justice educator.

Kelly Davio is the author of *Burn This House, It's Just Nerves,* and *The Book of the Unreal Woman.* She is a British American writer who lives in London, where she is a scientific director at a global communications agency.

Meg Day is the author of *Last Psalm at Sea Level,* winner of the Publishing Triangle's Audre Lorde Award. Day has been awarded the Amy Lowell Poetry Traveling Scholarship, the National Endowment for the Arts Fellowship in Poetry, and the 2024 Guggenheim Poet-in-Residence appointment. Day's recent work can be found in *Best American Poetry* and *The New York Times.* Day is an associate professor of English and creative writing in the MFA program at North Carolina State University.

Rigoberto González is the author of twenty books of poetry and prose. His most recent publication is *To the Boy Who Was Night: Poems Selected and New.* His awards include Lannan, Guggenheim, National Endowment for the Arts, New York Foundation for the Arts, and USA Rolón fellowships, as well as the PEN/Voelcker Award, the American Book Award from the Before Columbus Foundation, the Lenore Marshall Prize from the Academy of American Poets, and the Shelley Memorial Prize from the Poetry Society of America. He is a distinguished professor of English and the director of the MFA Program in Creative Writing at Rutgers-Newark, the State University of New Jersey.

torrin a. greathouse is a transgender cripple-punk poet and essayist. They have received fellowships from the National Endowment for the Arts, the Effing Foundation for Sex Positivity, the Ragdale Foundation, and the University of Arizona Poetry Center. She is the author of *DEED*, winner of a 2025 ALA Stonewall Book Award, and *Wound from the Mouth of a Wound*, a finalist for the Minnesota Book Award and CLMP Firecracker Award, and winner of the 2022 Kate Tufts Discovery Award. She teaches in the MFA program at Pacific Lutheran University.

Stephanie Heit (she/her) is a queer disabled poet, dancer, teacher, and codirector of Turtle Disco, a somatic writing space on Anishinaabe land in Ypsilanti, Michigan. She is bipolar, a shock/psych system survivor, a mad activist, and a member of the Olimpias, an international disability performance collective. Her poetry collections are *Psych Murders*, a book of hybrid memoir poems that explores the need for new futures of care beyond psychiatric wards and shock treatments, and *The Color She Gave Gravity*, which explores the seams of language, movement, and mental health difference.

Natalie E. Illum is a poet, disability activist, and singer-songwriter living in Washington, DC. She is a former Jenny McKean Moore Fellow, a recurring Pushcart and Best of the Net Nominee, and the 2013 Beltway DC Grand Slam Champion, as well as the recipient of multiple artist fellowship grants from the DC Commission for the Arts and Humanities. She was a founding board member of *mothertongue DC*, an LGBTQIA+ Open Mic series. Illum's band, *All Her Muses*, released *Not speaking in metaphor* in May 2022.

Andy Jackson is a poet and a lecturer in creative writing at the University of Melbourne. He has coedited disability-themed issues of *Southerly* and *Australian Poetry Journal* and the anthology *Raging Grace: Australian Writers Speak Out on Disability*. He has been featured at literary events and arts festivals across Australia, as well as on the Australian Broadcasting Corporation's Radio National and the 7.30 Report. He was the inaugural Writing the Future of Health Fellow in 2022. Jackson's latest poetry collection is *Human Looking*, which won the ALS Gold Medal and the Prime Minister's Literary Award for Poetry.

Camisha L. Jones (she/her) is the author of the poetry chapbook *Flare*. Her poems have been published at *Poets.org, The New York Times, The Deaf Poets Society, The Quarry: A Social Justice Poetry Database* at Split This Rock, *Typo, Button Poetry*, and elsewhere. With 30+ years providing organizational and programmatic leadership at nonprofits and higher education institutions, she has collaboratively cultivated access-centered gatherings and practices for arts organizations such as Split This Rock, Kinetic Light's LAB, and Zoeglossia. Jones is a 2022 Fellow of Disability Futures, a 2017 Lapine Poetry Fellow, and a Loft Literary Center 2017 Spoken Word Immersion Fellow.

Ilya Kaminsky was born in Odesa, Ukraine, and currently lives in New Jersey. He is the author of several books of poetry and translation, most recently *Deaf Republic*, which received the Los Angeles Times Book Prize and was listed as one of *The New York Times*'s Notable Books of the Year in 2019. Kaminsky teaches at Princeton.

Jill Khoury (she/her) is a disabled poet and a Western Pennsylvania Writing Project Fellow. She has taught poetry in high school, university, and enrichment settings. She holds an MFA from the Ohio State University and edits *Rogue Agent*, a journal of embodied poetry and art. Her poems have appeared in numerous venues, including *Copper Nickel, VerseDaily, CALYX*, and the Academy of American Poets' *Poem-A-Day*. Her second full-length collection, *earthwork*, won the Gatewood Prize from Switchback Books.

Travis Chi Wing Lau (he/him/his) is an assistant professor of English at Kenyon College. His research and teaching focus on eighteenth- and nineteenth-century British literature and culture, health humanities, and disability studies. Alongside his scholarship, he has published widely in venues of public scholarship and poetry, including three chapbooks—*The Bone Setter, Paring*, and *Vagaries*—and a full-length collection of poems, *What's Left Is Tender*.

Aurora Levins Morales is a cuir Puerto Rican-Ashkenazi feminist writer, artist, and movement elder who lives with disability and chronic illness. A former commissioned artist at the disability arts project *Sins Invalid,* her work has been widely anthologized and translated. She is the author of nine books, including *Kindling: Writings on the Body* and *The Story of What Is Broken Is Whole: An Aurora Levins Morales Reader.* She lives in Maricao, Puerto Rico.

Stephen Lightbown is a UK-based poet who lives in the city of Bristol. Paralyzed following an accident when he was sixteen, Lightbown uses his poems to give a voice to his disability. He is the author of two poetry collections for adults and one for children. His collection *And I Climbed, And I Climbed* was published in 2023 and has been widely hailed as essential reading for children. In 2022 and 2023, Lightbown represented England at the ISA World Para Surfing Championship.

Liv Mammone (she/her) is an editor and poet from Long Island. Her poetry has appeared in *Button Poetry* and *The Medical Journal of Australia,* on the Poetry Foundation's website, and elsewhere. In 2017, she competed for Union Square Slam to be on a New York national poetry slam team and was a finalist in the Capturing Fire National Poetry Slam in 2017. A Brooklyn Poets Fellow and Zoeglossia Fellow, she is currently an editor at Game Over Books. In 2022, her poem "On the Subway for the First Time" was one of the top ten most-read poems at Split This Rock's poetry database, *The Quarry.* Her first collection, *Fire in the Waiting Room,* was released in July 2025.

Lateef McLeod is a December 2024 graduate of the Anthropology and Social Change doctoral program at the California Institute of Integral Studies in San Francisco. In 2010, he published his first poetry book, *A Declaration of A Body of Love,* chronicling his life as a black man with a disability. In 2020, he published his second collection, *Whispers of Krip Love, Shouts of Krip Revolution.* In 2021, he coauthored a book of poetry titled *Studies in Brotherly Love.*

Constance Merritt is an American poet and social justice advocate. Born in 1966, Merritt is visually impaired and began her education at the Arkansas School for the Blind. Among other recognitions, she has won the Vassar Miller Prize in Poetry. Merritt is also dedicated to serving her community. She cofounded Bringing Justice Home, a nonprofit that fights food insecurity and fosters connection in Louisville.

Emily K. Michael is a blind poet, musician, and writing teacher from Jacksonville, Florida. Her work centers on ecology, disability, and music. She is the poetry editor for *Wordgathering: A Journal of Disability Poetry and Literature* at Syracuse University, and she curates the *Blind Academy* blog. She is the author of *Neoteny: Poems.*

Kobus Moolman was born with spina bifida sixty years ago. He has published seven collections of poetry, two collections of plays, a collection of short stories, and has edited an anthology of poetry, prose, and art by South African writers living with disabilities. He is a professor of creative writing and English literature in the department of English at the University of the Western Cape in South Africa. He has won numerous local and international awards.

Susannah Nevison is the author of the poetry collections *Lethal Theater* and *Teratology,* which won the 2014 Lexi Rudnitsky First Book Prize. With Molly McCully Brown, she is the coauthor of the poetry collection *In The Field Between Us.* Her work has appeared in the *Los Angeles Review of Books, Tin House, The New York Times,* and elsewhere. She lives and teaches in Virginia.

Cath Nichols started writing poetry in 2000 as the drag queen Daisy Buttercup. Their pamphlets are *Tales of Boy Nancy* and *Distance.* Their second poetry collection is *This is Not a Stunt.* Nichols has a PhD in creative writing and taught creative writing at the University of Leeds for twelve years. They were a queer journalist for print media and BBC Manchester radio in the 1990s. They now receive benefits and work from home. Nichols is disabled, autistic, and queer.

Emilia Nielsen is the author of two collections of poetry: *Body Work,* a finalist for a Lambda Literary Award and the League of Canadian Poets' Pat Lowther Memorial Award and third-place winner in the Fred Cogswell Award for Excellence in Poetry; and *Surge Narrows,* a finalist for the Gerald Lampert Memorial Award. Her scholarly text, *Disrupting Breast Cancer Narratives: Stories of Rage and Repair,* won an Elli Köngäs-Maranda Prize for superior work in feminist theory. She is an associate professor at York University in Toronto.

Michael Northen was the founder of *Wordgathering* and its editor from 2007 to 2019. He was an editor of the anthologies *Beauty is a Verb: The New Poetry of Disability* and *The Right Way to Be Naked and Crippled.* His book of poetry *The Only One in the Room in White Socks* will appear from Finishing Line Press in June

2026. For twelve years Northen facilitated the Inglis House Poetry Workshop for disabled writers in Philadelphia.

Naomi Ortiz (they/them) is a Disabled Mestize artist, poet, and author. Ortiz is a Reclaiming the US/Mexico Border Narrative Awardee and a 2022 United States Artist Disability Futures Fellow. Ortiz is the author of *Rituals for Climate Change: A Crip Struggle for Ecojustice* and *Sustaining Spirit: Self-Care for Social Justice.*

Leah Lakshmi Piepzna-Samarasinha is a nonbinary femme disabled writer and disability and transformative justice movement worker of Burgher and Tamil Sri Lankan, Irish, and Galician/Roma descent. They are the author and coeditor of ten books, including *The Future Is Disabled: Prophecies, Love Notes and Mourning Songs*; *Beyond Survival: Stories and Strategies from the Transformative Justice Movement* (coedited with Ejeris Dixon); *Tonguebreaker*; and *Care Work: Dreaming Disability Justice.* A Disability Futures Fellow, Lambda and Jeanne Córdova Award winner, and longtime disabled QTBIPOC space maker, they are currently building Living Altars, a cultural space by and for disabled QTBIPOC writers.

Jesse Rice-Evans is a housebound superfat white sick and disabled human. They have published several chapbooks as well as the full-length collection *The Uninhabitable.* Rice-Evans has taught writing since 2011 and worked at the City University of New York since 2015. Catch her on a heating pad.

David James "DJ" Savarese is a multi-genre writer, artful activist, and public scholar. He is the author of *Swoon* and *A Doorknob for the Eye*, and the coauthor of *Studies in Brotherly Love.* A three-time Pushcart Prize nominee, he publishes poetry, creative nonfiction, and scholarly essays in a range of literary journals and anthologies. Subject of the Peabody Award–winning documentary *Deej: Inclusion Shouldn't Be a Lottery*, as well as a 2022–23 Iowa Arts Fellow and Zoeglossia Fellow, he co-teaches inclusive, multigenerational, global poetry writing classes and directs the Lives-in-Progress Collective for the Alliance for Citizen Directed Supports.

Rachel Scoggins is a woman-of-color artist with intellectual and chronic pain disabilities. She paints portraits, draws in pencil and ink, and edits photos of her artwork, calling the process "photo manipulation." Scoggins also writes and performs poetry. Scoggins has worked as an advocate for the disability community for over twenty years. As someone with invisible disabilities who also grew up mixed-race, she knows how difficult it is to advocate for oneself.

Daniel Sluman is a poet and disability rights activist. He coedited the first major UK Disability poetry anthology *Stairs and Whispers: D/deaf and Disabled Poets Write Back*, and he has published three poetry collections. His most recent collection *single window* was released in 2021 and was shortlisted for the T. S. Eliot Prize.

Osimiri Sprowal (they/them) is an Afro-Indigenous, Trans, Queercrip poet and homeless-rights activist. Getting their start in youth slam, they are an internationally award-winning poet (CUPSI, 2018). Their book *Gemini: Duality of Self* won the 2019 Shockwire Micro Chapbook Contest. They have received fellowships with Till Arts and CoLab Arts. As a 2022 Marshall Scholar, they earned two degrees in the UK and staged their first play, *Perseus*. Presently, they are a Playwriting MFA candidate at Columbia University.

Jessica Suzanne Stokes is a disabled poet, performer, educator, and scholar, and cofounder of the HIVES Research Workshop on interdependent, multispecies disability community at Michigan State University. Stokes's work has appeared in *Wordgathering: A Journal of Disability Poetry and Literature*, *The Routledge Companion to Gender and Science Fiction*, and *Jacket2*. Their recent game, "Resurrecting Jatayu," created with collaborator Anuj Vaidya, was published in *Feminist Review*.

Gaia Thomas lectures on poetics and is the author of three chapbooks. In 2019, she was an inaugural fellow of Zoeglossia. Her manuscript *Serotine* was a finalist for the Carolyn Bush Award. She lives alone by the sea.

Viktora Valenzuela (she/her) is the associate publisher for Conocimientos Press. Her poetry has appeared on the Poetry Foundation website, in *Raising Mothers*, *Mutha Magazine*, and in anthologies such as *Puro Chicanx: Chicano Poets of the 21st Century*. Valenzuela suffers from the invisible disabilities of PTSD and fibromyalgia. She lives in San Antonio, Texas, with her husband, the Chicano poet Vincent Cooper, and their six children.

Liz Whiteacre is the author of *Hit the Ground* and *it could account for the panic*. Her poems have appeared in *Disability Studies Quarterly*, *Wordgathering*, *Kaleidoscope*, *Breath and Shadow*, and elsewhere. She was a recipient of a 2022–24 Center for Aging and Community Fellowship through which she worked with CICOA Aging and In-Home Services to research how writing poetry supports resilience in aging adults. Whiteacre is an associate professor and chair of English at the University of Indianapolis, where she teaches writing and publishing.

L. Lamar Wilson's poetics animate *Sacrilegion*, a Thom Gunn Award finalist; the stage production *The Gospel Truth*; and *The Changing Same*, a PBS/POV Short collaboration with Rada Film Group, for which he was associate producer. Scholarly and creative works have appeared in *Bigger Than Bravery: Black Resilience and Reclamation in a Time of Pandemic*, *Callaloo*, *The Los Angeles Times*, *The Nation*, *The New York Times*, *Oxford American*, *Obsidian*, and *south*. Wilson, the 2024-2025 Mohr Visiting Poet at Stanford University, has received fellowships from Cave Canem, Civitella Ranieri, and the Ragdale Foundation and teaches creative writing, African American poetics, and film studies at Florida State University and the Mississippi University for Women.